THAI
PHRASEBOOK

D0974303

Thai phrasebook
4th edition – September 1999

Published by
Lonely Planet Publications Pty Ltd A.C.N. 005 607 983
192 Burwood Rd, Hawthorn, Victoria 3122, Australia

Lonely Planet Offices
Australia PO Box 617, Hawthorn, Victoria 3122
USA 150 Linden St, Oakland CA 94607
UK 10a Spring Place, London NW5 3BH
France 1 rue du Dahomey, 75011 Paris

Cover illustration
Bustling Bangkok Bombards the Senses by Julian Chapple

ISBN 0 86442 658 5

text © Lonely Planet Publications 1999
cover illustration © Lonely Planet 1999

Printed by The Bookmaker Pty Ltd
Printed in China

All rights reserved. No part of this publication may be reproduced,
stored in a retrieval system or transmitted in any form by any means,
electronic, mechanical, photocopying, recording or otherwise, except
brief extracts for the purpose of review, without the written permission
of the publisher and copyright owner.

CONTENTS

4   Contents

ABOUT THE AUTHOR

Joe Cummings has been travelling and working in South-East Asia since the 1970s, enjoying stints as an English teacher, Thai translator–interpreter, movie extra and freelance writer. He has written over 30 original guidebooks, photographic books and phrasebooks, and atlases on countries in Asia and North America.

For Lonely Planet he has authored guides to *Thailand*, *Bangkok*, *Thailand's Islands & Beaches*, *Laos* and *Myanmar*, and various chapters in *South-East Asia on a Shoestring*, as well as the *Lao* phrasebook and the upcoming *World Food: Thailand*.

Joe has also published articles on culture, politics and travel in many print and online periodicals, including *Ambassador*, *Asia Magazine*, *Asian Wall Street Journal*, *Bangkok Post*, *Expedia*, *Fables*, *Geographical*, *The* Nation, *Outside*, *San Francisco Examiner*, *South China Morning Post* and *Via*.

FROM THE AUTHOR

Jeerapa Rugtuam prepared the Thai script for this phrasebook and was of great help with slang and other vocabulary questions. Conversations with Steve Martin, Ron Renard, Simon Robson, and Theerada Suphaphong were also helpful.

FROM THE PUBLISHER

This book was produced from the combined sweat of:

Peter D'Onghia, who coordinated the effort and helped out in any way he could.

Olivier Breton who, while fending off queries from the afore-mentioned about his sanity, edited.

Patrick Marris, who laid out with impressive cool.

Brendan Dempsey, who assisted with the layout and laid out the cover.

Renée Otmar, who assisted with editing and proofreading, and assembled the Hill Tribes chapter.

Julian Chapple, who created the illustrations and cover art.

Jeerapa Rugtuam, who graciously provided us with the Thai script.

Sally Steward, who oversaw production.

Quentin Frayne, the macro king.

INTRODUCTION สารบัญ

Thailand's official language is Thai (also known as Siamese) as spoken and written in central Thailand. Thai is spoken with various tonal accents and with slightly differing vocabularies as you move from one part of the country to the next, especially in a north to south direction; however, the central dialect has successfully become the lingua franca between all Thai and non-Thai ethnic groups in the kingdom, and provides the language used in this phrasebook.

All Thai dialects are members of the Thai half of the Thai-Kadai family of languages, and are closely related to languages spoken in Laos (Lao, Northern Thai, Thai Lü), northern Myanmar (Shan, Northern Thai), north-western Vietnam (Nung, Tho), Assam (Ahom) and pockets of southern China (Zhuang, Thai Lü). Thai-Kadai itself is part of the larger Austro-Thai group, one of the oldest language families in the world, even older than Sino-Tibetan or Indo-European.

Modern Thai linguists identify four basic dialects within Thailand: Central Thai (spoken as a first dialect through central Thailand and throughout the country as a second dialect, Northern Thai (spoken from Tak Province north to the Burmese border); North-Eastern Thai (in the north-eastern provinces toward the Lao and Cambodian borders), and Southern Thai (from Chumphon Province south to the Malaysian border). Each of these can be further divided into subdialects; North-Eastern Thai, for example, has nine regional varieties easily distinguished by those who know Thai well. There is also a number of Thai minority dialects such as those spoken by the Phu Thai, Thai Dam, Thai Daeng, Phu Noi, Phuan and other tribal Thais, most of whom reside in the north and north-east.

The Thai script, a recent development in comparison with the spoken language, consists of 44 consonants (but only 21 separate

INTRODUCTION

sounds) and 48 vowel and diphthong possibilities represented by 32 symbols. Experts disagree as to the exact origins of the script, but it was apparently developed around 800 years ago based on the Mon and possibly Khmer writing systems, both of which were in turn inspired by South Indian scripts. Like these languages, Thai is written from left to right, though vowel signs may be written before, above, below, 'around' (before, above and after), or after consonants, depending on the sign.

Though learning the alphabet is not difficult, combining the symbols is fairly complex, so unless you are planning a lengthy stay in Thailand it should perhaps be foregone in favour of learning to speak the language.

Most of the difficulty in mastering basic Thai comes from getting used to the new and different sounds. Once your ears become accustomed to the overall phonetic system the rest is fairly easy. The grammar is very straightforward; words do not change to signify tense, gender or plurality, and there are no articles.

So if you put aside your trepidations and take the plunge, you'll soon be getting by without a word of English. Your first attempts will no doubt meet with mixed success, but keep trying. Listen closely to the way Thais themselves speak. Half the struggle in learning is discovering the spirit of the language. Thais will often laugh at your pronunciation, but this is usually an expression of their appreciation for your efforts rather than a mocking sort of criticism. Don't give up!

This phrasebook also contains a brief chapter covering the more common languages spoken by peoples commonly referred to in Thailand as 'hill tribes'. This section should prove useful in those regions where Thai is less predominant.

ABBREVIATIONS USED IN THIS BOOK

adj	adjective	m	masculine
n	noun	f	feminine
pol	polite	inf	informal

HOW TO USE THIS PHRASEBOOK
You *Can* Speak Another Language

It's true – anyone can speak another language. Don't worry if you haven't studied languages before, or that you studied a language at school for years and can't remember any of it. It doesn't even matter if you failed English grammar. After all, that's never affected your ability to speak English! And this is the key to picking up a language in another country. You don't need to sit down and memorise endless grammatical details and you don't need to memorise long lists of vocabulary. You just need to start speaking. Once you start, you'll be amazed how many prompts you'll get to help you build on those first words. You'll hear people speaking, pick up sounds from TV, catch a word or two that you think you know from the local radio, see something on a billboard – all these things help to build your understanding.

Plunge In

There's just one thing you need to start speaking another language – courage. Your biggest hurdle is overcoming the fear of saying aloud what may seem to you to be just a bunch of sounds.

The best way to start overcoming your fear is to memorise a few key words. These are the words you know you'll be saying again and again, like 'hello', 'thank you' and 'how much?'. Here's an important hint though: right from the beginning, learn at least one phrase that will be useful but not essential. Such as 'good morning' or 'good afternoon', 'see you later' or even a conversational piece like 'lovely day, isn't it?' or 'it's cold today' (people everywhere love to talk about the weather). Having this extra phrase (just start with one, if you like, and learn to say it really well) will enable you to move away from the basics, and when you get a reply and a smile, it'll also boost your confidence. You'll find that people you speak to will like it too, as they'll understand that at least you've tried to learn more of the language than just the usual essential words.

Ways to Remember

There are several ways to learn a language. Most people find they learn from a variety of these, although people usually have a preferred way to remember. Some like to see the written word and remember the sound from what they see. Some like to just hear it spoken in context (if this is you, try talking to yourself in Thai, but do it in the car or somewhere private, to give yourself confidence, and so others don't wonder about your sanity!). Others, especially the more mathematically inclined, like to analyse the grammar of a language, and piece together words according to the rules of grammar. The very visually inclined like to associate the written word and even sounds with some visual stimulus, such as from illustrations, TV and general things they see in the street. As you learn, you'll discover what works best for you – be aware of what made you really remember a particular word, and if it sticks in your mind, keep using that method.

Kicking Off

Chances are you'll want to learn some of the language before you go. The first thing to do is to memorise those essential phrases and words. Check out the basics (page 39) ... and don't forget that extra phrase (see Plunge In!). Try the sections on making conversation or greeting people for a phrase you'd like to use. Write some of these words down on a separate piece of paper and stick them up around the place. On the fridge, by the bed, on your computer, as a bookmark – somewhere where you'll see them often. Try putting some words in context – the 'How much is it?' note, for instance, could go in your wallet.

Building the Picture

We include a chapter on grammar in our books for two main reasons.

Firstly, some people have an aptitude for grammar and find understanding it a key tool to their learning. If you're such a person, then the grammar chapter will help you build a picture of the language, as it works through all the basics.

The second reason for the grammar chapter is that it gives answers to questions you might raise as you hear or memorise some key phrases. You may find a particular word is always used when there is a question – check out the grammar heading on questions and it should explain why. This way you don't have to read the grammar chapter from start to finish, nor do you need to memorise a grammatical point. It will simply present itself to you in the course of your learning. Key grammatical points are repeated throughout the book.

Any Questions?

Try to learn the main question words (see page 32). As you read through different situations, you'll see these words used in the example sentences, and this will help you remember them. So if you want to hire a bicycle, turn to the Bicycles section in Getting Around (use the Contents or Index pages to find it quickly). You've already tried to memorise the word for 'where' and you'll see the word for 'bicycle'. When you come across the sentence 'Where can I hire a bicycle?', you'll recognise the key words and this will help you remember the whole phrase. If there's no category for your need, try the dictionary (the question words are repeated there too, with examples), and memorise phrases like 'What do you call this in Thai?' (page 57).

I've Got a Flat Tyre

Doesn't seem like the phrase you're going to need? Well in fact, it could be very useful. As are all the phrases in this book, provided you have the courage to mix and match them. We have given specific examples within each section. But the key words remain the same even when the situation changes. So while you may not be planning on any cycling during your trip, the first part of the phrase 'I've got ...' could refer to anything else, and there are plenty of words in the dictionary that, we hope, will fit your needs. So whether it's 'a ticket', 'a visa' or 'a condom', you'll be able to put the words together to convey your meaning.

INTRODUCTION

Finally

Don't be concerned if you feel you can't memorise words. On the inside front and back covers are the most essential words and phrases you'll need. You could also try tagging a few pages for other key phrases, or use the notes pages to write your own reminders.

PRONUNCIATION การสะกด

The following is a guide to the phonetic system used throughout this book. It is based on the Royal Thai General System of Transcription (RTGS), the most widely used system in Thailand, with some minor changes to help you to pronounce Thai as accurately as possible. See page 9 for details of how the two systems differ.

VOWELS   สระ

Most Thai vowels have approximate English equivalents. Those that do not will require careful listening and practice; a cursory knowledge of French and Italian vowels will help.

Take care to distinguish between long and short vowels, signified by doubling the vowel or addition of 'h': the distinction can change the meaning (just as 'ship' and 'sheep' depend on vowel length for meaning in English).

a	as the 'u' in 'but'
aa	as the 'a' in 'father'; twice as long as a
ae	as the 'a' in American 'bat'
ai	as the 'i' in 'pipe'
ao	as the 'ow' in 'now'
aw	as the 'aw' in 'jaw'
e	as the 'e' in 'hen'
eh	like 'a' in 'hay' but flat; twice as long as e
eu	as the 'i' in 'sir'
eua	eu + a
i	as the 'i' in 'it'
ii	as the 'ee' in 'feet'; twice as long as i
ia	as the 'ia' as in 'Fiat'
iaw	as the 'io' in 'Rio'
iu	i + u as the 'ew' in 'new'

o	as the 'o' in 'bone' but shorter
oh	as the 'o' in 'toe'; twice as long as o
oe	as the 'u' in 'hut' but more closed
oei	oe + i
u	as the 'u' in 'flute', but shorter
uu	as the 'oo' in 'food'; longer than u
ua	u + a
uay	u + ai

PRONUNCIATION

CONSONANTS   ตัวอักษร

If you hold your finger in front of your mouth as you make the English sounds 'k', 'p' and 't' you'll feel a slight puff of air. In Thai, you can produce each of these with or without breath to make different sounds. For example, the 'k' in lék has no breath; you have to 'swallow' the ending.

Breath is signified by the letter 'h'. For example, the 'k' in khǎo is pronounced with breath. So don't be confused by 'ph' (which means 'p' with breath, not the 'f' sound in 'photo'). Note, however, that the combination 'ch' is like in English 'chop'.

Other consonants which may cause difficulty:

ng	as the 'ng' in 'sing'; used as an initial consonant in Thai (practise by saying 'singer' without the 'si')
j	similar to 't' in 'rapture' or 'culture'
r	similar to the 'r' in 'run' but flapped (tongue touches palate); in everyday speech often pronounced like 'l' or even omitted entirely

TRANSLITERATION

Writing Thai in Roman script is a perennial problem; no truly satisfactory system has yet been devised to assure both consistency and readability. The Thai government uses the Royal Thai General System of Transcription for official government documents in English and for most highway signs. However, this system was not designed for people trying to learn Thai! It doesn't represent distinctions which are important for accurate pronunciation. For example, it does not differentiate between short and long vowel sounds; *o* and *aw* (both represented as 'o'); *u* and *eu* (both 'u'); or *ch* and *j* (both 'ch').

To top it off, many Thai words (especially people and placenames) have Sanskrit and Pali spellings but the actual pronunciation bears little relation to that spelling if Romanised strictly according to the original Sanskrit/Pali. Thus Nakhon Sǐi Thammarat, if transliterated literally, becomes Nagara Sri Dhammaraja. If you tried to pronounce it using this Pali transcription, very few Thais would be able to understand you.

Add to this the fact that local variations crop up on hotel signs, city street signs, menus and so on. Thawi, for example, is variously written as tavi, thawee, Thavi and Tavee. Thais often use English letters that have no equivalent sound in Thai: Faisal for phaisan, Bhumibol for phumiphon, vanich for wanit, Vibhavadi for wiphawadi. Sometimes they even mix literal Sanskrit transcription with Thai pronunciation, as in the King Bhumibol, which is pronounced phumiphon.

The following is a brief summary of common pitfalls you may encounter trying to pronounce transliterated words in Thailand.

- there is no 'v' sound in Thai so Sukhumvit is pronounced sukhumwit and Vieng sounds like wiang

- the letters 'l' and 'r' at the end of a word are always pronounced like an 'n'; hence, satul is pronounced satun and wihar, wihaan. The exception to this is when 'er' or 'ur' is used to indicate the sound 'oe', as in ampher, amphoe; or when 'or' is used for the sound aw as in porn, phawn.

PRONUNCIATION

- the sounds 'l' and 'r' are often used interchangeably in speech, and this shows up in some transliterations. For example, naliga, (clock) may appear as nariga and râat, (a type of noodle dish) might be rendered laat naa or lat na

- the letter u is often used to represent the short a sound, as in tam or nam, which may appear as tum and num. It is also used to represent the eu sound, as when beung 'swamp' is spelt bung.

- phonetically all Thai words end in a vowel (a, e, i, o, u), a semi-vowel (y, w) or one of three stops: p, t and k.

- words transcribed with ch, j, s or d endings like -panich, -raj, -chuanpis and -had should be pronounced as if they end in 't', as in -panit, 'rat', -chuanpit and 'hat'. Likewise 'g' should be pronounced 'k' (ralug is actually raluk) and 'b' is pronounced 'p' (thab becomes thap).

Here are some particular words commonly spelt in ways which encourage mispronunciation:

Common Spelling	Pronunciation	Meaning
bung	beung	pond/swamp
ko/koh	kàw	island
muang	meuang	city
nakhon/nakorn	nákhawn	large city
raja	usually râatchaa at the beginning of a word, râat the end	royal
sri	sĩi	sacred

Tones   เสียง

Tone, the pitch at which a syllable is pronounced, often determines its meaning. For example, depending on the tone, the syllable mái can mean 'new', 'burn', 'wood', 'not?' or 'not', from which we can make the sentence mái, mài mâi mâi mãi, 'new wood doesn't burn, does it?'

Thai has five different tones: level or mid, low, falling, high and rising. The range of all five tones is relative to each speaker's vocal range; there is no fixed musical pitch intrinsic to the language.

- the level or mid tone is pronounced 'flat' (ie doesn't move up or down) at the relative middle of the speaker's vocal range. No tone mark is used, as in dii, 'good'.

- the low tone is 'flat' like the mid tone, but pronounced at the relative bottom of one's vocal range, as in bàat, 'baht' (the Thai currency).

- the falling tone is pronounced as if you were emphasising a word, or calling someone's name from afar, as in mâi, 'no' or 'not'.

- the high tone is usually the most difficult for Westerners. It is pronounced near the relative top of the vocal range, as level as possible, as in níi, 'this'.

- the rising tone sounds like the inflection English speakers generally give to a question 'Yes?', as in sǎam, 'three'.

The tones can be represented like this:

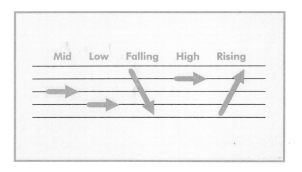

PRONUNCIATION

PRONUNCIATION

Even when we know what the correct tone in Thai should be, our tendency to denote emotion, verbal stress, the interrogative, and so on through tone modulation, often interferes with producing the correct tone. So the first rule in learning to speak Thai is to divorce emotions from your speech until you have learned the Thai way to express them without changing essential tone value.

Words in Thai that appear to have more than one syllable are usually compounds made up of two or more word units, each with its own tone. They may be words taken directly from Sanskrit, Pali or English, in which case each syllable must still have its own tone. Sometimes the tone of the first syllable is not as important as that of the last, so for these the tone mark has been omitted.

THEY MAY SAY ...

Like English, Thai has lots of interjectory expressions that have no discrete meaning but demonstrate emotions. A few of the most common:

ûay!/ohy!	Ouch!; Oh my God!
kâw	Well ... (expresses slight reluctance before saying something)
eh!	Hey!
oh-hōh	[surprise]
wáai	[stereotypical shriek imitation]
ùwáe	[imitating the sound of crying]
òey	[to indicate you made a mistake, eg a slip of the tongue]
éhw	[verbalising a sneer]
oék oék	[guffaw]

This chapter gives you a brief description of Thai grammar – enough to acquaint you with the general structure of the language and allow you to put together your own simple phrases and sentences.

SENTENCE STRUCTURE โครงสร้างประโยค

Word order in Thai is very significant: for instance dâi placed immediately before a verb marks the past tense, while the same word appearing immediately after the verb means 'can'.

To begin with, though, you can learn the basic word order in Thai sentences which, like English, is subject-verb-object:

We eat rice.	rao kin khâo
	(lit: we eat rice)
You study Thai.	khun rian phaasǎa thai
	(lit: you study language Thai)

However, it's not uncommon to place the object first for emphasis.

I don't like that bowl.	chaam nán phǒm mâi châwp
	(lit: bowl that I not like)
We don't have seafood.	aahǎan thaleh mâi mii
	(lit: food sea not have)

NOUNS   คำนาม

Nouns never vary. They do not change to indicate plurality, and they do not need articles like 'a' or 'the':

The house is large/	bâan yài
The houses are large.	(lit: house large)
I'm a soldier.	phǒm/dì-chǎn pen thahǎan
	(lit: I be soldier)
We're soldiers.	rao pen thahǎan
	(lit: we be soldier)

You can form nouns from verbs of physical action by adding kaan before the verb:

to travel	doen thaang
travel (n)/travelling	kaan doen thaang

You can form nouns from verbs of mental action, and from adjectives, by using khwaam.

to think	khít
thought (n)/thinking	khwaam khít
good	dii
goodness	khwaam dii

ADJECTIVES   คำคุณศัพท์

Adjectives always follow the nouns they describe. They do not change in any way to 'agree' with the noun.

big house	bâan yài
	(lit: house big)
small room	hâwng lék
	(lit: room small)
delicious food	aahăan aráwy
	(lit: food delicious)

Comparatives   การเปรียบเทียบขั้นกว่า

Basically any adjective in Thai can be used to make comparisons by adding kwàa to it (like English '-er'):

good	dii	better	dii-kwàa
cheap	thùuk	cheaper	thùuk-kwàa

GRAMMAR

Superlatives   การเปรียบเทียบขั้นสูงสุด

Any adjective may be made superlative by adding thîi-sùt.

delicious	aràwy
the most delicious	aràwy thîi-sùt
expensive	phaeng
the most expensive	phaeng thîi sùt

Equivalence   เท่ากัน, เหมือนกัน

To talk about two things being the same, use meŭan kan, '(is/are) the same', or meŭan kàp, '(is/are) the same as'.

Thai customs (are) not the same.   prà-phehnii thai mâi meŭan kan (lit: custom Thai not meŭan kan)

That kind is the same as this kind.   yáang nán meŭan kàp yàang níi (lit: kind that meŭan kàp kind this)

ADVERBS

Adjectives that can logically be used to modify action may function as adverbs in Thai. An adjective used adverbially is most often doubled, and always follows the verb.

slow (horse)	(máa) cháa
Drive slowly.	kháp cháa-cháa

Certain words and phrases function only as adverbs and, depending on the word or phrase, may either precede the verb or come at the end of the sentence.

Adverbs Which Come Before the Verb

ever	khoei
never	mâi khoei
perhaps	àat jà
probably	khong jà
rarely	mâi khâwy jà
usually	mák jà
yet	yang

Adverbs Which End a Sentence

also	dûay
always	samõe
immediately	than thii
often	bawy-bawy
only	thâo-nán

GRAMMAR

THIS/THAT/THESE/THOSE   นี่, นั่น

The words nîi (this) and nân (that) are spoken with falling tone when used alone as pronouns.

this	nîi	What's this?	nîi a-rai?
that	nân	How much is that?	nân thâo-rai?

However, when used with a noun, they are spoken with a high tone (nán, níi); and like adjectives, they follow the noun they refer to:

this bus	rót níi
that plate	jaan nán

The addition of láo makes níi and nân plural.

these	láo níi
those	láo nán
these chickens	kài láo níi

PERSONAL PRONOUNS   สรรพนาม

Thai has eight common personal pronouns. They aren't used as frequently as their English equivalents, since the subject of a sentence is often omitted after the first reference, or when it is clear from context. There is no distinction between subject and object pronouns (such as 'I' and 'me').

I/me (males)	phŏm
I/me (females)	di-chăn
you	khun/thâan (pol)
	/thoe (inf)
we/us	rao
he/him/she/her/they/them	khăo
it (inanimate objects and animals)	man

First Person   บุรุษที่หนึ่ง

The pronouns phŏm (used by males) and dì-chăn (used by females) are polite forms of 'I/me', appropriate for all situations, formal and informal. Close friends (males and females) use chăn.

Second Person   บุรุษที่สอง

The general all-purpose 'you' is khun.

When addressing someone substantially older than you, or a person of high social position such as a monk or government official, you should use the word thâan.

With an intimate friend or lover, use thoe.

GRAMMAR

Other terms of address you may hear include lung (uncle) and pâa (aunt) for middle-aged Thais, as well as phîi (elder sibling) and náwng (younger sibling), which are used informally among friends and social equals. However, none of these kinship terms are appropriate for use by a foreigner with an elementary command of Thai.

Third Person   บุรุษทีสาม

The third person pronoun khǎo encompasses all people; there are no distinctions for gender or number.

The word thâan, as well as being a respectful form of 'you', can also refer to people of high position in the third person, for example:

How many rainy seasons   thâan pen phrá kìi
    has he been a monk?   phansǎa láew?
                             (lit: thâan is monk how many
                                 rainy season?)

GRAMMAR

POSSESSION   การแสดงความเป็นเจ้าของ

The word khǎwng is used to denote possession and is roughly the same as the preposition 'of' or the verb 'belongs to' in English

my bag   krapǎo khǎwng phǒm
                            (lit: bag khǎwng me)

his/her seat   thîi nâng khǎwng khǎo
                            (lit: seat khǎwng him/her)

Does this belong to you?   nîi khǎwng khun rēu plào?
                            (lit: this khǎwng you or not?)

khăwng can also be used as a noun to mean 'stuff' or 'things'

She went to buy some things.   khăo pai séu khăwng
                                (lit: she go buy khăwng)

For 'whose' use khăwng khrai:

Whose plate is this?   jaan níi khăwng khrai?
                        (lit: plate this khăwng khrai)

VERBS   คำกริยา

Thai verbs don't change according to tense. Thus the sentence
khăo thaan kài can mean 'she/he eats; ate; has eaten; will eat
chicken'. Context will often tell you what time is being referred
to. Otherwise you can do one of the following:

• specify the time with a word like wan-níi, 'today', mêua-waan-
  níi 'yesterday' and so on (see page 79 for more time words):

She/he ate chicken   mêua-waan-níi khăo
    yesterday.   thaan kài
                          (lit: yesterday she/he
                          eat chicken)

• add one of the words listed below to indicate whether an action is ongoing, completed or to-be-completed.

Ongoing Action   กริยาที่กำลังดำเนินอยู่

The word kamlang is used before the verb to mark ongoing or
progressive action, a bit like the English 'am/are/is doing'. However,
it is not used unless the speaker feels it is absolutely necessary to
express the continuity of an action, as in this reply to the question sák
sêua-phâa láew rěu yang? 'Have you washed the clothes yet?'

I'm washing the clothes now!   kamlang sák sêua-phâa
                                láew!
                                (lit: kamlang wash
                                clothes now)

Completed Action
กริยาที่ดำเนินการเสร็จสิ้นแล้ว

The most common way of expressing completed action in Thai is by using the word láew at the end of the sentence.

We went to Bangkok.	rao pai Krung Thêp láew
	(lit: we go Bangkok láew)
I spent the money.	phŏm/dì-chān jai ngoen láew
	(lit: I spend money láew)

The marker láew can also refer to a current condition that began a short time ago.

I'm hungry (already).	phŏm/dì-chān hĭu khâo láew
	(lit: I hungry rice láew)

The marker dâi also shows past tense but, unlike láew, never refers to a current condition. It immediately precedes the verb, and is often used in conjunction with láew. It is more commonly employed in negative statements than in the affirmative.

Our friends didn't go to Chiang Mai.	phêuan rao mâi dâi pai Chiang Mài
	(lit: friend us no dâi go Chiang Mai)

To-Be-Completed Action
กริยาที่จะเสร็จสิ้นในอนาคต

The word já is used to mark an action to be completed in the future. It always appears directly before the verb.

She/he will buy rice.	khăo já séu khâo
	(lit: she/he já buy rice)

Making Requests & Giving Commands
การขอร้อง

The word khăw is used to make polite requests. Depending on the context, it's roughly equivalent to 'Please give me a ...' or 'May I ask for a ...'. Khăw always comes at the beginning of a sentence,

and is often used in conjunction with the added 'polite' word
náwy, literally 'a little', spoken with a low tone instead of the
usual high tone, at the end of the sentence.

| Can I have some rice? | khǎw khâo nàwy?
(lit: khǎw rice nàwy) |

To ask someone to do something, you can politely preface the
sentence with chûay 'help' or choen 'I invite you'. In English the
closest equivalent is 'please'.

| Please close the window. | chûay pìt nâa daang
(lit: chûay close window) |

| Please sit down. | choen nâng
(lit: choen sit) |

To express a greater sense of urgency, use sí at the end of the sentence:

| Close the door! | pìt prátuu sí!
(lit: close door sí) |

TO BE   ต้องเป็น

The verb pen is the closest Thai equivalent to English 'to be',
but with some important differences. It is used to join nouns
and/or pronouns:

| I am a teacher. | phǒm/dì-chǎn pen khruu
(lit: I pen teacher) |

| This train is an express train. | rót níi pen rót dùan
(lit: train this pen train express) |

However, it cannot be used to join pronouns and adjectives;
the adjective simply follows the noun directly, with no verb.
So the English sentence 'The house is red' is said literally as
'house red'.

| That person is tall. | khon nán sǔung
(lit: person that tall) |

The word pen also has other meanings, such as 'to have' when describing a person's condition:

I have a fever.	phŏm/dì-chǎn pen khài. (lit: I pen fever)
She has a cold.	khǎo pen wàt (lit: she pen cold)

KEY VERBS

Thai verbs don't have 'infinitive' forms. There is no grammatical distinction between finite or infinitive verbal situations.

to be	pen
to bring	ao maa
to come	maa
to depart	àwk
to do	tham
to go	pai
to have	mii
to know (someone)	rúu-jàk
to know (something)	rúu; sâap
to like	châwp
to live (somewhere)	yùu
to make	tham
to meet	phóp
to need	tâwngkaan
to say	bàwk
to speak	phûut
to stay (overnight)	phák
to take	ao pai
to understand	khâo jai
to want (something)	ao; yàak dâi
to want (to do something)	yàak

GRAMMAR

It can be used to show ability:

She knows how to play guitar.	khǎo lên kiitaa pen (lit: she play guitar pen)

One question you'll hear quite often in Thailand is khun thaan aahǎan thai pen mǎi? (lit: can you eat Thai food), which ultimately means 'can you tolerate spicy food?'

If you want to say 'there is' or 'there are', to describe the existence of something somewhere, the verb mii, literally 'have', is used instead of pen. You can use it in such sentences as:

In Bangkok there are many cars.	thîi Krung Thêp mii rót yon mâak (lit: in Bangkok mii car many)
At Wat Pho there is a large Buddha image.	thîi Wát Phoh mii phrá phútthá-rûup yài (lit: in Wat Pho mii Buddha image large)

TO HAVE   ต้องมี

As mentioned above, mii is equivalent to 'to have':

I have a bicycle.	phǒm/dì-chǎn mii rót jákráyaan (lit: I mii bicycle)
Do you have fried noodles?	mii kǔaytǐaw phàt mǎi? (lit: mii noodle fry mǎi?)

QUESTIONS   คำถาม

Thai has two ways of forming questions: through the use of a question word like 'who', 'how', 'what', or through the addition of a tag like 'isn't it?' to the end of the sentence.

Question Words   คำที่เป็นคำถาม

Many English speakers instinctively place an English question inflection to the end of a Thai question; try to avoid doing this as it will usually interfere with the tones.

GRAMMAR

In Thai, question tags alone signify the interrogative. The one exception is the question word for 'where' (nǎi), which features a rising tone in Thai, very much like the question tone used by some English speakers.

Note the placement of Thai question words in a sentence. Some come at the beginning of the question, others at the end.

what	a-rai
how	yang-ngai
who	khrai
when	mêua-rai
why	thammai
how much	thâo rai
where	thîi nǎi
which	nǎi

What do you need?	khun tâwng-kaan a-rai?
How do you do it? (How is it done?)	tham yang-ngai?
Who is sitting there?	khrai nâng thîi nân?
When will you go to Chiang Mai?	mêua-rai jà pai Chiang Mái?
Why are you quiet?	thammai ngîap?
How much is this?	nîi thâo rai?
Where is the bathroom?	hâwng náam yùu thîi nǎi?
Which one do you like?	châwp an nǎi?

Question Tags

mǎi makes a statement into a question:

Is the weather hot?	aakàat ráwn mǎi? (lit: weather hot mǎi)

GRAMMAR

châi mǎi asks for confirmation of something we think is true, similar to English similar to 'aren't you?' or 'isn't it?'

You're a student, aren't you?	khun pen nák-rian châi mǎi?
	(lit: you are student châi mǎi)

rǔu?, mening 'eh?/yeah?' is a similar way of turning a statement into a question, often used in the combinations rǔu pláo and rǔu mǎi, 'or not?'

Do you want to go	yàak pai thîaw rǔu pláo?
out or not?	(lit: want go out rǔu pláo)

láew rǔu yáang asks if something has happened yet:

Have you eaten yet?	thaan khâo láew rǔu yang?
	(lit: you eat láew rǔu yang)

Answers   คำตอบ

To answer a question, just repeat the verb, with or without the negative particle (pláo, yáng, mǎi, mâi châi). Informally, a negative particle will do for a negative reply.

Do you want a beer?	ao bia mǎi?
Yes.	ao
No.	mâi ao
Are you well?	sabai dii rǔu?
Yes.	sabai dii
No.	mâi sabai
Have you eaten yet?	thaan khâo láew rǔu yang?
Yes.	thaan láew
No.	yáng
You're a teacher, aren't you?	khun pen khruu châi mǎi?
Yes.	châi
No.	mâi châi
Are you angry?	kròht rǔu plào?
Yes.	kròht
No.	plào

NEGATIVES   ปฏิเสธ

The main negative marker in Thai is mâi. Any verb or adjective may be negated by the insertion of mâi immediately before it. You can also use pláo but only in conjunction with questions that use the pláo tag.

She/he isn't thirsty.	khǎo mâi hǔu náam (lit: she/he mâi thirsty)
I don't have any cash.	phǒm/dì-chǎn mâi mii tàang (lit: I mâi have cash)
We're not French.	rao mâi pen khon faràngsèht (lit: we mâi be person France)
John has never gone to Chiang Mai.	John mâi khoei pai Chiang Mài (lit: John mâi never go Chiang Mai)
We won't go to Ubon tomorrow.	phrûng-níi rao mâi pai Ubon (lit:tomorrow we mâi go Ubon)

MODALS

Modals are words like the English 'should', 'want to', 'must' or 'can' used in conjunction with verbs to express obligation, want, need and ability as in 'you *should* study harder' or 'I *want* to go'.

Obligation   ความจำเป็น

The words khuan and nâa serve as 'should' or 'ought to', usually in conjunction with jà, the marker for to-be-completed action.

You should eat.	khun khuan jà thaan khâo (lit: you khuan jà eat rice)
We ought to go.	rao nâa jà pai (lit: we nâa jà go)
She/he shouldn't do that.	khǎo mâi khuan tham yang nán (lit: she/he not khuan do that)

Want   ต้องการ

The words yàak jà are placed in front of the verb. In informal
conversation já may be omitted.

The dog wants to eat.	māa yàak jà kin khâo
	(lit: dog yàak jà want eat rice)
I don't want to walk.	phǒm/dì-chǎn mâi yàak doen
	(lit: I not yàak walk)

You can't put a noun straight after yàak jà; you need to use either
ao 'take' or yàak dâi 'want to get':

I want bananas.	phǒm/dì-chǎn ao klûay
	(lit: I ao banana)
Tom wants a shirt.	Tom yàak dâi sêua
	(lit: Tom yàak dâi shirt)

Must/Need to   ต้อง

The word tâwng (or the long form, jam pen jà tâwng) comes
before verbs to give the meaning 'must' or 'need to'.

I must go to Phetburi.	phǒm/dì-chǎn tâwng pai Phetburi
	(lit: I tâwng go Phetburi)
We need to look for a house.	rao tâwng hǎa bâan
	(lit: we tâwng search house)
You don't have to stay here.	khun mâi tâwng phák thîi nîi
	(lit: you not tâwng stay at this)

The word for 'need' before a noun is tâwng-kaan.

I need a map.	phǒm/dì-chǎn tâwng-kaan phǎen thîi
	(lit: I tâwng-kaan map)

GRAMMAR

Can สามารถ

Thai has three ways of expressing 'can': dâi, pen and wǎi.

- dâi means 'to be able to' or 'to be allowed to' and is the more general equivalent of the English 'can'. It always follows the verb (and its object, if any).

Can you go?	pai dâi mǎi?
	(lit: go dâi mǎi?)
(I) can't go.	pai mâi dâi
	(lit: go not dâi)
(I) can't eat pork.	thaan mǔu mâi dâi
	(lit: eat pork not dâi)

- The verb pen may mean 'can' in the sense of 'to know how to'. Like dâi, it ends the verb phrase:

S/he knows how to play guitar.	khǎo lên kiitaa pen
	(lit: she play guitar pen)

The word wǎi is used as 'can' to express physical possibility or ability:

I can't lift that vehicle.	phǒm/dì-chǎn yók rót nán mâi wǎi
	(lit: I lift vehicle that not wǎi)

CLASSIFIERS ลักษณะนาม

Occasionally in English you can't just put a number with a noun: you use an extra word which 'classifies' the noun. These are also known as counters. For example, you don't just say 'three breads' or 'three papers'; you have to say 'three loaves of bread' and 'three sheets of paper'.

In Thai, whenever you specify a particular number of any noun you must use a classifier. The classifier you choose depends on the physical appearance of the noun. First you name the thing, then the number, and finally the appropriate classifier. So five oranges is sôm hâa lûuk, 'orange five fruit'.

Some Common Classifiers

If you don't know (or forget) the appropriate classifier, an may be used for almost any small object. Alternatively, Thais sometimes repeat the noun rather than not use a classifier at all.

animals, furniture, clothing	tua
books, candles	lêm
children, young animals, fruit, balls	lûuk
eggs	fawng
glasses (of water, tea, etc)	kâew
houses	lǎng
letters, newspapers (flat sheets)	chàbàap
monks, Buddha images	rûup
pairs of items (people, things)	khûu
people	khon
pieces, slices (cakes, cloth)	chín
pills, seeds, small gems	mét
plates (food)	jaan
rolls (toilet paper, film)	múan
round hollow objects	bai
royal persons, stupas	ong
sets of things	chút
stamps, planets, stars	duang
small objects, miscellaneous things	an
trains (whole)	khabuan
vehicles (bikes, cars, train carriages)	khan

GRAMMAR

CONJUNCTIONS   คำบุพบท

and	kàp (can also mean 'with') or láe
because	phráw wâa
but	tàe
or	rěu
so	phráw-cha-nán
so that (in order to)	phêua

PREPOSITIONS

คำบุพบท

above	nĕua
across from	trong khâam kàp
adjacent to	tìt kàp
around	râwp
at	thîi
at the edge of	rim kàp
behind	lăng
beside	khâang
from	jàak
in	nai
in front of	nâa
inside	phai-nai
of	khăwng
on	bon
opposite	trong khâam
under	tâi
with	kàp

YOU SHOULD KNOW   สที่ควรรู้

Hello.	sawàt-dii (khráp/khâ)	สวัสดี
Goodbye.	laa kàwn	ลาก่อน
Excuse me.	khǎw thôht	ขอโทษ
Please.	kàwrúnaa	กรุณา
Thank you.	kháwp khun (khráp/khâ)	ขอบคุณ
Many thanks.	kháwp khun mâak (khráp/khâ)	ขอบคุณมาก

KHRÁP/KHÂ   ครับ/ค่ะ

As a normal courtesy, Thai speakers end their sentences with a politening syllable: khráp (if the speaker is male) or khâ (if the speaker is female). You should follow this convention or you may appear abrupt and aggressive. Always use khráp/khâ after sawàt-dii 'Hello', khàwp khun, 'Thank you' and in small talk. However, if your conversation is a long one (let's be ambitious!), you can drop the khráp/khâ after a few lines.

These words are also used to answer 'yes' to a question, to show agreement, or simply to acknowledge that you're listening. (Thai has an equivalent of 'uh-huh', anh, but it's not nearly as polite.)

In everyday speech, the 'r' in khráp is dropped to produce the simplified kháp.

Women should pronounce their kha with a high tone khá instead of the usual falling tone (khâ) when forming questions.

Are you going to eat?
thaan khâo mǎi khá?   ทานข้าวไหมคะ

(Yes) I'm going to eat.
thaan khâo khâ   ทานข้าวค่ะ

GREETINGS/HELLO   การทักทาย

The all-purpose Thai greeting (and farewell) is sawàt-dii (khráp/khâ). It's often accompanied by a wâi, the palms-together gesture of respect (see Body Language, page 43). Its literal meaning derives from the Sanskrit words su, meaning 'happiness', plus asti, 'is'; hence it has the general meaning of wishing happiness or well-being on the listener.

If someone says sawàt-dii (khráp/khâ) to you, you should reply with the same phrase.

Other common greetings, especially when meeting someone on the street, are pai nǎi? 'Where are you going?' and thaan khâo láew rěu yang?, 'Have you eaten yet?'. As with the English 'How are you?', the answer doesn't usually matter. If you're just out for a stroll, a common reply to pai nǎi? is pai thîaw, which roughly translates as 'I'm just out for fun'. The greeting thaan khâo láew rěu yang? carries an implicit invitation to dine together (even for just a quick bowl of noodles), hence you choose the reply based on whether you'd like to spend time with the person. Answer yang, 'Not yet' if you're willing to accept a possible meal invitation; answer thaan láew, 'I've eaten already' if you'd rather be on your way.

GOODBYES   ลาก่อน

As mentioned previously, a simple sawàt-dii (khráp/khâ) can be used as a farewell, especially if both speakers are leaving at the same time.

If you are leaving and the person you're speaking to is staying behind, you can say laa kàwn, literally 'leaving first' or pai kàwn, 'going first' as a rough equivalent of 'goodbye'. If you're the one staying, you bid farewell by saying chôhk dii 'good luck'.

Whether you're staying or going, you can also say phóp kan mài, meaning 'We'll meet again', roughly equivalent to 'See you later'.

HEART TO HEART

One of the most important and frequently used words in Thai is jai, which literally means 'heart' but, as in English, may also connote 'mind' with regard to emotional states. Hundreds of Thai phrases containing the word jai are used to express all kinds of mental feelings, perceptions and attitudes in one's personal and social life. In Thai, for example, your heart can be cool or hot, wet or dry, small or wide, single or paired, or any of several hundred other metaphorical variations.

Below are a few of the most common and useful jai expressions. Think of each of these expressions as beginning with 'feeling', as in 'feeling trust', 'feeling confident', 'feeling deferential' and so on. You can express the opposite of each of these feelings by adding mâi (not) in front of the phrase, as in mâi nâe jai, 'feeling uncertain'.

calm, easy-going	'cool heart'	jai yen
certain	'certain heart'	nâe jai
confident	'steady heart'	mân jai
deferential	'awe heart'	krehng jai
easily upset	'hot heart'	jai ráwn
good-hearted	'good heart'	jai dii
happy, at ease	'heart comfortable'	sabaai jai
pitiless	'black heart'	jai dam
sensitive	'little heart'	jai náwy
shocked	'fall heart'	tòk jai
sorry	'spoil heart'	sǐa jai
straightforward, sincere	'true heart'	jing jai
surprised	'strange heart'	plàek jai
trust	'trust heart'	wái jai

MEETING PEOPLE

CIVILITIES

How are you?	pen yang-ngai	เป็นยังไง
	sabai-dii rĕu?	สบายดีหรือ
I'm fine.	sabàay dii	สบายดี
Thank you.	khàwp khun	ขอบคุณ
Thank you very much.	khàwp khun mâak	ขอบคุณมาก
It's nothing; Never mind; Don't bother.	mâi pen rai	ไม่เป็นไร
Excuse me.	khăw thôht	ขอโทษ

FORMS OF ADDRESS   การเขียนที่อยู่

Thais often address each other using their first names with the honorific khun or other title preceding it. Other formal terms of address include naai, 'Mr' and naang, 'Ms/Miss/Mrs'. Friends often use nicknames or kinship terms like phîi 'elder sibling', náwng, 'younger sibling', mâe, 'mother' or lung, 'uncle' depending on the age differential. Young children can be called lăan, 'nephew/niece'.

The following list includes kinship terms commonly used as forms of address for non-relatives, based on relative age difference from the speaker. (For more kinship terms, see page 99).

elder sibling	phîi	พี่
younger sibling	náwng	น้อง
mother	mâe	แม่
father	phâw	พ่อ
uncle	lung	ลุง
aunt	pâa	ป้า
grandfather	taa	ตา
grandmother	yaai	ยาย
niece/nephew	lăan	หลาน

BODY LANGUAGE   ภาษากาย

Nonverbal behaviour or body language is more important in
Thailand than in most Western countries.

If you're inside and you walk in front of someone who's sitting
down you should stoop a little as a sign of respect.

The feet are the lowest part of the body (spiritually as well as
physically), so don't point your feet at people or point at things
with your feet. In the same context, the head is regarded as the
highest part of the body, so don't touch a Thai person on the head.

USEFUL PHRASES

Just a minute.	raw diaw	รอเดี๋ยว
It's OK. (OK is also widely understood.)	mâi pen rai	ไม่เป็นไร
It's important.	sǎmkhan	สำคัญ
It's not important.	mâi pen rai/mâi sǎmkhan	ไม่เป็นไร/ ไม่สำคัญ
It's possible.	pen pai dâi	เป็นไปได้
It's not possible.	pen pai mâi dâi	เป็นไปไม่ได้
Look!	duu sí!	ดูซิ
Listen/Listen to this!	fang sí!	ฟังซิ
I'm ready.	rîap ráwy láew/ phráwm láew	เรียบร้อยแล้ว/ พร้อมแล้ว
Are you ready?	rîap ráwy láew rěu yang?/ phráwm láew rěu yang?	เรียบร้อยแล้ว หรือยัง/พร้ อมแล้วหรือยัง
Good luck!	chôhk dii	โชคดี
Just a second!	páep diaw	แป๊บเดียว

MEETING PEOPLE

Temples   วัด

To enter a temple you must be neatly dressed (no shorts or sleeveless shirts) and you must take your shoes off when you enter any building that contains a Buddha image. Buddha images are sacred objects, so don't pose in front of them for pictures and definitely do not clamber upon them.

Monks are not supposed to touch or be touched by women. If a woman wants to hand something to a monk, the object should be placed within reach of the monk, not handed directly to him.

When sitting in a religious edifice, keep your feet pointed away from any Buddha images or monks. The usual way to do this is to sit in the 'mermaid' pose in which your legs are folded to the side, with the feet pointing backwards.

Social Gestures   การเข้าสังคม

Traditionally, Thais greet each other not with a handshake but with a prayer-like palms-together gesture known as a *wâi*. If someone uses it with you, you should *wâi* back (unless used by a child).

In Bangkok and large cities, the western-style handshake is commonly offered to foreigners.

FIRST ENCOUNTERS   การพบกันครั้งแรก

Hello/Greetings.	sawàt-dii (khráp/khâ)	สวัสดี
Are you well?	sabaai-dii rĕu?	สบายดีหรือ
I'm fine.	sabaai-dii	สบายดี
What's your name?	khun chêu arai?	คุณชื่ออะไร
My name is ...	phŏm chêu ... (m)	ผมชื่อ...
	dì-chăn chêu ... (f)	ดิฉันชื่อ...
Pleased to meet you.	yin-dii thîi dâi rúujàk	ยินดีที่ได้รู้จัก

MEETING PEOPLE

MAKING CONVERSATION การสร้างบทสนทนา

We're friends.
   rao pen phêuan kan — เราเป็นเพื่อนกัน

We're relatives.
   rao pen phîi-náwng kan — เราเป็นพี่น้องกัน

I've come on business.
   phõm/dì-chãn maa tham thúrá — ผม/ดิฉันมาทำธุระ

I've come on pleasure.
   phõm/dì-chãn maa thîaw — ผม/ดิฉันมาเที่ยว

Nice weather, isn't it?
   aakàat dii chái mãi? — อากาศดีใช่ไหม

It's quite hot in Thailand.
   meuang thai ráwn mâak — เมืองไทยร้อนมาก

I like it here.
   phõm/dì-chãn châwp thîi nîi — ผม/ดิฉันชอบที่นี่

May I have; ask for your address?
   khãw thî-yùu khãwng khun — ขอที่อยู่ของคุณได้ไหม
   dâi mãi?

This is my address.
   nîi pen thî-yùu khãwng chãn — นี่เป็นที่อยู่ของฉัน

Do you live here?
   khun phák thîi nîi mãi? — คุณพักที่นี่ใช่ไหม

Where are you going?
   pai nãi? — ไปไหน

What are you doing?
   tham á-rai? — ทำอะไร

What do you think (about ...)?
   (rèuang ...) khít wâa yang-ngai? — (เรื่อง...) คิดว่ายังไง

Can I take a photo (of you)?
   tháai rûup dâi mãi? — ถ่ายรูปได้ไหม

What is this called?
   nîi rîak wâa á-rai? — นี่เรียกว่าอะไร

Beautiful, isn't it?
   sũay mãi? — สวยไหม

We like it here very much.
    rao châwp thîi nîi mâak   เราชอบที่นี่มาก

What a cute baby!
    lûuk nâa rák jang!   ลูกน่ารักจัง

Are you waiting too?
    khun kamlang raw dûay rēu?   คุณกำลังรอด้วยหรือ

That's strange!
    pláek!   แปลก

That's funny (amusing).
    tàlòhk   ตลก

Are you here on holiday?
    maa thîi nîi phêua maa thîaw rēu?   มาที่นี่เพื่อมาเที่ยวหรือ?

I'm here ...   maa thîi nîi phêua ...   มาที่นี่เพื่อ...
    for a holiday   thîaw   เที่ยว
    on business   tham thúrá   ทำธุระ
    to study   rian năng su   เรียนหนังสือ

How long are you here for?
    já yùu thîi nîi naan thâo rai?   จะอยู่ที่นี่นานเท่าไร

I'm/We're here for ... weeks/days.
    jà yùu thîi nîi ... aathít/wan   จะอยู่ที่นี่...อาทิตย์/วัน

Do you like it here?
    châwp thîi nîi māi?   ชอบที่นี่ไหม

I/We like it here very much.
    châwp thîi nîi mâak   ชอบที่นี่มาก

address	thîi yùu	ที่อยู่
clear/clearly	chát	ชัด
fluent	khláwng	คล่อง
friend	phêuan	เพื่อน
language	phaasăa	ภาษา
phone number	boe thorásàp	เบอร์โทรศัพท์
study/learn	rian	เรียน

USING 'I'

Thai is what's known as a 'subject weak' language. This is particularly true when it comes to the use of personal pronouns. Most Thais seldom use them at all in everyday conversation, although since they're used to hearing English speakers fill their beginning Thai with personal pronouns, Thais will often respond in kind! The commonly known first-person pronouns, phŏm and dì-chăn, are actually quite formal and are used sparingly in everyday speech.

More typically Thais will use no pronoun, or insert the person's name (even their own name, when talking about themselves). Friends often use kinship terms (eg phîi, elder sibling, or náwng, younger sibling), even if unrelated by blood.

Joe speaking to Somchai, a new acquaintance:
somchai jà pai năi?

Somchai replying to Joe:
somchai jà pai tàlàat. joe yàak pai dûay măi?
Joe replying to Somchai: yàak pai dûay

Joe speaking to Pia, a close friend younger then himself: náwng châwp kin aahăan phèt rĕu plào?
Pia replying to Joe: châwp mâak. phîi châwp aahăan phèt măi?

NATIONALITIES   สัญชาติ/เชื้อชาติ

Unfortunately we can't list all countries here however, you'll find that many country names in Thai are similar to English. Remember though; even if a word looks like the English equivalent, it will have a Thai pronunciation.

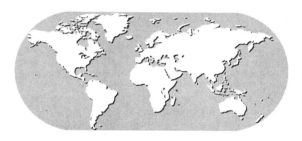

Where do you come from?

   Maa jàak thîi nǎi?   มาจากที่ไหน

I am a/an ...

   phǒm/dì-chǎn pen khon ...   ผม/ดิฉันเป็นคน...

I come from ...   phǒm/dì-chǎn   ผม/ดิฉันมาจาก...
                         maa jàak ...

Australia	aw-sàtreh-lia	ออสเตรเลีย
Canada	khaenaadaa	แคนาดา
China	jiin	จีน
Denmark	denmàak	เดนมาร์ก
England	angkrìt	อังกฤษ
France	faràngsèht	ฝรั่งเศส
Germany	yoe-ra-man	เยอรมัน
Holland	hawlandaa	ฮอลันดา
India	india	อินเดีย
Italy	italii	อิตาลี

Japan	yîi-pùn	ญี่ปุ่น
Singapore	sĭnkha-poh	สิงคโปร์
Spain	sàpehn	สเปน
Sweden	sàwiiden	สวีเดน
Switzerland	sàwit-soelaen	สวิสเซอร์แลนด์
Taiwan	tâiwăn	ไต้หวัน
Thailand	meuang thaai	เมืองไทย
the USA	sàhàrát amehrikaa	สหรัฐอเมริกา

I live in/at ...	bâan phŏm/ dì-chăn yúu nai ...	บ้านผม/ ดิฉันอยู่ใน...
the city	meuang	เมือง
the countryside	chonàbót	ชนบท
the mountains	phuu khăo	ภูเขา
the seaside	fáng tháleh	ฝั่งทะเล
the suburbs of ...	râwp nâwk meuang ...	รอบนอกเมือง...
a village	mùu bâan	หมู่บ้าน

CULTURAL DIFFERENCES
ความแตกต่างทางวัฒนธรรม

How do you do this in your country?
   tham yang-ngai thîi
   meuang thai?
ทำยังไงที่เ
มืองไทย

Is this a local or national custom?
   níi pen pràphenii phéun
   bâan rĕu pràjam châat?
นี่เป็นประเพณีพื้น
บ้านหรือประจำชาติ

I don't want to offend you.
   phŏm/dì-chăn mâi
   yàak róp kuan
ผม/ดิฉันไม่อ
ยากรบกวน

I'm sorry, it's not the custom in my country.

khǎw thôht, mâi châi	ขอโทษ,ไม่ใช
pràphenii khǎwng	ประเพณี
phǒm/dì-chān	ของผม/ดิฉัน

I'm not accustomed to this.

| phǒm/dì-chān mâi chin | ผม/ดิฉันไม่ชิน |

I don't mind watching, but
I'd prefer not to participate.

| phǒm/dì-chān duu chōei | ผม/ดิฉันดูเฉย |
| chōei táe mâi tham | ๆแต่ไม่ทำ |

AGE   อายุ

Asking someone's age is a common question in Thailand. It's not
considered rude to ask strangers their age.

How old are you?

| khun aayúu thâo rai? | คุณอายุเท่าไร |

| I'm ... years old. | phǒm/dì-chān | ผม/ดิฉันอายุ...ปี |
| | aayúu ... pii | |

| Very young! | nùm mâak! | หนุ่มมาก |
| Very old! | kàe mâak! | แก่มาก |

END OF QUESTION

Unlike in English, which usually places question words like what,
when or where in front of the question, in Thai such question words
come at the end of the question.

so say ...	raakhaa thâo rai
	(lit: price how much)
not	thâo rai raakhaa

PEN

Probably the most prevalent mistake English-speaking foreigners make when learning Thai is trying to use pen – the Thai word for 'be'– with the many Thai adjectives that function as stative verbs. Such words act as both adjectives and verbs.

so say ...	phŏm/dì-chān nèuay
	(lit: I tired)
	I'm tired.
not	phŏm/dì-chān pen nèuay

OCCUPATIONS   อาชีพ

I'm (a/an) ...	phŏm/dì-chān pen ...	ผม/ดิฉันเป็น...
actor	nák-sadāeng	นักแสดง
businessperson	nák thúrákìt	นักธุรกิจ
diplomat	nák kaan-thûut	นักการ ทูต
doctor	phâet, māw	แพทย์,หมอ
engineer	wítsàwakawn	วิศวกร
farmer	chao-naa	ชาวนา
journalist	nák nāng sēu phim	นักหนังสือพิมพ์
lawyer	thanai-khwaam	ทนายความ
military	thahāan	ทหาร
missionary	phûu sāwn sàat-sanāa	ผู้สอนศาสนา
musician	nák dontrii	นักดนตรี
pilot/flyer	nák-bin	นักบิน
secretary	lehkhāanúkaan	เลขานุการ
student	nák-sèuksāa	นักศึกษา
teacher	khruu	ครู
traveller/tourist	nák thâng thîaw	นักท่องเที่ยว

MEETING PEOPLE

volunteer	aasāasamàk	อาสาสมัคร
worker	kamma-kawn	กรรมกร
unemployed	wâang ngaan	ว่างงาน

What are you studying?

| khun rian àrai? | คุณเรียนอะไร |

I'm studying ...	phōm/dì-chān rian ...	ผม/ดิฉันเรียน...
art	sìlàpà	ศิลปะ
arts/humanities	mánútsàat	มนุษยศาสตร์
business	kaan bawríhāan thúrákìt	การบริหารธุรกิจ
teaching	kaan sèuk-sāa	การศึกษา
engineering	wísáwákam	วิศวกรรม
languages	phāasāasàat	ภาษาศาสตร์
law	wíchaa kòtmāai	วิชากฎหมาย
medicine	phâethàyásàat	แพทย์ศาสตร์
science	wítháyaasàat	วิทยาศาสตร์

EXPRESSING FEELINGS   การแสดงความรู้สึก

Thais are much less apt to express their feelings or emotions to strangers than most Westerners. Exercise discretion. Any display or expression of strong emotion means a potential loss of face for both speaker and listener. Talking loudly is also perceived as rude behaviour, whatever the situation.

I feel ...	phŏm/dì-chǎn rúusèuk ...	ผม/ดิฉันรู้สึก...
angry	kròht	โกรธ
excited	tèun tên	ตื่นเต้น
happy	dii jai	ดีใจ
lonely	ngǎo	เหงา
nervous	ngùt ngìt;	หงุดหงิด;
	khîi tók jai	ขี้ตกใจ
sad	sǐa jai	เสียใจ
satisfied	phaw jai	พอใจ
sleepy	ngûang nawn	ง่วงนอน
surprised	pràlàat jai	ประหลาดใจ
tired	nèuay	เหนื่อย
upset	mâi sabaai-jai;	ไม่สบายใจ;
	náwy jai	น้อยใจ
(I'm) bored.	bèua	เบื่อ
(This is) fun!	sanùk dii!	สนุกดี

DID YOU KNOW ...

A person who wipes out a good deed by immediately following it with ill action is said to khǐan dûay meu, lóp dûay tháo. Literally this means 'Write with the hand, erase with the foot', using the lowly position of the feet in the Thai corporal hierarchy to emphasise the point.

MEETING PEOPLE

LOVE & SEX

Like any language, Thai has a large vocabulary for expressing romance and desire. Here are a few common ones:

broken-hearted	òk hàk
darling	thîi rák
dear	jāa; ōey
(usually spoken after a name or pronoun, as in 'dear child')	lûuk ōey,
dirty old man	thâo hūa nguu
fickle	jai loh leh
in love	phlâwt rák
horny	bâa tanhāa
(lit: crazed with desire)	
intimate	sànit kan
to lose one's virginity	jàwk khài daeng
(idiom, lit: break the yolk)	
to love	rák
love (n)	khwaam rák
lovesick	khâi jai
to make love/(slang)	fan
(slang, slightly vulgar)	éup
to miss	khít thēung
obscene	bàt sīi
sweetheart	wāan jai
transvestite	kàthoei
turned on/aroused	sàyīn/wāam

EXPRESSING OPINIONS
การแสดงความคิดเห็น

I feel that ...
   phōm/dì-chán rúusèuk
   wâa ...
                            ผม/ดิฉันรู้สึกว่า...

I think that ...
   phōm/dì-chán khít wâa ...
                            ผม/ดิฉันคิดว่า...

I agree.
   hēn dûay
                            เห็นด้วย

I disagree.
   mâi hēn dûay
                            ไม่เห็นด้วย

(In) my opinion ...
   khwaam khít-hēn khāwng
   phōm/dì-chán ...
                            ความคิดเห็
นของผม/ดิฉัน

As for me ...
   sāmràp phōm/dì-chán ...
                            สำหรับผม/ดิฉัน...

(It's) not important.
   mâi sāmkhan
                            ไม่สำคัญ

LANGUAGE DIFFICULTIES
ความมญฎฎขฮงภษษษ

I can't speak Thai.
   phōm/dì-chán phûut
   phaasāa thai mâi dâi
                            ผม/ดิฉันพูดภาษาไทยไม่ได้

I can speak only a little Thai.
   phōm/dì-chán phûut
   phaasāa thai dâi nít nàwy
   thâo nán
                            ผม/ดิฉันพูดภาษาไทยได้
นิดหน่อยเท่านั้น

I can't speak Thai well.
  phŏm/dì-chăn phûut phaasăa
  thai mâi kèng
  ผม/ดิฉันพูดภาษาไทยไม่เก่ง

I don't speak very much Thai.
  phŏm/dì-chăn phûut phaasăa
  thai dâi mâi mâak
  ผม/ดิฉันพูดภาษาไทยได้
  ไม่มาก

Can you speak English?
  khun phûut phaasăa angkrìt
  dâi măi?
  คุณพูดภาษาอังกฤษได้ไหม

A little.
  nít nàwy
  นิดหน่อย

I speak ...
  phŏm/dì-chăn phûut
  phaasăa ...
  ผม/ดิฉันพูดภาษา...

Please speak slowly.
  kawrúnaa phûut cháa-cháa
  nàwy
  กรุณาพูดช้าๆหน่อย

Please repeat.
  phûut ìik thii sí
  พูดอีกทีซิ

Sorry, I don't understand.
  khăw thôht phŏm/dì-chăn
  mâi khâo jai
  ขอโทษผม/ดิฉันไม่เข้าใจ

(I) don't understand.
  mâi khâo jai
  ไม่เข้าใจ

Do you understand?
  khun khâo jai măi?
  คุณเข้าใจไหม

What?
  á-rai ná?
  อะไรนะ

What did you say?
  khun phûut wâa à-rai?
  คุณพูดว่าอะไร

Can you teach me Thai?
  khun săwn phaasăa thai hâi
  phŏm/dì-chăn dâi măi?
  คุณสอนภาษาไทยให้
  ผม/ดิฉันได้ไหม

What do you call this in Thai?
  níi phaasăa thai rîak wâa à-rai?
  นี่ภาษาไทยเรียกว่าอะไร

DOPE

fin	opium
kanchaa	marijuana
khîi yaa	addicted/addict (slang)
mǔu (pork)	heroin (slang)
néua (beef)	marijuana (slang)
phíi néua	smoke pot (slang)
phŏng khǎo	heroin
yaa kheh	cocaine
yaa love; ii	ecstasy
yaa máa (horse medicine);	amphetamines (slang)
yaa bâa (crazy medicine)	
yaa sèhp tìt	addictive drugs

GETTING AROUND   ไปเที่ยว

FINDING YOUR WAY   ถามเส้นทาง

Excuse me, can you help me?
khǎw thôht chûay phǒm/
dì-chǎn dâi mǎi?
ขอโทษช่วยผม/
ดิฉันได้ไหม

I want to go to ...
phǒm/dì-chǎn yàak pai ...
ผม/ดิฉันอยากไป...

I'm looking for ...
phǒm/dì-chǎn hǎa ...
ผม/ดิฉันหา...

Is it far from/near here?
yùu klai jàak thîi nîi mǎi?
อยู่ไกลจากที่นี่ไหม

Can we walk there?
doen pai dâi mǎi?
เดินไปได้ไหม

Can you show me the way?
bàwk thaang hâi rúu dâi mǎi?
บอกทางให้รู้ได้ไหม

Are there other means of getting there?
mii ìik thaang pai mǎi?
มีอีกทางไปไหม

Where's the ...	... yùu thîi nǎi?	...อยู่ที่ไหน
bus station	sathǎanii khǒn sòng	สถานีขนส่ง
bus stop	thîi jàwt rót	ที่จอดรถประจำ
	pràjam thaang;	ทาง;
	pâai rót meh	ป้ายรถเมล์
map	phaen thîi	แผนที่
railway station	sathǎanii rót fai	สถานีรถไฟ
taxi stand	thîi jàwt rót tháek-sîi	ที่จอดรถแท็กซี่

Which ... is this?	thîi nîi ... a-rai?	ที่นี่...อะไร
alley	tràwk	ตรอก
city	meuang	เมือง
lane (soi)	sawy	ซอย
province	jang-wàt	จังหวัด
street	thanǒn	ถนน
village	mùu bâan	หมู่บ้าน

GETTING AROUND

When will the ... leave?	... jà àwk mêua-rai?	...จะออกเมื่อไร
aeroplane	khrêuang bin	เครื่องบิน
air-conditioned bus	rót ae	รถแอร์
boat	reua	เรือ
minivan	rót tûu	รถตู้
(ordinary) bus	rót thammadaa	รถธรรมดา
train	rót fai	รถไฟ

DIRECTIONS   ทิศทาง

Excuse me, I'm looking for ...
    khǎw thôht phǒm/dì-chǎn hǎa ...
    ขอโทษผม/ดิฉันหา...

Turn ...	líaw ...	เลี้ยว...
left	sáai	ซ้าย
right	khwǎa	ขวา

Straight ahead.	trong pai	ตรงไป
Turn around.	thawy klàp	ถอยกลับ
Turn back (return).	klàp	กลับ

How far?	klai thâo rai?	ไกลเท่าไร

How many kilometres from here?
    kìi ki-loh-mêt jàak thîi níi?   กี่กิโลเมตรจากที่นี่

east	thít tàwan àwk	ทิศตะวันออก
(not) far	(mâi) klai	(ไม่) ไกล
(not) near	(mâi) klâi	(ไม่) ใกล้
north	thít něua	ทิศเหนือ
north-east	thít tàwan àwk chǐang něua	ทิศตะวันออกเฉียง เหนือ
south	thít tâi	ทิศใต้
south-west	thít tàwan tòk chǐang tâi	ทิศตะวันออกเฉียงใต้
west	thít tàwan tòk	ทิศตะวันออก

ADDRESSES

Many Thai street addresses show a string of numbers divided by slashes and hyphens, for example 48/3-5 Soi 1, Thanon Sukhumvit. This is because undeveloped property is originally bought and sold in lots. The number before the slash (tháp in Thai) refers to the original lot number; the numbers following the slash indicate buildings (or entrances to buildings) constructed within that lot. The pre-slash numbers appear in the order in which they were added to city plans, while the post-slash numbers are arbitrarily assigned by developers. As a result numbers along a given street don't always run consecutively.

The Thai word thanŏn is used for any large thoroughfare; so you may see thanŏn ratchadamnoen referred to as Ratchadamnoen Rd, St or Ave.

A Soi (pronounced sawy) is a small street or lane that runs off a larger street. In our example, the address referred to as 48/3-5 Soi 1, Thanon Sukhumvit will be located off Sukhumvit Rd on Soi 1. Alternative ways of writing the same address include 48/3-5 Sukhumvit Rd Soi 1, or even just 48/3-5 Sukhumvit 1. Some Sois have become so large that they are also called a thanŏn.

Smaller than a Soi is a Trok (pronounced tràwk) or alley.

48/3-5 Soi 1, Sukhumvit Rd
sìi-sìp-pàet tháp săam
théung hâa sawy nèung
thanŏn sùkhumwit

สี่สิบแปดทับสาม
ถึงห้าซอยหนึ่ง
ถนนสุขุมวิท

GETTING AROUND

BUYING TICKETS

ซื้อตั๋ว

How many departures are there ...?	... mii kìi thîaw?	...มีกี่เที่ยว
today	wan níi	วันนี้
tomorrow	phrûng níi	พรุ่งนี้

Where can I buy a ticket?	séu tǔa thîi nǎi?	ซื้อตั๋วที่ไหน
I'd like a ticket.	yàak dâi tǔa	อยากได้ตั๋ว
Are there any tickets to ...?	mii tǔa pai ...?	อยากได้ตั๋ว วสองใบมีตั๋วไป...
We want to go to ...	yàak pai ...	อยากไป...

How much per place/seat/berth
thîi-lá thâo rai? ที่ละเท่าไร

Do I need to book?
tâwng jawng thîi nâng ต้องจองที่นั่งก่อนไหม
kàwn mǎi?

I'd like to book a seat to ...
yàak jawng thîi nâng อยากจองที่นั่งไป...
pai ...

We'd like to reserve ... places/seats/berths.
rao yàak jà jawng thîi เราอยากจองที่นั่ง...ที่
nâng ... thîi

It's full.
tem láew; mòt láew เต็มแล้ว

I'd like to change my ticket.
yàak plìan tǔa อยากเปลี่ยนตั๋ว

I'd like a refund on my ticket.
yàak kheun tǔa อยากคืนตั๋ว

Sorry, I've changed my mind.
khǎw thôht plìan ขอโทษเปลี่ยนใจแล้ว
jai láew

I'd like ...	phǒm/dì-chǎn yàak dâi ...	ผม/ดิฉันอยากได้...
a one-way ticket	tǔa thîaw diaw	ตั๋วเที่ยวเดียว
a return ticket	tǔa pai klàp	ตั๋วไป–กลับ
two tickets	tǔa sǎwng bai	ตั๋วสอ๋ใบ

1st class	chán nèung	ชั้นหนึง
2nd class	chán sǎwng	ชั้นสอง
3rd class	chán sǎam	ชั้นสาม

In Thailand instead of stand-by tickets, there are waiting lists which you can ask to be put on.

Can I get on the waiting list?
long chêu nai wait list dâi mǎi?   ลงชื่อในเวสลิสได้ไหม

AIR   เครื่องบิน

Thai Airways International, Bangkok Airways and Angel Airways handle all domestic flights in Thailand. You can purchase domestic tickets and make reservations at airline offices or travel agencies all over the country. International flights are best handled at airline offices or travel agencies in Bangkok, Chiang Mai or Phuket, where English-speaking staff are always on hand.

What time will the plane leave?
khrêuang bin jà àwk kìi mohng?   เครื่องบินจะออกกี่โมง

aeroplane	khrêuang bin	เครื่องบิน
aeroplane tickets	tǔa khrêuang bin	ตั๋วเครื่องบิน
airline	kaan-bin	การบิน
airport	sanǎam bin	สนามบิน
departures/flights	thîaw	เที่ยว

THEY MAY SAY ...

mâi mii thîi nâng	There are no seats.
tem láew	Full.
jawng thîi nâng mâi dâi	You can't reserve a seat.
tǔa khǎai mòt láew	The tickets are sold out.
jà mii thîi nâng	Seats will be
phrûng níi	available tomorrow.

BUS   รถบัส

Various classes of buses travel all over the kingdom with great frequency. Ordinary buses are the least expensive, but slowest, since they tend to stop many times along their routes. Air-condtioned buses cost one-third to one-half more than the average ordinary bus fare but are usually faster and more comfortable. If possible, always have a look at the bus you wish to take before purchasing a ticket. The most reliable buses are those that run from the government bus stations.

Along some routes you have a choice between 2nd and 1st class Air-condtioned buses. The latter are usually newer and more comfortable. VIP buses, which travel only at night, have fewer seats (usually 24 to 30 total) than 2nd and 1st class buses so they offer extra room to recline.

How many departures are there today/tomorrow?
    wan-níi/phrûng-níi mii kìi thîaw?   วันนี้/พรุ่งนี้มีกี่เที่ยว
What time will the bus leave?
    rót jà àwk kìi mohng?   รถจะออกกี่โมง

air-conditioned bus	rót ae (rót thua)	รถ
1st class	chán nèung	ชั้นหนี
government bus station	sathãanii baw khãw sãw	สถานีบ.ข.ส.
ordinary bus	rót thamadaa	รถธรรมดา
2nd class	chán sãwng	ชั้นสอง
VIP bus	rót nawn (rót wii-ai-phii)	รถ (รถวีไอพี)

REMEMBER

End your sentence with the politening syllable khráp (if you're male) or khâ (if you're female) (see page39).

TRAIN
รถไฟ

Thailand has an extensive rail network. Third class seats are cheaper than ordinary buses but are available only on the slow, ordinary trains. Second class seating costs about the same as a 1st-class air-conditioned bus, but is much more spacious.

First and second-class sleeping berths are available on long-distance rapid and express trains. In 2nd class, upper berths are smaller and less expensive than lower berths.

What time will the train leave?
    rót jà àwk kìi mohng?   รถจะออกกี่โมง
What time will the train arrive?
    rót jà thĕung kìi mohng?   รถจะถึงกี่โมง?

express train	rót dùan	รถด่วน
lower	lâang	ล่าง
ordinary train	rót thammadaa	รถธรรมดา
rapid train	rót rehw	รถเร็ว
sleeper	rót nawn	รถนอน
sleeping berth	thîi nawn	ที่นอน
stationmaster	naai sathăanii	นายสถานี
train station	sathăanii rót fai	สถานีรถไฟ

TAXI
แท็กซี่

Bangkok has both metered and non-metered auto taxis. With non-metered taxis you'll have to bargain for the fare.

In other towns in Thailand there are very few auto taxis for city travel, but share taxis, long-distance taxis in which four to seven passengers (depending on the size of the auto) pay separate fares to a common destination, may be available. Share taxi fares are set, so bargaining usually isn't necessary.

taxi	rót tháek-sîi	รถแท็กซี่
metered taxi	tháek-sîi mii-toe	แท็กซี่มิเตอร์
Turn on the meter.	pòet mii-toe	เปิดมิเตอร์
How much to ...?	pai ... thâo rai?	ไป...เท่าไร?

GETTING AROUND

Too expensive. How about ... baht?
  phaeng pai ... bàat dâi mãi?   แพงไป...บาทได้ไหม?
Agreed. Let's go.
  tòklong láew, pai   ตกลงแล้ว,ไป
Drive slowly please.
  kawrúnaa khàp rót cháa-cháa nàwy   กรุณาขับรถช้าๆหน่อย
Stop here.
  jàwt thîi nîi   จอดที่นี่

HIRE   จ้าง

Cars and motorcycles can be hired in most provincial capitals.
Except in Bangkok, Chiang Mai, Phuket and Hat Yai, traffic is
fairly light, though driving styles will take some getting used to.
Bicycles are a good way of getting around in smaller towns and
rural areas.

I'd like to hire a ...	phõm/dì-chãn	ผม/ดิฉันอยากเช่า...
	yàak châo ...	ยากเช่า...
car	rót yon	รถยนต์
motorcycle	rót maw-toe-sai	รถมอเตอร์ไซค์
bicycle	rót jàkràyaan	รถจักรยาน

How much ...?	... thâo rai?	...เท่าไร?
per day	wan-lá	วันละ
per week	aathít-lá	อาทิตย์ละ
per month	deuan-lá	เดือนละ
for three days	sãam wan	สามวัน

Can you lower the price?
  lót raakhaa dâi mãi?   ลดราคาได้ไหม?
Does the price include insurance?
  raakhaa ruam pràkan mãi?   ราคารวมประกันไหม?
Can you repair it?
  sâwm dâi mãi?   ซ่อมได้ไหม?

CAR   รถยนต์

air	lom	ลม
battery	baettoerii	แบตเตอรี่
brakes	brehk;	เบรค;
	khrêuang hâam láw	เครื่องห้ามล้อ
clutch	khlát	คลัช
driver's licence	bai anúyâat khàp rót	ใบอนุญาตขับรถ
engine	khrêuang	เครื่อง
garage	ûu rót	อู่รถ
indicator	khrêuang chíi	เครื่องชี้
insurance	pràkan	ประกัน
leaded/regular	bensiin thammadaa	เบนซินธรรมคา
lights	fai	ไฟ
main road	thanŏn yài	ถนนใหญ่
mechanic	châang sâwm rót	ช่างซ่อมรถ
motor oil	náam-man khrêuang	น้ำมันเครื่อง
oil	náam-man khrêuang	น้ำมันเครื่อง
petrol (gasoline)	náam-man rót yon	น้ำมันรถยนต์
	(ben-siin)	(เบนซิน)
petrol station	pôem náam-man	ปั๊มน้ำมัน
puncture	rûa	รั่ว
radiator	mâw náam rót	หม้อน้ำรถ
roadmap	phăen thîi thanŏn	แผนที่ถนน
seatbelt	khêm khàt niraphai	เข็มขัดนิรภัย
speed limit	kamnòt khwaam rehw	กำหนดความเร็ว
tyre	yaang rót	ยางรถ
unleaded	bensiin ráisăan	เบนซินไร้สาร
wheel	láw	ล้อ
windscreen	kràjòk bang lom	กระจกบังลม

Car Problems   ปัญหาเกี่ยวกับรถยนต์

We need a mechanic.	tâwngkaan châang	ต้องการช่าง
What make is it?	pen yîi-hâw àrai?	เป็นยี่ห้ออะไร?
The car broke	rót sĭa thîi …	รถเสียที่...
down at ...		
The battery is flat.	baettoerii sĭa	แบตเตอรี่เสีย

GETTING AROUND

The radiator is leaking.	mâw náam rót rûa	หม้อน้ำรถยนต์
I have a flat tyre.	yaang rót rûa	ยางรถรั่ว
It's overheating.	khrêuang ráwn koen pai	เครื่องร้อนเกินไป
It's not working.	mâi tham ngaan	ไม่ทำงาน
I've lost my car keys.	kunjae rót hāai	กุญแจรถหาย
I've run out of petrol.	náam man mòt	น้ำมันหมด

BICYCLE   จักรยาน

Is it within cycling distance?
thìip rót jàkràyaan thêung thîi nân dâi māi?   ถีบรถจักรยานถึงที่นั่นได้ไหม

Where can I hire a bicycle?
châo rót jàkràyaan dâi thîi nāi   เช่ารถจักรยานได้ที่ไหน

Where can I find secondhand bikes for sale?
séu rót jàkràyaan meu sāwng dâi thîi nāi   ซื้อรถจักรยานมือสองได้ที่ไหน

I've got a flat tyre.
yaang rûa   ยางรั่ว

How much is it for ...?	... thâo rai?	...เท่าไร
an hour	nèung chûa mohng	หนึ่งชั่วโมง
the morning	tawn cháo	ตอนเช้า
afternoon	tawn baai	ตอนบ่าย
the day	nèung wan	หนึ่งวัน

bike	rót jàkràyaan	รถจักรยาน
brakes	bréhk	เบรค
to cycle	thìip rót jàkràyaan	ถีบรถจักรยาน
gear stick	dâam kia	ด้ามเกียร์
handlebars	meu thêu	มือถือ
helmet	mùak niraphai	หมวกนิรภัย
inner tube	yaang nai	ยางใน

lights	fai	ไฟ
mountain bike	rót jàkràyaan sǎmràp khêun khǎo	รถจักรยานสำ หรับขึ้นเขา
padlock	kunjae	กุญแจ
pump	khrêuang sùup	เครื่องสูบ
puncture	rûa; jàw	รั่ว,เจาะ
racing bike	rót jàkràyaan bàep wîng khàeng	รถจักรยานแบบ วิ่งแข่
saddle	thîi nâng	ที่นั่ง
tyre	yaang	ยาง
wheel	láw	ล้อ

BOAT   เรือ

River, lagoon, gulf, sea and canal transport is plentiful in the kingdom. One of the most common types of craft along rivers, canals and coastal waterways is the reua hǎang yao or 'longtail boat', a vessel named for the lengthy propeller shaft extending from its engine. The motor itself, which varies from a small marine engine to a large car engine, is mounted on gimbals and the whole unit is swivelled to steer the boat.

boat	reua	เรือ
boat taxi (hire boat)	reua jâang	เรือจ้าง
Chinese junk	reua sǎm phao	เรือสำเภา
cross-river ferry	reuan khâam fâak	เรือข้ามฟาก
express boat	reua dùan	เรือด่วน
longtail boat	reua hǎang yao	เรือหางยาว
sampan	reua sǎmpân	เรือสำปั้น

Where do we get on the boat?
  long reua thîi nǎi?   ลงเรือที่ไหน
What time does the boat leave?
  reua jà àwk kìi mohng?   เรือจะออกกี่โมง
What time does the boat arrive?
  reua jà thěung kìi mohng?   เรือจะถึงกี่โมง

SONGTHAEWS, SAMLORS & TUK-TUKS
สองแถว,สามล้อ & ตุ๊กตุ๊ก

Outside Bangkok, the most common form of public city transport is the songthaew (sǎwng-thǎew), literally 'two rows'. These are trucks, usually small Japanese pickups, with two parallel benches in the back where passengers sit. A third, middle row may be improvised from tiny wooden stools.

Often there are two kinds of songthaews in the same town: the rót pràjam which run along regular routes like buses and the rót mǎo which must be chartered for each trip. On the rót pràjam you pay a flat per person fare while for a rót mǎo you must negotiate a fee.

The samlor, sǎam-láw, literally 'three wheels', is a pedicab in which one or two passengers ride in a small carriage behind the front half of a bicycle. Some cities, like Hua Hin, have standard, posted samlor fares, but in most places you must negotiate the fare.

A túk-túk, named for the sound of its two-stroke engine, is a motorised, somewhat larger version of the samlor that can carry three to eight passengers, depending on the size of the vehicle (and the passengers!). Typically you must negotiate a fare, though in some cities (Ayuthaya, for example) tuk-tuks which run along regular routes may be available for set fares.

songthaew	sāwng-thǎew	สองแถว
samlor	sǎam-láw	สามล้อ
tuk-tuk	túk-túk	ตุ๊กตุ๊ก

USEFUL WORDS & PHRASES
คำและวลีที่ควรรู้

What time do we; does it leave here?
  jà àwk jàak thîi níi kìi mohng?　จะออกจากที่นี่กี่โมง?

What time do we; does it arrive there?
  jà thěung thîi nôhn kìi mohng?　จะถึงที่โน่นกี่โมง?

What time does the first vehicle leave?
  khan râek jà àwk kìi mohng?　คันแรกจะออกกี่โมง?

What time does the last vehicle (bus, songthaew, etc) leave?
  khan sùt-tháai jà àwk kìi mohng?　คันสุดท้ายจะออกกี่โมง

What's the fare?
  khâa doisǎan thâo rai?　ค่าโดยสารเท่าไร

How much per person?
  khon-lá thâo rai?　คนละเท่าไร

(I/we) don't want to charter a vehicle.
  mâi yàak mǎo rót　ไม่อยากเหมารถ

(I/we) want to charter a vehicle.
  yàak mǎo rót　อยากเหมารถ

Can you lower the price?
  lót raakhaa dâi mǎi?　ลดราคาได้ไหม

Can you lower (the price) more?
  lót ìik dâi mǎi?　ลดอีกได้ไหม

Where does the vehicle depart from?
  rót àwk jàak thîi nǎi?　รถออกจากที่ไหน

Where can we get on the vehicle?
  khêun rót thîi nǎi dâi?　ขึ้นรถที่ไหนได้

Is there anyone sitting here?
  mii khrai nâng thîi níi mǎi?　มีใครนั่งที่นี่ไหม

May I sit here?
  nâng thîi níi dâi mǎi?　นั่งที่นี่ได้ไหม

Can I put my bag here?
  waang kràpǎo thîi níi dâi mǎi?　วางกระเป๋าที่นี่ได้ไหม

Can you wait for me?
  khawy phŏm/dì-chān dâi măi?　　คอยผม/ดิฉันได้ไหม
Can you wait here?
  khawy thîi nîi dâi măi?　　คอยที่นี่ได้ไหม
Where are you going?
  pai năi?　　ไปไหน
I want to go to ...
  phŏm/dì-chān yàak pai ...　　ผม/ดิฉันอยากไป
I'll get out here.
  phŏm/dì-chān jà long thîi nîi　　ผม/ดิฉันจะลงที่นี่
Which vehicle goes to ...?
  rót năi pai ...?　　รถไหนไป...
When the vehicle arrives in ... please tell me.
  mêua thĕung ...　　เมื่อถึง...
  kawrúnaa bàwk dûay　　กรุณาบอกด้วย
Can we stop over in ...?
  long phák thîi ... dâi măi?　　ลงพักที่นี่ได้ไหม

to arrive	thĕung	ถึง
bridge	saphaan	สะพาน
bypass	thaang âwm	ทางอ้อม
charter vehicle	rót măo	รถเหมา
coast	fàng thaleh	ฝั่งทะเล
daily	pràjam wan (thúk wan)	ประจำวัน
detour	thaang biang	ทางเบี่ยง
drive	khàp	ขับ
early	cháo	เช้า
express	dùan	ด่วน
hire	jâang	จ้าง
leave	àwk	ออก
pier/dock	thâa reua	ท่าเรือ
rapid	rehw	เร็ว
seat	thîi nâng	ที่นั่ง
slow	cháa	ช้า
stop/park	jàwt	จอด
truck	rót banthúk	รถบรรทุก

ACCOMMODATION

ที่พัก

ACCOMMODATION

FINDING ACCOMMODATION   การหาที่พัก

Thailand has a large and varied choice of places to stay. Standard, old-fashioned Thai-Chinese hotels are usually found on main streets near bus or train stations. Newer, more expensive hotels may be on the outskirts of town. Traditionally, a 'single' means a room with one large bed that will sleep two, while a 'double' has two large beds. The price is usually set according to the number of beds a room has, not the number of people who will be using it. On the other hand, at newer Western-style hotels rates increase according to the number of guests per room.

An 'ordinary room' (hâwng thamadaa) usually means a less expensive room with a fan rather than with air-conditioning.

In areas where backpackers and budget travellers congregate you'll find inexpensive family-run guesthouses. Guesthouses are often good places for picking up information from fellow travellers, but are usually not so good for practising Thai or absorbing local culture.

Whether at hotels or guesthouses, rates for room rates may be negotiable for long-term stays or during the tourist low season.

In villages where there are no hotels or guesthouses you may be able to stay with local residents. Sometimes this entails money, sometimes not, but you should always offer a useful gift, such as food or something needed in the household, to your host family.

Excuse me, is there a hotel nearby?
    khăw thôht mii rohng raem klâi thîi nîi măi?
ขอโทษมีโรงแรมใกล้ที่นี่ไหม
Is this a hotel?
    nîi rohng raem châi măi?   นี่โรงแรมใช่ไหม
Is this a guesthouse?
    nîi bâan phák châi măi?   นี่บ้านพักใช่ไหม

73

ACCOMODATION

Is there a place to stay here?
mii thîi phák thîi nîi mãi?   มีที่พักที่นี่ไหม
We need a place to stay.
rao tâwng-kaan thîi phák   เราต้องการที่พัก
Can (I/we) stay here?
phák thîi nîi dâi mãi?   พักที่นี่ได้ไหม
Can (I/we) sleep here?
nawn thîi nîi dâi mãi?   นอนที่นี่ได้ไหม

guesthouse	bâan phák (kèt háo)	บ้านพัก (เกสต์เฮ้าส์)
hotel	rohng raem	โรงแรม

BOOKING AHEAD   จองล่วงหน้า

I'd like to book a room.
yàak jawng hâwng   อยากจองห้อง
Do you have any rooms available?
mii hâwng wâang mãi?   มีห้องว่างไหม?

How much for ...?	... thâo rai?	...เท่าไร?
one night	nèung kheun (kheun diaw)	หนึ่งคืน(คืนเดียว)
three nights	sãam kheun	สามคืน
a week	nèung aathít (aathít diaw)	หนึ่งอาทิตย์ (อาทิตย์เดียว)
two people	sãwng khon	สองคน
a month	deuan-lá	เดือนละ

We will be arriving at ...	jà thĕung ...	จะถึง...
My name is ...	phõm/ dì-chãn chêu ...	ผม/ดิฉันชื่อ...

ACCOMMODATION

AT THE HOTEL
Checking In

การลงทะเบียนเข้าพัก

Do you have a room?		
	mii hâwng wâang măi?	มีห้องว่างไหม
How many people?	kìi khon?	กี่คน
one person	nèung khon	หนึ่งคน
	(khon diaw)	(คนเดียว)
two people	săwng khon	สองคน
How much ...?	... thâo rai?	...เท่าไร
per night	kheun-lá	คืนละ
per week	aathít-lá	อาทิตย์ละ
for three nights	săam kheun	สามคืน
Too expensive.		
	phaeng pai	แพงไป
(I/we) will stay two nights.		
	jà phák săwng kheun	จะพักสองคืน

WHAT?

When forming a question, avoid the normal English tonal
patterns used to indicate a question. In Thai, question tags
alone signify the interrogative. Resist the urge to alter the
tone of the final word in the system to conform to the
English question tones (which differ from country to country, but always interfere with Thai comprehension).

so say ...	rót fai jà àwk kii mohng?
	(lit: train will leave what time)
not	rót fai jà àwk kii mŏhng?

The one exception to this is the question word for 'where'
(năi), which features a rising tone Thai, very much like
the question tone used by some English speakers.

ACCOMODATION

Can you lower the price?
  lót raakhaa dâi mãi?   ลดราคาได้ไหม
Can (I/we) look at the room?
  duu hâwng dâi mãi?   ดูห้องได้ไหม
Do you have any other rooms?
  mii hâwng ìik mãi?   มีห้องอีกไหม
(I/we) want an ordinary room.
  ao hâwng thamadaa   เอาห้องธรรมดา

We need a ...	rao tâwng-kaan	เราต้องการห้อง...นี้
room than this.	hâwng ... níi	
cheaper	thùuk-kwàa	ถูกกว่า
larger	yài-kwàa	ใหญ่กว่า
smaller	lék-kwàa	เล็กกว่า
quieter	ngîap-kwàa	เงียบกว่า

Useful Words

air-conditioning	pràp aakàat (ae)	ปรับอากาศ
bathroom	hâwng náam	ห้องน้ำ
fan	phát lom	พัดลม
hot water	náam ráwn	น้ำร้อน
not vacant	mâi wâang	ไม่ว่าง
room	hâwng	ห้อง
toilet	sûam	ส้วม
vacant	wâang	ว่าง

CHECK

It's a good idea to look at a room before checking in. To make sure you get what you're paying for, check to see that the air-conditioning and hot water work if your room is supposed to come with these amenities.

REQUESTS & COMPLAINTS
ความต้องการ & การบ่น

Is there a/any ...?	mii ... mãi?	มี...ไหม
hot water	náam ráwn	น้ำร้อน
telephone	thohrásàp	โทรศัพท์

(I/we) need (a) ...	tâwng-kaan ...	ต้องการ...
another bed	tiang ìik	เตียงอีก
blanket	phâa hòm	ผ้าห่ม
pillow	mãwn	หมอน
sheet	phâa puu thîi nawn	ผ้าปูที่นอน
soap	sabùu	สบู่
towel	phâa chêht tua	ผ้าเช็ดตัว

Can you clean the room?
tham khwaam-sa-àat
hâwng dâi mãi?
ทำความสะอาดห้องได้ไหม

This room isn't clean.
hâwng níi mâi sa-àat
ห้องนี้ไม่สะอาด

There is no hot water.
mâi mii náam ráwn
ไม่มีน้ำร้อน

Can you repair it?
sâwm dâi mãi?
ซ่อมได้ไหม

CHECKING OUT   เช็คเอ็าท์

Can I pay with a travellers cheque?
jaai pen chék doen
thaang dâi mãi?
จ่ายเป็นเช็คเดินทางได้ไหม

Bring the bill please.
kèp tàng dûay
เก็บตังค์ด้วย

There's a mistake in the bill.
bin phìt láew
บิลผิดแล้ว

(I/we) will return in two weeks.
ìik sãwng aathít jà klàp
อีกสองอาทิตย์จะกลับ

Can I store my bags here?
fàak kràbão wái
ฝากกระเป๋าไว้ที่นี่ได้ไหม

ACCOMODATION

ACCOMODATION

bill (check)	bin	บิล
checkout	chék-aó	เช็คเอ๊าท์
receipt	bai sèht ráp ngoen	ใบเสร็จรับเงิน
service charge	khâa bawrikaan	ค่าบริการ
tax	phaa-si	ภาษี

LAUNDRY   บริการซักรีด

Can you wash these clothes?
  sák sêua phâa níi dâi mãi?   ซักเสื้อผ้านี้ได้ไหม
Where can I wash my clothes (myself)?
  phõm/dì-chán sák sêua   ผม/ดิฉันซักเสื้อผ้าเองได้ที่ไหน
  phâa ehng dâi thîi nãi?

| No starch. | mâi long pâeng | ไม่ลงแป้ง |
| Add starch. | long pâeng | ลงแป้ง |

Is there a laundry service near here?
  mii bawrikaan sák   มีบริการซักรีดใกล้ที่นี่ไหม
  rîit klâi thîi nîi mãi?
These clothes aren't very clean.
  sêua phâa níi mâi sa-àat thâo rai   เสื้อผ้านี้ไม่สะอาดเท่าไร
Please wash (them) again.
  karúnaa sák ìik thii   กรุณาซักอีกที

dry clean	sák hâeng	ซักแห้ง
an iron	tao rîit	เตารีด
to iron	rîit	รีด
laundry service	bawrikaan sák rîit	บริการซักรีด

BATHROOMS

Cheaper hotels and some guesthouses may not put towels or soap in the room, but if you ask for them they are usually cheerfully supplied.

USEFUL WORDS

accommodation	thîi phák	ที่พัก
air-conditioning	pràp aakàat	ปรับอากาศ
bathe	àap náam	อาบน้ำ
bed	tiang nawn	เตียงนอน
bedroom	hâwng nawn	ห้องนอน
breakfast	aahǎan cháo	อาหารเช้า
electricity	kaan fai fáa	การไฟฟ้า
entrance	thaang khâo	ทางเข้า
exit	thaang àwk	ทางออก
fan	phát lom	พัดลม
food	aahǎan	อาหาร
key	lûuk kun-jae	ลูกกุญแจ
lift (elevator)	líf	ลิฟท์
lights	fai	ไฟ
lock	kunjae	กุญแจ
mosquito coil	yaa kan yung bàep jùt	ยากันยุงแบบจุด
soap	sabùu	สบู่
toilet	sûam	ส้วม
toilet paper	kràdàat cham-rá	กระดาษชำระ
towel	phâa chêht tua	ผ้าเช็ดตัว
water (cold/hot)	náam (yen/ráwn)	น้ำ(เย็น/ร้อน)

PAPERWORK   เอกสาร

name	chêu	ชื่อ
address	thîi yùu	ที่อยู่
date of birth	wan kòet	วันเกิด
place of birth	sathǎan thîi kòet	สถานที่เกิด
age	aayú	อายุ
sex	phêht	เพศ
nationality	sǎnchâat	สัญชาติ
religion	sàat-sa-nǎa	ศาสนา
profession/work	aachîip	อาชีพ
reason for travel	jùt pràsǒng	จุดประสงค์
marital status	sathǎaníkaan sǒmrít	สถานะการสมรส

ACCOMODATION

single	sòht	โสด
married	taeng-ngaan láew	แต่งงานแล้ว
divorced	yàa ráang	หย่าร้าง
widow/widower	phâw mâai/mâe mâai	พ่อหม้าย/แม่หม้าย
identification	bàt pràjam tua	บัตรประจำตัว
passport number	mãay-lêhk	หมายเลข
	nãng-sẽu doen thaang	หนังสือเดินทาง
visa	wii-sâa	วีซ่า
driving licence	bai ànúyâat khàp rót	ใบอนุญาตขับรถ
customs	dàan	ด่าน
immigration	khâo meuang	เข้าเมือง
purpose of visit	jùt pràsõng	จุดประสงค์
holiday	maa thîaw	มาเที่ยว
business	maa tham thúrá	มาทำธุระ
visiting relatives	maa yîam yâat	มาเยี่ยมญาติ
visiting the homeland	klâp bâan meuang	กลับบ้านเมือง

THEY MAY SAY ...

hâwng dìaw	'single room', usually one bed, for one or two people
hâwng khûu	'pair room', usually two beds, for two to four people
kìi kheun?	How many nights?
sên chêu thîi nîi	Sign here.
tèm láew	Full.

| Where's the ...? | yùu thîi nǎi? | อยู่ที่ไหน |
| How far is ...? | ... klai thâo rai? | ...ไกลเท่าไร |

I'm looking for a/the ...	phǒm/dì-chǎn hǎa ...	ผม/ดิฉันหา...
bank	thanaakhaan	ธนาคาร
barber shop	ráan tàt phǒm	ร้านตัดผม
Buddhist temple/ monastery	wát	วัด
cemetery	sùsǎan	สุสาน
church	bòht khrít	โบสถ์คริสต์
cinema	rohng phâaphayon (rohng nǎng)	โรงภาพยนตร์ (โรงหนัง)
factory	rohng ngaan	โรงงาน
monument	anú-sǎa-warii	อนุสาวรีย์
museum	phíphíthaphan	พิพิธภัณฑ์
national park	wana-ùthayaan hàeng châat	วนอุทยานแห่งชาติ
park (garden)	sǔan	สวน
post office	thîi tham-kaan praisanii	ที่ทำการไปรษณีย์
school	rohng rian	โรงเรียน
shrine (usually Chinese)	sǎan jâo	ศาลเจ้า
tourist office	sǎmnák-ngaan thâwng thîaw	สำนักงานท่องเที่ยว
Tourist Authority of Thailand	kaan thâwng thîaw hàeng pràthêt thai	การท่องเที่ยวแห่งประเทศไทย
zoo	sǔan sàt	สวนสัตว์

THEY MAY SAY ...

| yùu nôhn | It's over there (often spoken with a sweep of the arm, indicating general direction). |

AT THE BANK   ที่ธนาคาร

The basic unit of Thai currency is the baht (bàat). There are 100 satang (satàng) in 1 baht; coins include 25 satang and 50 satang pieces, plus baht in 1B, 5B and 10B coins. Paper currency comes in denominations of 10B (brown), 20B (green), 50B (blue), 100B (red), 500B (purple) and 1000B (beige) denominations. Large denominations 500B and especially 1000B bills can be hard to change in small towns.

Banks or legal moneychangers offer the best exchange rate. Automatic teller machines (ATMs) are available in every provincial capital. Most banks are open 8.30 am to 3.30 pm. A few have special foreign exchange booths open as late as 8 pm.

Plastic money has become increasingly popular in Thailand and many shops, hotels and restaurants now accept credit as well as debit cards.

I need to change money
   phõm/dì-chãn tâwng lâek ngoen   ผม/ดิฉัน
Can (I/we) change money here?
   lâek ngoen thîi nîi dâi mãi?   แลกเงินที่นี่ได้ไหม

I have ...	phõm/dì-chãn mii ...	ผม/ดิฉันมี...
US $	dawn-lâa sàhàrát	คอลลาร์สหรัฐฯ
UK £	pawn angkrìt	ปอนด์อังกฤษ
Australian $	dawn-lâa aw-satreh-lia	คอลลาร์ออสเตรเลีย
HK $	dawn-lâa hâwng kong	คอลลาร์ฮ่องกง
Deutschmarks	mâak yoe-raman	มาร์คเยอรมัน
Japanese ¥	yen yîipùn	เย็นญี่ปุ่น

What's the exchange rate?
   àtraa lâek plian thâo rai?   อัตราแลกเปลี่ยนเท่าไร
Can I get smaller change?
   khãw lâek ngoen plìik dâi mãi?   ขอแลกเงินปลีกได้ไหม
Can I use my credit card to withdraw money?
   chái bàt khrehdìt   ใช้บัตรเครดิต
   thãwn ngoen dâi mãi?   ถอนเงินได้ไหม
Please write it down.
   khĩan hâi dâi mãi?   เขียนให้ได้ไหม

The automatic teller swallowed my card.
khrêuang eh-thii-em   เครื่องเอทีเอ็ม
kin bàt láew   กินบัตรแล้ว

Can I transfer money here from my bank?
ohn ngoen jàak thánaakhaan   โอนเงินจากธนาคาร
khǎwng phǒm/dì-chǎn   ของผม/ดิฉัน
maa thîi nîi dâi mǎi?   มาที่นี่ได้ไหม

How long will it take to arrive?
chái wehlaa naan thâo   ใช้เวลานานเท่า
rai já maa thěung thîi nîi ?   ไรจะมาถึงที่นี่

money	ngoen	เงิน
change (n)	ngoen thǎwn	เงินทอน
to change	lâek plìan	แลกเปลี่ยน
cheque	chék	เช็ค
exchange rate	àtraa lâek plìan	อัตราแลกเปลี่ยน

AT THE POST OFFICE ที่ที่ทำการไปรษณีย์

Almost every town in Thailand has a post office. Most are open
Monday to Friday 8.30 am to 4.30 pm. Post offices in provincial
capitals are also open Saturdays 8.30 am to midday. A few main
offices in larger cities are also open 8.30 am to midday on Sundays
and holidays.

AROUND TOWN

Is this the post office?
nîi pen thîi-tham-kaan   นี่เป็นที่ทำการ
praisanii châi mǎi?   ไปรษณีย์ใช่ไหม

I want to send (a/an) ...	phǒm/dì-chǎn yàak sòng ...	ผม/ดิฉันอยากส่ง...
aerogram	jòt-mǎai aakàat	จดหมายอากาศ
letter	jòt-mǎai	จดหมาย
postcard	praisanii bàt	ไปรษณียบัตร
parcel	phátsàdù	พัสดุ
telegram	thohralêhk	โทรเลข

May I have (a/an/some) ...	khǎw ...	ขอ...
stamps	sataem;	แสตมป์;
	duang traa praisanii	ดวงตราไปรษณีย์
envelope	sawng jòt-mǎai	ซองจดหมาย
insurance	pràkan	ประกัน
registered receipt	bai thábian	ใบทะเบียน

How much does it cost to send this to ...?
sòng pai ... raakhaa thâo rai?   ส่งไป...ราคาเท่าไร

Send it by ...	sòng thaang ...	ส่งทาง...
air (mail)	thaang aakàat	ทางอากาศ
express (mail)	dùan	ด่วน
surface (mail)	thamadaa	ธรรมดา

This letter is going to the USA.
jòt-mǎai níi pai amerikaa   จดหมายนี้ไปอเมริกา

How much to send this letter to England?
sòng jòt-mǎai níi pai   ส่งจดหมายนี้ไปอังกฤษราคาเท่าไร
angkrìt raakhaa thâo rai?

I want to send this package by air mail.
phǒm/dì-chǎn yàak sòng   ผม/ดิฉันอยากส่งห่อนี้ทางอากาศ
hàw níi thaang aakàat

I want a registered receipt.
phǒm/dì-chǎn yàak   ผม/ดิฉันอยากได้ใบลงทะเบียน
dâai bai long thábian

I'd like four 10 baht stamps, please.
khǎw sataem duang-lá   ขอแสตมป์ดวงละสิบบาทสี่ดวง
sìp bàat sìi duang

Is there any mail for me?
mii jòt-mǎai sǎmràp   มีจดหมายสำหรับผม/ดิฉันไหม
phǒm/dì-chǎn mǎi?

My last name is ...
naam sàkun ...   นามสกุล...

to mail	sòng jòt-mǎai	ส่งจดหมาย
to register	long thábian	ลงทะเบียน

TELECOMMUNICATIONS การติดต่อสื่อสาร

The telephone system in Thailand, operated by the government subsidised Telephone Organisation of Thailand (TOT) under the Communications Authority of Thailand (CAT), is quite efficient. From Bangkok or other provincial capitals you can usually direct dial most major centres with little difficulty.

Hotels generally add surcharges (sometimes as much as 30% on top of the TOT rate) for international long-distance calls, so it's always cheaper to call abroad from a CAT telephone office. These offices are almost always attached to a city's main post office, often on the building's 2nd floor, around the side or just behind. Typically they offer international phone services daily 7 am to 10 or 11 pm. The main CAT office in Bangkok (behind the main post office on Thanon Charoen Krung) is open 24 hours.

Except for collect calls, you must estimate in advance the time you'll be on the phone and pay a deposit equal to the time/distance rate. There is always a minimum three-minute charge, refunded if your call doesn't go through.

I'd like to make an international collect call.

   phŏm/dì-chān yàak   ผม/ดิฉันอยาก
   thohrásàp ráwàang pràthêt โทรศัพท์ระหว่างประเท
   kèp plai thaang   ศเก็บปลายทาง

How much does it cost to call (name of country or city)?

   thoh pai ... raakhaa thâo rai? โทรไป...ราคาเท่าไร

I'd like to speak for 10 minutes.

   phŏm/dì-chān yàak   ผม/ดิฉันอยาก

collect (call)		
kèp plaai thaang		เก็บปลายทาง
international call	thohrásàp	โทรศัพท์ระหว่าประเทศ
	ráwàang pràthêt	
long distance	thaang klai	ทางไกล
(domestic)		
minute(s)	naa-thii	นาที
telephone	thohrásàp	โทรศัพท์

TEMPLE ARCHITECTURE

Technically speaking, a wát (from the Pali-Sanskrit avasatha or 'dwelling for pupils and ascetics') is a Buddhist compound where men or women can be ordained as monks or nuns. Virtually every village in Thailand has at least one wát, while in towns and cities they're quite numerous. Without an ordination area (designated by sěma, or stone ordination markers), a monastic centre where monks or nuns reside is simply a săm-nák sŏng (Sangha residence). The latter are often established as meditation retreat facilities in forest areas, sometimes in conjunction with larger wát pàa (forest monasteries).

The typical wát compound in Thailand will contain at the very least an uposatha, a consecrated chapel where monastic ordinations are held, and a wiháan, where important Buddha images are housed. Classic Thai wiháan and uposatha architecture usually involves a steeply pitched roof system tiled in green, gold and red and often constructed in tiered series of three levels, representing the triratna or triple gems – the Buddha, the Dhamma and the Sangha. Partial fourth and fifth tiers may also be included to shade porticoes at the front, rear or sides of the building. The front of the wiháan/uposatha, at a minimum, will feature an open veranda; often the veranda will extend around the entire perimeter of the building. Generally speaking, wát buildings in north-eastern Thailand will feature a narrower front profile, while southern Thai temples – perhaps subtly influenced by Malay or Sumatran mosque architecture, will have a broader profile.

TEMPLE ARCHITECTURE

Another classic component of temple architecture throughout the country is the presence of one or more chedi or jedi (from the Pali-Sanskrit *cetiya*), also known by the more generic term stupa, a solid cone-shaped monument that pays tribute to the enduring stability of Buddhism. Chedis come in a myriad of styles, from simple inverted bowl-shaped designs imported from Sri Lanka to the more elaborate multi-sided chedis of northern Thailand, heir to the great Thai-Lao kingdoms of Lan Na and Lan Chang (Lan Xang). Many chedis are believed to contain 'relics' (pieces of bone) belonging to the historical Buddha. In north-eastern Thailand and in Laos such chedis are known as thâat.

Other structures typically found in wát compounds include one or more sala (sǎalaa) or open-sided shelters for community meetings and Dhamma (Buddhist teachings) lectures; a number of kùti or monastic quarters; a hǎw trai or tripitaka library where Buddhist scriptures are stored; a hǎw klawng or drum tower (sometimes with a hǎw rákhang or bell tower); various chedis or stupas (the smaller squarish stupas are thâat kràdùk or bone reliquaries), where the ashes of worshippers are interred); plus various ancillary buildings – such as schools or clinics that differ from wát to wát according to local community needs. Many wát also have a hǎw phǐi wát or 'spirit house' for the temple's reigning earth spirit.

Making a Call   โทรศัพท์

Hello, is ... there?	hello, ... yùu mǎi?	ฮัลโหล...อยู่ไหม
Hello? (answering a call)	hello?	ฮัลโหล
I'd like to speak to ...	khǎw phûut kàp ...	ขอพูดกับ...
Who's calling?	jàak nǎi?	จากไหน
It's ...	jàak ...	จาก...
Yes, he/she is here.	yùu	อยู่
One moment, (please).	raw sàk khrûu	รอสักครู่

I'm sorry, he's not here.
   khǎw thôht, mâi yùu   ขอโทษ,ไม่อยู่
What time will she be back?
   jà klàp mêua rai?   จะกลับเมื่อไร
Can I leave a message?
   fàak khâw khwaam dâi mǎi?   ฝากข้อความได้ไหม
Please tell her I called.
   kawrúnaa bàwk wâa phǒm/   กรุณาบอกว่าผม/
   dì-chǎn thohrásàp maa hǎa khǎo   ดิฉันโทรศัพท์มาหาเขา
I'll call back later.
   phǒm/dì-chǎn jà   ผม/ดิฉันจะโ
   thohrásàp maa mài   ทรศัพท์มาใหม่

SIGNS

HOT/COLD	RÁWN/YEN	ร้อน/เย็น
ENTRANCE	THAANG KHÂO	ทางเข้า
EXIT	THAANG ÀWK	ทางออก
NO ENTRY	HÂAM KHÂO	ห้ามเข้า
NO SMOKING	NGÓT SÙUP BÙRII	งดสูบบุหรี่
OPEN/CLOSED	PÒET/PÌT	เปิด/ปิด
PROHIBITED	HÂAM	ห้าม
TOILETS	HÂWNG SÙAM	ห้องส้วม

FIRE IN THE LOTUS

Over the centuries, traditional Thai artists have taken the principle drama in Theravada Buddhism – the overcoming or taming of human passions via the practice of Buddhism – and made it an integral part of the artistic outcome. Buddhism offers a way to cool the passions through the practice of morality and mental development, an effect that if followed to conclusion will result in the extinguishing of that fire, the defeat of the existential angst produced by the human condition.

In its most simple artistic manifestation, the cooling effect of Buddhism is represented by the lotus, a motif seen throughout Thai Buddhist art, from such obvious examples as the lotus seat upon which Buddha figures sit to the less obvious lotus-bud shapes at the tip of classical Sukhothai chedis.

Less obvious still are the many shapes that combine the lotus bud motif with that of a flame to produce a unitary symbol – a peculiarly Thai innovation that brings human fire into contact with Buddhist cool. You can find this motif everywhere in Thai Buddhist art, and even in much traditional secular art, from the gold-leaf prints dotting lacquered temple walls to the unfurling tails of the kinnari and other mythical creatures painted into murals or standing in sculpted form on wiháan porticoes. Even the Buddha's ushnisha – the flame atop the head, representing in this case both the burning out of the passions and the light of self realisation – in Thai sculpture often features aspects of the lotus bud.

Look closely at some of the most common prints found on traditional cotton pháasin, the sarong once universally worn by Thai women and still worn by some in rural Thailand, and you'll see perhaps dozens of variations on this simple but highly evocative motif.

Fax & Telegraph

แฟ็ก & โทรเลข

CAT telephone offices (often attached to post offices) throughout the country offer fax and telegraph services in addition to the regular phone service. There's no need to bring your own paper, as the post offices supply their own forms. A few TOT offices also have fax services.

Larger hotels with business centres offer the same telecommunication services but always at higher rates.

How much per page?	phàen-lá thâo rai?	แผ่นละเท่าไร
How much per word?	kham-lá thâo rai?	คำละเท่าไร
fax	fáek/thohrásǎan	แฟ็กซ์/โทรสาร
telegraph	thorálêhk	โทรเลข

Internet

อินเตอร์เน็ต

Is there a local Internet centre/café?
thǎew níi mii sǔn intoe-net mǎi?
แถวนี้มีศูนย์อินเตอร์เนตไหม

I need to get Internet access.
phǒm/dì-chǎn tâwng khâo intoe-net
ผม/ดิฉันต้อเข้าอินเตอร์เนต

I need to check my email.
phǒm/dì-chǎn tâwng chék email
ผม/ดิฉันอยากต้อเช็คอีเมล์

Sightseeing

ไปเที่ยวดูสถานที่ต่างๆ

Where is the tourist office?
sǎmnák-ngaan tháwng thîaw yùu thîi nǎi?
สำนักงานท่อเที่ยวอยู่ที่ไหน

Do you have a local map?
mii phǎen thîi meuang mǎi?
มีแผนที่เมือไหม

I'd like to see ...
... yàak jà duu
...อยากจะด

What time does it open?
jà pòet kìi mohng?
จะเปิดกี่โมง

What time does it close?
jà pìt kìi mohng?   จะปิดกี่โมง

What is that building?
nán tèuk àrai?   นั่นตึกอะไร

What is this monument?
nîi aanúsǎawarii àrai?   นี่อนุสาวรีย์อะไร

May we take photographs?
thàai rûup dâi mǎi?   ถ่ายรูปได้ไหม

I'll send you the photograph.
phǒm/dì-chǎn jà sòng rûup maa   ผม/ดิฉันจะส่งรูปมา

Could you take a photograph of me?
thàai rûup hâi phǒm/   ถ่ายรูปให้ผม/
dì-chǎn dâi mǎi?   ดิฉันได้ไหม

Buddhist temple/ monastery	wát	วัด
cinema	rohng phâaphayon	โรงภาพยนตร์
concert	kaan sadāeng dontrii	การแสดงดนตรี
crowded	khon nâen	คนแน่น
temple ruins	wát ráang	วัดร้าง
statue	rûup salàk	รูปสลัก
university	mahǎawítháyálai	มหาวิทยาลัย

COMMON INTERESTS
การเอาใจใส่เบื้องต้น

What do you do in your spare time?
châwp tham àrai wehlaa wâang?
ชอบทำอะไรเวลาว่าง?

I like ...	châwp ...	ชอบ...
I don't like ...	mâi châwp ...	ไม่ชอบ...
Do you like ...?	châwp ... mãi?	ชอบ...ไหม?
films	duu phâaphayon	ดูภาพยนตร์
	(duu nãng)	(ดูหนัง)
hiking	doen pàa	เดินป่า
music	fang dontrii	ฟังดนตรี
playing soccer	lên fút-bawn	เล่นฟุตบอล
playing sport	lên kiilaa	เล่นกีฬา
reading books	àan nãng sẽu	อ่านหนังสือ
shopping	sẽu khãwng	ซื้อของ
travelling	doen thaang	เดินทาง
watching TV	duu thii-wii	ดูทีวี
art	sìlàpà	ศิลปะ
dancing	tên ram	เต้นรำ
cooking	tham aahãan	ทำอาหาร
drawing	wâat rûup	วาดรูป
painting	khĩan rûup	เขียนรูป
photography	thàai rûu	ถ่ายรูป
the theatre	lákhawn	ละคร
sewing	yèp phâa	เย็บผ้า
writing	khĩan	เขียน

SPORT
กีฬา

Do you like sport?	châwp kiilaa mãi?	ชอบกีฬาไหม?
I like playing sport	châwp lên kiilaa	ชอบเล่นกีฬา

I prefer to watch rather than play sport.
   châwp duu kiilaa mâak   ชอบดูกีฬามาก
   kwàa lên kiilaa   กว่าเล่นกีฬา
Do you play ...?
   lên … mǎi?   เล่น...ไหม?
Would you like to play ...?
   yàak lên … mǎi?   อยากเล่น...ไหม?

Useful Words

baseball	beht-bawn	เบสบอล
basketball	bae-sakèt-bawn	บาสเกตบอล
cricket	khrík-kit	คริกเกต
diving	dam náam	ดำน้ำ
football	fút-bawn amehlikan	ฟุตบอลอเมริกัน
gymnastics	kaai kam	กายกรรม
hockey	hawkîi	ฮอกกี้
international boxing	muay sǎakon	มวยสากล
keeping fit	àwk kamlang kaai	ออกกำลังกาย
martial arts	muay	มวย
rugby	rák-bii	รักบี้
soccer	fút-bawn	ฟุตบอล
surfing	tham soef	กระดานโต้คลื่น
swimming	wâai náam	ว่ายน้ำ
skiing	sàkii	สกี
takraw	tàkrâw	ตะกร้อ
tennis	tennit	เทนนิส
Thai boxing	muay thai	มวยไทย

FAMILY

ครอบครัว

Thailand is a very family-oriented society so questions about family are quite common. If you are asked about your plans concerning marriage and children, it is customary to use the Thai for 'not yet' rather than 'never' or 'no way'!

Thai has no specific word for 'cousin' – to refer to this relationship, preface the appropriate Thai word for aunt or uncle with lûuk khǎwng (child of).

How many brothers and sisters do you have?
mii phîi-náwng kěi khon?   มีพี่น้องกี่คน?
I have ... brothers and sisters.
mii phîi-náwng ... khon   มีพี่น้อง...คน
Are you married (yet)?
tàeng-ngaan láew rěu yang?   แต่งงานแล้วหรือยัง?
Yes, I'm married.   tàeng láew   แต่งแล้ว
Not yet.   yang mâi tàeng-ngaan   ยังไม่แต่งงาน
(I'm) single.   pen sòht   เป็นโสด
Do you have any children (yet)?
mii lûuk láew rěu yàng?   มีลูกแล้วหรือยัง?
Not yet.
yang mâi mii lûuk   ยังไม่มีลูก
I have ... child/children.
mii lûuk ... khon làew   มีลูก...คนแล้ว

TRADITIONAL MUSIC

Throughout Thailand you'll find a wide variety of musical genres and styles, from the serene court music that accompanies classical dance-drama to the chest-thumping house music played at Bangkok's latest discos. Even in Thai monasteries – where music is proscribed by the vinaya or monastic discipline – the chanting of the monks exhibits musical qualities.

Traditional Music

Classical Central Thai music is spicy, like Thai food, and features an incredible array of textures and subtleties, hair-raising tempos and pastoral melodies.

The classical orchestra is called the pìi-phâat, which might include as few as five players or more than 20. Among the more common instruments is the pìi, a woodwind instrument which has a reed mouthpiece; it is heard prominently at Thai boxing matches. The pìi is a relative of a similar Indian instrument, while the phin, a stringed instrument whose name comes from the Indian *vina*, is considered native to Thailand. A bowed instrument, similar to ones played in China and Japan, is aptly called the saw. The ranâat èk is a bamboo-keyed percussion instrument resembling the xylophone, while the khlui is a wooden flute.

One of the more amazing Thai instruments is the kháwng wong yài; tuned gongs arranged in a semicircle. There are also several different kinds of drums, some played with the hands,

TRADITIONAL MUSIC

some with sticks. The most important Thai percussion instrument is the tà-phon (or thon), a double-headed hand-drum that sets the tempo for the ensemble. Prior to a performance, the players make offerings of incense and flowers to the tà-phon, which is considered to be the 'conductor' of the music's spiritual content.

The pìi-phâat ensemble was originally developed to accompany classical dance-drama and shadow theatre but can be heard in straightforward performance these days, in temple fairs as well as concerts. One reason classical Thai music may sound strange to the western ear is that it does not use the tempered scale. The standard Thai scale does feature an eight-note octave but it is arranged in seven full-tone intervals, with no semi-tones. Thai scales were first transcribed by Thai-German composer Peter Feit (Phra Chen Duriyanga), who also composed Thailand's national anthem in 1932.

In the North and North-East there are several popular reed instruments with multiple bamboo pipes, which function basically like a mouth-organ. Chief among these is the khaen, which originated in Laos; when played by an adept musician it sounds like a rhythmic, churning steam organ. The funky lûuk thûng (literally 'children of the fields') or country style, which originated in the North-East, has become a favourite throughout Thailand.

Muay Thai

Muay Thai, or Thai kickboxing, is without a doubt the most popular spectator sport in Thailand and one of growing interest around the world. No one trained in any other martial art has been able to defeat a ranking Thai nák muay (fighter trained in muay thai) and many martial art aficionados consider the Thai style the ultimate in hand-to-hand fighting. On one famous occasion, Hong Kong's top five kung fu masters were dispatched in less than six and a half minutes cumulative total, all knockouts.

chá-ná	win
chók!	Come out fighting! (spoken by the referee at the beginning of each round)
faai daeng	red corner
faai náam ngoen	blue corner
kamakaan	referee
khanãen	score
khào	knee
mòt yók	end of a round
náwk-áo	knockout
ram muay	'kickboxing dance', the ritualised series of gestures and body movements performed by each boxer in rhythm to the ringside musical accompaniment before a match begins
sanãam muay	boxing stadium
sàwk	elbow
tàwy	punch
tè	kick
weh-thii	ring
yók	round

Kinship Terms

การลำดับญาติ

relatives	yâat	ญาติ
family	khrâwp krua	ครอบครัว
child/children	lûuk	ลูก
daughter	lûuk săo	ลูกสาว
son	lûuk chaai	ลูกชาย
younger sister	náwng săo	น้องสาว
younger brother	náwng chaai	น้องชาย
older sister	phîi săo	พี่สาว
older brother	phîi chaai	พี่ชาย
parents	phâw-mâe	พ่อแม่
mother	mâe	แม่
father	phâw	พ่อ
husband	săami	สามี
wife	phanráya	ภรรยา
aunt/uncle (father's younger sister/ brother)	aa	อา
aunt/uncle (mother's younger sister/brother)	náa	น้า
aunt (older sister of either parent)	pâa	ป้า
uncle (older brother of either parent)	lung	ลุง
grandfather (father's side)	pùu	ปู่
grandfather (mother's side)	taa	ตา
grandmother (father's side)	yâa	ย่า
grandmother (mother's side)	yaai	ยาย
elder sibling	phîi	พี่
younger sibling	náwng	น้อง
niece/nephew	lăan	หลาน

FAMILY & INTERESTS

SPIRIT HOUSES

Every Thai house or building has to have a spirit house to go with it – a place for the spirits of the site (phrá phum), to live in. Without this vital structure you're likely to have the spirits living in the house with you, which can cause all sorts of trouble. A spirit house looks rather like a birdhouse-sized Thai temple mounted on a pedestal – at least your average spirit house does. A big hotel may have a shrine covering 100 sq metres or more.

How do you ensure that the spirits take up residence in your spirit house rather than in the main house with you? Mainly by making the spirit house a more auspicious place to live in than the main building, through daily offerings of food, flowers, candles and incense. The spirit house should also have a prominent location and should not be shaded by the main house. Thus its position has to be planned from the very beginning and installed with due ceremony. If your own house is improved or enlarged then the spirit house should be as well. The local phâw khru or mâe khruu (father or mother teacher) usually presides over the initial installation as well as later improvements.

An abandoned or damaged spirit house can't simply be tossed aside like a broken appliance, left to rot or dismantled for firewood. Instead, it should be deposited against the base of a sacred banyan tree or in the corner of a sympathetic wát where benevolent spirits will watch over it.

SHOPPING การซื้อของ

BARGAINING การต่อรองราคา

Your success at shopping in Thailand will depend to a certain extent on your ability to bargain. Bargaining is common practice and will become easier the more you indulge.

Anything bought in a market should be bargained for. However, prices in department stores and most non-tourist shops are fixed. One may need to bargain hard in heavily touristed areas, since many first-time visitors pay whatever's asked, creating an artificial price zone between the local and tourist markets.

On the other hand, the Thais aren't always trying to rip you off, so use some discretion when going for the bone on a price. There's a fine line between bargaining and niggling. Getting hot under the collar over a few baht makes both seller and buyer lose face.

How much?	thâo rai?	เท่าไร
How many baht?	kìi bàat?	กี่บาท
Do you have something cheaper?		
mii thùuk-kwàa níi mãi?		มีถูกกว่านี้ไหม
The price is very high.		
raakhaa phaeng mâak		ราคาแพงมาก
I think that's too much.		
khít wâa phaeng pai		คิดว่าแพงไป
Can you bring the price down?		
lót raakhaa dâi mãi?		ลดราคาได้ไหม
Can you lower it more?	lót ìik dâi mãi?	ลดอีกได้ไหม
How about ... baht?	... bàat dâi mãi?	บาทได้ไหม
I don't have much money.		
mâi mii ngoen mâak thâo rai.		ไม่มีเงินมากเท่าไร
I won't give more than ... baht.		
hâi mâi koen ... bàat		ให้ไม่เกิน...บาท
If (I/we) buy two ...	thâa séu sãwng ...	ถ้าซื้อสอง...
(+ classifier, see page 36)	lót dâi mãi?	ลดได้ไหม

SHOPPING

The quality is not very good.
khunaphâap mâi khâwy dii ··· คุณภาพไม่ค่อยดี

What's your lowest price?
raakhaa tàm sùt thâo rai? ··· ราคาต่ำสุดเท่าไร

MAKING A PURCHASE ··· การสั่งซื้อ

Do you have any ...?	mii ... mãi?	มี...ไหม
Please give me ...	khãw ...	ขอ...
I'm looking for ...	phõm/dii-chán hãa ...	ผม/ดิฉันหา...
Do you have any more?	mii ìik mãi?	มีอีกไหม
I'd like to see another style.	khãw duu ìik bàep nèung	ขอดูอีกแบบหนึ่ง
Can I try this on?	long sài dâi mãi?	ลองใส่ได้ไหม

How much (for) ...?	... thâo rai?	...เท่าไร
this	níi	นี้
per fruit	lûuk-lá	ลูกละ
per piece	chín-lá	ชิ้นละ
three pieces	sãam chín	สามชิ้น
per metre	mêt-lá	เมตรละ
both	tháng sãwng	ทั้งสอง

How much altogether?	tháng mòt thâo rai?	ทั้งหมดเท่าไร

ESSENTIAL GROCERIES ··· ของใช้ที่จำเป็น

Where can I buy ...?	séu ... dâi thîi nãi?	ซื้อ...ได้ที่ไหน

I'd like ...	yàak dâi ...	อยากได้...
batteries	baet-toerii	แบตเตอรี่
bread	khanõm bang	ขนมปัง
butter	noei	เนย
cheese	noei khãeng/chiis	เนยแข็ง/ชีส
chocolate	cháwk-koh-lêht	ช็อกโกเลต
eggs	khài	ไข่
flour	pâeng	แป้ง

gas cylinder	thăng káat	ถังแก๊ส
ham	haem	แฮม
honey	náam phêung	น้ำผึ้ง
margarine	noei thiam	เนยเทียม/มาการีน
matches	mái khìit fai	ไม้ขีดไฟ
milk	nom	นม
pepper (black)	phrík thai	พริกไทย
salt	kleua	เกลือ
shampoo	chaemphuu	แชมพู
soap	sàbuu	สบู่
sugar	náam-taan	น้ำตาล
toilet paper	kràdàat chamrá	กระดาษชำระ
toothpaste	yaa sii fan	ยาสีฟัน
washing powder	phŏng sák fâwk	ผงซักฟอก
yoghurt	nom prîaw	นมเปรี้ยว

SOUVENIRS & CRAFTS
ของที่ระลึก & การฝีมือ

Before leaving Thailand, you must obtain an export licence for any antiques or objects of art you want to take with you. An antique is any 'archaic movable property whether produced by man or by nature, or any part of an ancient structure, human skeleton or animal carcass, which by its age or characteristic of production or historical evidence is useful in the field of art, history or archaeology'. An object of art is a 'thing produced by craftsmanship and appreciated as being valuable in the field of art'.

Application can be made by submitting two front-view photos of the object(s) (no more than five objects to a photo) and a photocopy of your passport, along with the object(s) in question, to one of three locations in Thailand: the Bangkok National Museum, the Chiang Mai National Museum or the Songkhla National Museum. You need to allow three to five days for the application and inspection process to be completed.

Thailand has special regulations for taking a Buddha or other deity image (or any part thereof) out of the country. These require not only a licence from the Department of Fine Arts but a permit from the Ministry of Commerce as well. The one exception to this are the small Buddha images (phrá phim or phrá khreûang) that are meant to be worn on a chain around the neck – these may be exported without a licence as long as the reported purpose is religious.

baskets	tà-kràa	ตระกร้า
classical dance-drama mask	hǔa khǒn	หัวโขน
handicrafts	ngaan fǐi-meu (hàttakam)	งานฝีมือ

Sawankhalok (Sangkhalok) style ceramics
   khrêuang thûay chaam   เครื่องถ้วยชาม
   (Sāngkhàlôk)   (สังคโลก)
Thai umbrellas   rôm thai   ร่มไทย

Materials   วัสดุ

What's this made of?   níi tham dûay àrai?   นี่ทำด้วยอะไร

It's made of....
aluminium	aluminium	อลูมิเนียม
brass	thawng lĕuang	ทองเหลือง
bronze	thawng sām-rīut	ทองสัมฤทธิ์
cloth	phâa	ผ้า
copper	thawng daeng	ทองแดง
gold (pure)	thawng kham	ทองคำ
gold-plated	thawng chúp	ทองชุบ
leather	nãng	หนัง
silver	ngoen	เงิน
stone	hĩn	หิน
teak	mái sàk	ไม้สัก
wood	mái	ไม้

Textiles   สิ่งทอ

baggy fishermen's pants
   kaang kehng chao leh   กางเกงชาวเล
   (kaang kehng jiin)   (กางเกงจีน)

batik	paa-tìk	บาติก
cotton	phâa fâai	ผ้าฝ้าย
denim farmer's shirt	sêua mâw hâwm	เสื้อหม้อฮ่อม
embroidery	phâa pàk	ผ้าปัก
ikat-style tie-dyed cloth	mát-mìi	มัดหมี่
shoulder bag	yâam	ย่าม
silk	phâa mãi	ผ้าไหม
traditional long	phâa sîn	ผ้าซิ่น
sarong for women	(phâa nûng)	(ผ้านุ่ง)
traditional short	phâakhāomáa	ผ้าขาวม้า
sarong for men		
triangular 'axe' pillow	māwn khwāan	หมอนขวาน

SHOPPING

Gems & Jewellery   อัญมณี

Thailand is the world's largest trade and production centre for precious stones, gems and ornaments, and both the International Colorstones Association (ICA) and World Federation of Diamond Bourses maintain offices in Bangkok.

Although rough stone sources in Thailand itself have decreased dramatically, stones are now imported from Australia, Sri Lanka and other countries to be cut, polished and traded here. If you know what you are doing you can get some really good buys in both unset gems and finished jewellery. Gold ornaments are sold at a good rate as labour costs are low. The best bargains in gems are jade, rubies and sapphires. Buy from reputable dealers only, unless you're a gemologist.

bracelet	sâwy khâw meu	สร้อยข้อมือ
diamond	phéht	เพชร
emerald	mawrákòt	มรกต
gems	phlawy	พลอย
gold (pure)	thawng kham	ทองคำ
gold-plated	thawng chùp	ทองชุบ
jade	yòk	หยก
necklace	sâwy khaw	สร้อยคอ
ring	wăen	แหวน
ruby	tháp thim	ทับทิม
sapphire	phlawy phailin	พลอยไพลิน
silver	ngoen	เงิน

WARNING

Warning: be wary of special deals that are one-day only or which set you up as a courier in which you're promised large profits. Many visitors end up losing big. Shop around and don't be hasty. There's no such thing as a government sale or a factory price at a gem or jewellery shop; the Thai government does not own or manage any gem or jewellery shops.

THEY MAY SAY ...

lót raakhaa dâi	(I) can lower (the price).
lót ìik mâi dâi	(I) can't lower (the price) any further.
jà hâi raakhaa phí-sèht	(I'll) give you a special price.
thùuk mâak	Very cheap.
khǎai mòt laew	All sold out.

CLOTHING เสื้อผ้า

The general Thai word for clothing is sêua phâa. The word sêua itself can mean 'shirt', blouse', 'dress' or 'jacket'; phâa means 'cloth'.

hat	mùak	หมวก
shirt/blouse/jacket/dress	sêua	เสื้อ
shoes	rawng tháo	รองเท้า
skirt	kràprohng	กระโปรง
socks	thǔng tháo	ถุงเท้า
tailor/seamstress	châang tàt sêua	ช่างตัดเสื้อ
trousers	kaang kehng	กางเกง
underwear	kaang kehng nai	กางเกงใน
Can you make ...?	tàt ... dâi mǎi?	ตัดได้ไหม
The sleeves are too ...	khǎen ... pai	แขน...ไป
long	yao	ยาว
short	sân	สั้น

Fabrics ผ้า

Synthetic materials and Western fabric weaves use the same names as in English (polyester, dacron, serge, gaberdine).

cotton	phâa fâai	ผ้าฝ้าย
leather	nǎng	หนัง
linen	phâa línin	ผ้าลินิน
silk	phâa mǎi	ผ้าไหม
wool	phâa sàkàlàat	ผ้าสักหลาด

SHOPPING

COLOURS

black	sǐi dam	สีดำ
blue	sǐi náam-ngoen	สีน้ำเงิน
brown	sǐi náam-taan	สีน้ำตาล
green	sǐi kzaw	สีเขียว
grey	sǐi thao	สีเทา
off-white	sǐi phèuak	สีเผือก
pink	sǐi chomphuu	สีชมพู
purple	sǐi mûang	สีม่วง
red	sǐi daeng	สีแดง
sky blue	sǐi fáa	สีฟ้า
white	sǐi khǎo	สีขาว
yellow	sǐi léuang	สีเหลือง
dark	kàe	แก่
light	àwn	อ่อน

Do you have another colour?
mii sǐi èun mǎi? มีสีอื่นไหม

TOILETRIES อุปกรณ์ห้องน้ำ

brush	praeng	แปรง
comb	wǐi	หวี
deodorant	yaa kamjàt klìn tua	ยาระงับกลิ่นตัว
condoms	thǔng yaang anaamai	ถุงยางอนามัย
razor	mîit kohn	มีดโกน
razor blades	bai mîit kohn	ใบมีดโกน
sanitary napkins	phâa anaamai	ผ้าอนามัย
shampoo	yaa sà phǒm (chaemphuu)	ยาสระผม (แชมพู)
soap	sa-bùu	สบู่
toilet paper	kràdàat cham-rá	กระดาษชำระ
toothbrush	praeng sǐi fan	แปรงสีฟัน
toothpaste	yaa sǐi fan	ยาสีฟัน

FOR THE BABY

ของใช้สำหรับเด็ก

tinned (canned)	aahǎan dèk	อาหาร
baby food	kràpǎwng	เด็กกระป๋อง
baby powder	pâeng dèk	แป้งเด็ก
bib	iáam	เอี๊ยม
disposable nappies	phâa âwm/	ผ้าอ้อม
(diapers)	pràdawng jàt kaan dâi	
feeding bottle	khùat nom	ขวดนม
nappy (diaper)	phâa âwm/pràdawng	ผ้าอ้อม
powdered milk	nom phǒng	นมผง

STATIONERY & PUBLICATIONS
เครื่องเขียน & สิ่งพิมพ์

Is there an English-language bookshop here?
mii ráan nǎng sěu phaasǎa
angkrìt thîi nǐi mǎi?
มีร้านหนังสือภาษา
อังกฤษที่นี่ไหม

Do you/they sell English-language books?
khǎai nǎng sěu phaasǎa
angkrìt mǎi?
ขายหนังสือภาษา
อังกฤษไหม

book	nǎng sěu	หนังสือ
bookshop	ráan nǎng sěu	ร้านหนังสือ
envelope	sawng jòt-mǎai	ซองจดหมาย
guidebook	khûu meu thâwng thîaw	คู่มือท่องเที่ยว
ink	mèuk	หมึก
magazine	nítàyasǎan	นิตยสาร
newspaper	nǎng su phim	หนังสือพิมพ์
notebook	sàmùt	สมุด
pen	pàak-kaa	ปากกา
pencil	din-sǎw	ดินสอ
stationery	khrêuang khǐan	เครื่องเขียน
writing paper	kràdàat	กระดาษ
	sǎm ràp khǐan	สำหรับเขียน

SHOPPING

MUSIC

ดนตรี

I'm looking for a ... CD.
  hǎa CD khāwng ...

หาซีดีของ...

Do you have any ...?
  mii ... mǎi?

มี...ไหม

What's his/her best recording?
  chút àrai dii thîi sùt?

ชุดอะไรดีที่สุด

I heard a band/singer called ...
  phǒm/
  dii-chán fang wong dontrii/
  nák ráwng chêu ...

ผม/
ดิฉันฟังวงดนตรี/
นักร้องชื่อ...

Can I listen to this CD here?
  fang CD níi thîi nîi dâi mǎi

ฟังซีดีที่นี่ได้ไหม

I need a blank tape.
  tâwngkaan thêp plào

ต้องการเทปเปล่า

PHOTOGRAPHY

การถ่ายภาพ

camera	klâwng thàai rûup	กล้องถ่ายรูป
develop	láang fim	ล้างฟิล์ม
film	fim	ฟิล์ม
colour	sǐi	สี
B&W	khǎo dam	ขาวดำ
lens	lehn	เลนส์
photograph	rûup (phâap)	รูป(ภาพ)
to photograph	thàai rûup	ถ่ายรูป
slide film	fim sàlai	ฟิล์มสไลด์
How many days?	kìi wan?	กี่วัน

SMOKING

การสูบบุหรี่

A packet of cigarettes, please.
  khǎw bùrìi nèung sawng

ขอบุหรี่หนึ่งซอง

Are these cigarettes strong?
  bùrìi níi raeng mǎi?

บุหรี่นี่แรงไหม

Do you have a light?
　mii fai chék mãi?　　　　　　　มีไฟแช็คไหม

Please don't smoke.
　kawrúnaa ngòt sùup bùrìi　　กรุณางดสูบบุหรี่

Do you mind if I smoke?
　sùup bùrìi dâi mãi?　　　　　สูบบุหรี่ได้ไหม

I'm trying to give up.
　kamlang phayaayaam　　　　กำลังพยายาม
　loêk sùup bùrìi　　　　　　　เลิกสูบบุหรี่

cigarettes	bùrìi	บุหรี่
cigarette papers	kràdàat muan bùrìi	กระดาษมวนบุหรี่
filtered	krawng	กรอง
lighter	fai chék	ไฟแช็ค
matches	mái khìit fai	ไม้ขีดไฟ
menthol	men-thawn	เมนทอล
pipe	klâwng sùup yaa	กล้องสูบยา
tobacco	yaa sùup	ยาสูบ

WEIGHTS & MEASURES　การชั่ง & การวัด

Dimensions and weight are usually expressed using the metric system in Thailand. The exception is land measure, which is usually quoted using the traditional Thai system of waa, ngaan and râi.

　Gold jewellery is often measured in baht (bàat).

gram	kram	กรัม
kilogram	kìloh-kram	กิโลกรัม
litre	lít	ลิตร
kilolitre	kìloh-lít	กิโลลิตร
metre	mêht	เมตร
kilometre	kìloh-mêht	กิโลเมตร

SHOPPING

Sizes & Comparisons ขนาด & การเปรียบเทียบ

size	khanàat	ขนาด
too large	yài pai	ใหญ่ไป
too long	yao pai	ยาวไป
too short	sân pai	สั้นไป
too small	lék pai	เล็กไป
too tight	kháp pai	คับไป
too wide	kwâang pai	กว้างไป

Do you have anything ... than this?

mii ... níi mãi?		มี...นี่ไหม
larger	yài-kwàa	ยาวกว่า
smaller	lék-kwàa	เล็กกว่า

USEFUL WORDS & PHRASES

buy	séu	ซื้อ
cheap	thùuk	ถูก
cigarettes	bùrìi	บุหรี่
expensive	phaeng	แพง
good enough	phaw dii	พอดี
matches	mái khìit fai	ไม้ขีดไฟ
mosquito repellant	yaa kan yung	ยากันยุง
quality	khunáphâap	คุณภาพ
sell	khãai	ขาย
style	bàep	แบบ

I'd like to see ...

yàak duu ...		อยากดู...
this one	an níi	อันนี้
that one	an nán	อันนั้น

FOOD

Thai meals are usually ordered family style: that is, diners serve themselves from dishes placed in the centre of the table. Traditionally, the party orders one of each kind of dish, maybe a curry, a vegetable dish and a soup. One dish is generally large enough for two people. One or two extras may be ordered for a large party. Dishes are not served in courses; the whole meal is served more or less at once (or as fast as the kitchen can prepare them; if there's only one wok the dishes may arrive sequentially). Soup most often is not served in individual bowls. You serve yourself from the common bowl, spooning broth and ingredients over your rice or into your own spoon.

Most Thai dishes are eaten with a fork and tablespoon. The fork (sáwm) is held in the left hand and used to push food onto the spoon (cháwn) from which you eat. To the Thais, pushing a fork into one's mouth is as uncouth as putting a knife into the mouth would be in Western countries. Exceptions to the fork-and-spoon routine are noodle soups, eaten with spoon and chopsticks, and sticky rice (common in the north and north-east), which is rolled into balls and eaten with the right hand, along with the food accompanying it.

When serving yourself from a common platter, put no more than one or two spoonfuls onto your own plate at a time. It's customary at the start of a shared meal to eat a spoonful of plain rice first – a gesture that recognises rice as the most important part of the meal. If you're being hosted by Thais, they'll undoubtedly encourage you to eat less rice and more curries, seafood and so on as a gesture of their generosity (since rice costs comparatively little). The humble guest, however, takes rice with every spoonful.

Always leave some food on the serving platters as well as on your plate. To clean your plate and leave nothing on the serving platters would be a grave insult to your hosts. This is why Thais tend to over-order at social meal occasions – the more food is left on the table, the more generous the host appears.

FOOD

Some people take to the food in Thailand immediately, while others don't. Thai dishes can be pungent and spicy. Lots of garlic and chillies are used, especially phrík khîi nǔu (lit: mouse-dropping peppers), these are the small torpedo-shaped devils which can be pushed aside if you are timid about red-hot curries.

The best antidote to an overpowering bite of chillies or curry is plain steamed rice (preferably cooled). Water or beer will spread the fire around your mouth; rice will absorb some of the caustic oils. After the initial shock, strong tea may be helpful in scouring away remaining oils and washing them down.

Although Thais have words for morning meal (aahǎan cháo), noon meal (aahǎan thîang) and evening meal (aahǎan yen), there is little differentiation between the types of dishes eaten at different times of day. Curries, fried rice, noodles, omelettes and so on are eaten whenever the individual prefers.

AT THE RESTAURANT ที่ภัตตาคาร

Please bring (a/the) ...	khǎw ...	ขอ...
bill (cheque)	bin	บิล
bowl	chaam	ชาม
chopsticks	tà-kìap	ตะเกียบ
fork	sâwm	ส้อม
glass	kâew	แก้ว
knife	mîit	มีด
menu	meh-nuu;	เมนู;
	raaikaan aahǎan	รายการอาหาร
plate	jaan	จาน
spoon	cháwn	ช้อน

(I) can eat Thai food.
thaan aahǎan thai pen ทานอาหารไทยเป็น
(I) like it hot and spicy.
châwp phèt ชอบเผ็ด
(I) don't like it hot and spicy.
mâi châwp phèt ไม่ชอบเผ็ด

Do you have ...?	mii ... mǎi?	มี...ไหม
It's delicious.	aràwy	อร่อย
What do you have that's special?		
mii a-rai phí-sèt?		มีอะไรพิเศษ
I didn't order this.		
níi phǒm/dii-chǎn mâi dâi sàng		นี่ผม/ดิฉันไม่ได้สั่ง

RICE SPOILED FISH ROTTEN

Food plays an important role in Thai idioms and proverbs whose intended meaning have nothing to do with eating.

khâo bùut plaa ráa 'rice spoiled fish rotten', a reference to a long-term marriage or relationship gone sour
khâo mài plaa man 'new rice, moist fish', the honeymoon phase of a relationship
kin hǎew 'eat water chestnuts', to fail at something.
kwàa thùa jà sùk ngaa kâw mâi 'Before the peanuts are done, the sesame will burn,' an admonition to do things in the proper order. This saying offers added poetry in the way all words in the first clause - 'before the peanuts are done' - are spoken in parallel low tones, while two out of the three of the tones in the second clause – 'the sesame will burn' – are falling tones.
mâi kin sên 'not eating noodles', when two people refuse to speak to one another due to a falling out
phàk chii rohy nâa 'coriander leaf sprinkled on top', performing a deed for appearances only
sên yài 'big noodle', important person
wǎan yen 'sweet cool' (a type of iced Thai dessert), easy-going

FOOD

FOOD

VEGETARIAN MEALS   อาหารมังสวิรัติ

With some effort you can avoid eating any animal products while in Thailand. The number of vegetarian restaurants throughout the country is increasing, thanks largely to Bangkok's ex-Governor Chamlong Srimuang, whose strict vegetarianism has inspired a non-profit chain of vegetarian restaurants in Bangkok and several provincial capitals. Look for a green sign outside with one or two large Thai numerals, as the restaurants are numbered according to the order in which they were established. The food at these restaurants is usually served buffet-style and is very inexpensive.

Another handy, though less widespread, venue for vegetarian meals are Indian restaurants, which usually feature a vegetarian section on the menu. These are most prevalent in Bangkok, Chiang Mai, Pattaya and Phuket's Patong Beach. Chinese restaurants are also a good bet since many Chinese Buddhists eat vegetarian food during Buddhist festivals, especially in southern Thailand.

More often than not, however, visiting vegetarians are left to their own devices at the average Thai restaurant. In Thai the magic words 'I eat only vegetarian food' are phŏm kin jeh (for men) or dii-chăn kin jeh (women). It might be necessary to follow with the explanation phŏm/dii-chăn kin tàe phàk, 'I eat only vegetables.'

Most Thai restaurants these days prepare stir-fried dishes with vegetable oil. If in doubt, ask.

I eat only vegetarian food.
　　phŏm/dii-chăn kin jeh　　　　　　ผม/ดิฉันกินเจ
I can't eat pork.
　　phŏm/dii-chăn kin mǔu mâi dâi　　ผม/ดิฉันกินหมูไม่ได้
I don't want any meat at all.
　　phŏm/dii-chăn　　　　　　　　　ผม/ดิฉัน
　　mâi ao nɨ́a sàt loei　　　　　　　ไม่เอาเนื้อสัตว์เลย
No fish or chicken.
　　mâi sài plaa rɨ̌u kài.　　　　　　ไม่ใส่ปลาหรือไก่
(I/we) want vegetables only.

	ao phàk thâo nán.	เอาผักเท่านั้น
Please don't use fish sauce.		
	karúnaa mâi sài náam plaa	กรุณาไม่ใส่น้ำปลา
Please don't use MSG.		
	karúnaa mâi sài phŏng chuu-rót	กรุณาไม่ใส่ผงชูรส
soy sauce	náam sii-yíw	น้ำซีอิ๊ว
tofu (soybean curd)	tâo-hûu	เต้าหู้
vegetable oil	náam-man phêut	น้ำมันพืช
vegetarian restaurant	ráan aahǎan	ร้านอาหารมังสวิรัต

FOOD

WHEN'S AND WHERE'S OF CHOPSTICKS

If you're not offered chopsticks (tàkìap), don't ask for them. When foreigners ask for chopsticks to eat Thai food, it only puzzles the restaurant proprietors. For white rice, use the fork (sâwm) and spoon (cháwn), provided (fork in the left hand, spoon in the right, or the reverse for left-handers). An even more embarrassing act is trying to eat sticky rice (popular in Northern and North-Eastern Thailand) with chopsticks. Use your right hand instead to pinch off balls of sticky rice and sop up the food using the rice balls. Chopsticks are reserved for eating Chinese-style food from bowls (such as noodles) or, for eating in all-Chinese restaurants. In either case you will be supplied with chopsticks without having to ask. Unlike their counterparts in many Western countries, restaurateurs in Thailand won't assume you don't know how to use them.

STAPLES
อาหารจานหลัก

beef	néua; néua wua	เนื้อ;เนื้อวัว
chicken	kài	ไก่
fish	plaa	ปลา
pork	mǔu	หมู
prawns/shrimp	kûng	กุ้ง
rice	khâo	ข้าว
seafood	aahǎan thaleh	อาหารทะเล
vegetables	phàk	ผัก

Rice Dishes
อาหารประเภทข้าว

khâo sǔay	ข้าวสวย	steamed white rice (lit: beautiful rice)
khâo nǐaw	ข้าวเหนียว	sticky rice
khâo man kài	ข้าวมันไก่	boned, sliced Hainan-style chicken with broth-marinated rice
khâo nâa kài	ข้าวหน้าไก่	sliced chicken with gravy over rice
khâo nâa pèt	ข้าวหน้าเป็ด	roast duck over rice
khâo mǔu daeng	ข้าวหมูแดง	red pork (char siu) with rice
khâo kaeng	ข้าวแกง	curry over rice
khâo lǎam	ข้าวหลาม	sticky rice, coconut milk & black beans steamed in bamboo
jók	โจ๊ก	broken rice porridge (congee)
fried rice with ...	khâo phàt ...	ข้าวผัด...
chicken	kài	ไก่
crab	puu	ปู
pork	mǔu	หมู
shrimp/prawns	kûng	กุ้ง

FOOD

Noodles & Wonton   ก๋วยเตี๋ยว & เกี๊ยว

Noodles are widely available in restaurants and in small, casual noodle shops called **ráan kŭaytǐaw**. The word **kŭaytǐaw** refers to flat noodles made with rice flour; you'll often be given a choice of **sên lék** (thin noodles) or **sên yài** (wide noodles). Heavier wheat noodles – sometimes made with egg, sometimes not – are known as **bà-mìi**. You'll often be able to choose either chicken, beef or pork with your noodles; smaller shops may serve only beef or only pork.

Many of the same shops that serve noodles, especially those with **bà-mìi**, also serve wonton (**kíaw**, a rice-flour 'ravioli' typically stuffed with crab or pork). More elaborate Chinese noodle restaurants may serve Chinese dumplings (**khanŏm jìip**, a rice-flour dumpling stuffed with a variety of meats) for dim sum, a late morning Chinese breakfast. Because of their Chinese origins, noodles, wonton and dumplings are usually eaten with chopsticks (and a spoon if served in a broth).

FOOD

kŭaytǐaw náam	ก๋วยเตี๋ยวน้ำ	rice noodle soup with vegetables & meat
kŭaytǐaw hâeng	ก๋วยเตี๋ยวแห้ง	rice noodles with vegetables & meat
râat nâa	ราดหน้า	rice noodles with gravy
kŭaytǐaw phàt sii-yíw	ก๋วยเตี๋ยวผัดซีอิ๊ว	fried rice noodles with soy sauce
phàt thai	ผัดไทย	thin rice noodles fried with tofu, pork, vegetables, dried shrimp, egg & peanuts
bà-mìi náam	บะหมี่น้ำ	egg noodle soup with vegetables & meat

bà-mìi hâeng	บะหมี่แห้ง	egg noodles with vegetables & meat
kíaw	เกี๊ยว	wonton
kíaw kràwp	เกี๊ยวกรอบ	fried wonton
kíaw náam	เกี๊ยวน้ำ	wonton soup
bà-mìi kíaw	บะหมี่เกี๊ยว	wonton soup with egg noodles
khanǒm jìip	ขนมจีบ	Chinese dumplings

Eggs   ไข่

In Thailand, egg dishes can be ordered at any meal; in fact they're more commonly eaten in the afternoon or evening than the morning. The Thai-style omelette (khài jiaw) is considerably more well-cooked than the Western version. It is often eaten as a side dish with larger meals.

egg	khài	ไข่
hard-boiled egg	khài tôm	ไข่ต้ม
coddled egg	khài lûak	ไข่ลวก
fried egg	khài dao	ไข่ดาว
plain omelette	khài jiaw	ไข่เจียว
omelette stuffed with vegetables & pork	khài yát sài	ไข่ยัดไส้
scrambled egg	khài kuan	ไข่คน

APPETISERS (DRINKING FOOD)   อาหารว่าง

Thais have a category of dishes called kàp klâem, which are meant to be eaten during the consumption of alcoholic beverages. On some menus these are translated as 'snacks' or 'appetisers'.

Any of these dishes may also be ordered as accompaniments to a regular meal.

thùa thâwt	ถั่วทอด	fried peanuts
mét má-mûang	เม็ดมะม่วง	fried cashews
hìmáphaan thâwt	หิมพานต์ทอด	

man faràng thâwt	มันฝรั่งทอด	fried potatoes
thâwt man plaa	ทอดมันปลา	fried fish cakes
thâwt man kûng	ทอดมันกุ้ง	fried shrimp cakes
khâo krìap kûng	ข้าวเกรียบกุ้ง	shrimp chips
kài sãam yàang	ไก่สามอย่าง	'three kinds of chicken' (chopped ginger, peanuts, chilli peppers and bits of lime to be mixed and eaten by hand)
mìi kà-thí	หมี่กะทิ	rice noodles in coconut milk
paw pía thâwt	ปอเปี๊ยะทอด	fried spring rolls
paw pía sòt	ปอเปี๊ยะสด	fresh spring rolls
mũu pîng	หมูปิ้ง	toasted pork

FOOD

THAI SALAD

yam	ยำ	yam

Thai-style salad (made with lots of chillies and lime juice) with:

cellophane noodles	yam wún sên	ยำวุ้นเส้น
grilled beef	yam nêua	ยำเนื้อ
squid	yam plaa mèuk	ยำปลาหมึก
grilled eggplant	yam mákhẽua yao	ยำมะเขือยาว
cashew nuts	yam mét má-mûang	ยำเม็ดมะม่วง
fried eggs	yam khài dao	ยำไข่ดาว
pomelo	yam sôm-oh	ยำส้มโอ
mango	yam má-mûang	ยำมะม่วง
fried, shredded catfish & peanuts	yam plaa dùk fuu	ยำปลาดุกฟู

SOUP
ชุป/แกงจืด

kaeng jèut	แกงจืด	mild soup with vegetables & pork
kaeng jèut tâo-hûu	แกงจืดเต้าหู้	mild soup with vegetables, pork & bean curd
tôm khàa kài	ต้มข่าไก่	soup with chicken, galanga root & coconut
tôm yam kûng	ต้มยำกุ้ง	prawn & lemon grass soup with mushrooms
kaeng jèut lûuk chín	แกงจืดลูกชิ้น	fish ball soup
pèt tǔn	เป็ดตุ๋น	duck stew
kài tǔn	ไก่ตุ๋น	chicken stew
pó tàek	โป๊ะแตก	'broken fish-trap' (with fresh shellfish & other seafood)
khâo tôm ...	ข้าวต้ม...	rice soup with ...
kài	ไก่	chicken
plaa	ปลา	fish
kûng	กุ้ง	shrimp

'OVER RICE'

For persons eating alone, it is best to order a rice plate or noodle dish. Also, almost any standard dish can be ordered râat khâo 'over rice'. The dish kài phàt bai kràphrao râat khâo, for example is 'chicken fried in holy basil on rice'. For simple meat-on-rice dishes, the word nâa is used, and the word order is reversed; khâo nâa pèt is 'duck on rice'. Curry (kaeng) on rice is simply called khâo kaeng.

FOOD

CURRIES

แกง

The word kaeng in Thai roughly translates as 'curry' but refers to any soupy, spicy concoction, whether it conforms to the English notion of curry or not. Basic Thai curries can be made with chicken, beef, pork or prawns.

Certain curries tend to be hotter than others, though the heat very much depends on the cook. Even the mildest Thai curries will seem hot if you're not used to chillies; the following comments in parentheses are intended for the chilli-initiated!

kaeng phèt	แกงเผ็ด	red Thai curry (usually very hot)
kaeng mátsàmàn	แกงมัสมั่น	rich & spicy Muslim-style curry (can be relatively mild or very hot)
kaeng khĭaw-wăan	แกงเขียวหวาน	green-sweet curry (medium hot)
phánaeng	แพนง	mild, savoury curry
kaeng pàa	แกงป่า	very hot curry without coconut extract (jungle curry)
kaeng kari	แกงกะหรี่	mild, Indian-style curry
kaeng sôm	แกงส้ม	hot & sour fish & vegetable ragout
kaeng kài nàw mái	แกงหน่อไม้	hot chicken curry with bamboo shoots
kaeng plaa dùk	แกงปลาดุก	hot catfish curry
kaeng pèt yâang	แกงเป็ดย่าง	roast duck curry (mild to hot)

FOOD

STIR-FRIED DISHES   อาหารประเภทผัด

plaa dùk phàt phèt	ปลาดุกผัดเผ็ด	catfish fried in fresh chili paste & basil
kài phàt mét má-mûang	ไก่ผัดเม็ดมะม่วง	chicken with cashews
kài phàt khĭng	ไก่ผัดขิง	chicken with ginger
kài phàt bai kà-phrao	ไก่ผัดใบกระเพรา	chicken fried with holy basil and chillies
kài phàt phrík	ไก่ผัดพริก	chicken fried with chillies
kài phàt hèt	ไก่ผัดเห็ด	chicken with mushrooms

FOOD

WAITER!

Most waiters in Thai restaurants, cafés are beckoned by calling out the word meaning either 'elder sibling' (if they are older than you) or 'younger sibling' (when younger). Gender doesn't matter.

younger sibling	nàwng
older sibling	phîi

If the person is much younger – say a child (in many family-owned restaurants in Thailand children help wait tables) – than you may use nŭu, a term of endearment that literally means 'mouse'.

mŭu prîaw wăan	หมูเปรี้ยวหวาน	sweet & sour pork
nĕua phàt	เนื้อผัดน้ำมันหอย	beef in oyster sauce
náam-man hăawy		
phàt phàk ruam	ผัดผักรวม	stir-fried mixed vegetables
phàt phàk khánáa	ผัดผักคะน้า	stir-fried greens (similar to collard)
phàt phàk bûng	ผัดผักบุ้งไฟแดง	water spinach
fai daeng		fried in garlic & bean sauce

SEAFOOD   อาหารทะเล

puu nêung	ปูนึ่ง	steamed crab
kâam puu nêung	ก้ามปูนึ่ง	steamed crab claws
hŭu chalăam	หูฉลาม	shark fin soup
plaa thâwt	ปลาทอด	crisp-fried fish
kûng phàt phrík phăo	กุ้งผัดพริกเผา	prawns stir-fried with roasted chillies
kûng thâwt	กุ้งทอด	fried prawns
kûng chúp	กุ้งชุบแป้งทอด	batter-fried prawns
pâeng thâwt		
kûng phăo	กุ้งเผา	grilled prawns
plaa nêung	ปลานึ่ง	steamed fish
plaa phăo	ปลาเผา	grilled fish
plaa jïan	ปลาเจี๋ยน	whole fish cooked in ginger & chillies
plaa prîaw wăan	ปลาเปรี้ยวหวาน	sweet & sour fish
hàw mòk	ห่อหมก	ground fish curry mixed with curry paste & steamed in banana leaves
puu òp wûn-sên	ปูอบวุ้นเส้น	cellophane noodles baked with crab
plaa mèuk phàt phèt	ปลาหมึกผัดเผ็ด	squid stired fried with chillies & basil

FOOD

FOOD

plaa mèuk yâang	ปลาหมึกย่าง	roast squid
hãwy thâwt	หอยทอด	oysters fried in heavy egg batter
plaa dùk	ปลาดุก	catfish
plaa	ปลา	fish
plaa lãi	ปลาไหล	freshwater eel
hãwy malaeng phùu	หอยแมลงภู่	green mussel
hãwy naang rom	หอยนางรม	oyster
plaa lòt	ปลาหลด	saltwater eel
hãwy kraeng	หอยแครง	scallop
kúng	กุ้ง	shrimp
kûng mangkon	กุ้งมังกร	spiny lobster
plaa mèuk	ปลาหมึก	squid
plaa nin	ปลานิล	tilapia

MENU DECODER

APPETISERS

ถั่วทอด	thùa thâwt	fried peanuts
เม็ดมะม่วง	mét má-mûang	fried cashews
หิมพานต์ทอด	himáphaan thâwt	
มันฝรั่งทอด	man faràng thâwt	fried potatoes
ทอดมันปลา	thâwt man plaa	fried fish cakes
ทอดมันกุ้ง	thâwt man kûng	fried shrimp cakes
ข้าวเกรียบกุ้ง	khâo krìap kûng	shrimp chips
ไก่สามอย่าง	kài sǎam yàang	'three kinds of chicken (chopped ginger, peanuts, chilli peppers and bits of lime to be mixed and eaten by hand)
หมี่กะทิ	mìi kà-thí	rice noodles in coconut milk
ปอเปี๊ยะทอด	paw pía thâwt	fried spring rolls
ปอเปี๊ยะสด	paw pía sòt	fresh spring rolls
หมูปิ้ง	mǔu pîng	toasted pork

SOUP

แกงจืด	kaeng jèut	mild soup with vegetables & pork
แกงจืดเต้าหู้	kaeng jèut tâo-hûu	mild soup with vegetables, pork & bean curd

FOOD

MENU DECODER

ต้มข่าไก่	tôm khàa kài	soup with chicken, galanga root & coconut
ต้มยำกุ้ง	tôm yam kûng	prawn & lemon grass soup with mushrooms
แกงจืดลูกชิ้น	kaeng jèut lûuk' chín	fish ball soup
เป็ดตุ๋น	pèt tǔn	duck stew
ไก่ตุ๋น	kài tǔn	chicken stew
โป๊ะแตก	pó tàek	'broken fish-trap' (with fresh shellfish & other seafood)
ข้าวต้ม...	khâo tôm ...	rice soup with ...
ไก่	kài	chicken
ปลา	plaa	fish
กุ้ง	kûng	shrimp

RICE DISHES

ข้าวสวย	khâo sǔay (lit: beautiful rice)	steamed white rice
ข้าวเหนียว	khâo nǐaw	sticky rice
ข้าวมันไก่	khâo man kài	boned, sliced Hainan-style chicken with broth-marinated rice
ข้าวหน้าไก่	khâo nâa kài	sliced chicken with gravy over rice
ข้าวหน้าเป็ด	khâo nâa pèt	roast duck over rice

FOOD

MENU DECODER

ข้าวหมูแดง	khâo mǔu daeng	red pork (*char siu*) with rice
ข้าวแกง	khâo kaeng	curry over rice
ข้าวหลาม	khâo lǎam	sticky rice, coconut milk & black beans steamed in bamboo
โจ๊ก	jók	broken rice porridge (congee)
ข้าวผัด	khâo phàt ...	fried rice with ...
ไก่	kài	chicken
ปู	puu	crab
หมู	mǔu	pork
กุ้ง	kûng	shrimp/prawns

THAI SALAD

ยำ	yam	yam

Thai-style salad (made with lots of chillies and lime juice) with:

ยำวุ้นเส้น	yam wún sên	cellophane noodles
ยำเนื้อ	yam núa	grilled beef
ยำปลาหมึก	yam plaa mèuk	squid
ยำมะเขือยาว	yam mákhěua yao	grilled eggplant
ยำเม็ดมะม่วง	yam mét má-mûang	cashew nuts
ยำไข่ดาว	yam khài dao	fried eggs
ยำส้มโอ	yam sôm-oh	pomelo
ยำมะม่วง	yam má-mûang	mango
ยำปลาดุกฟู	yam plaa dùk fuu	fried, shredded catfish & peanuts

FOOD

FOOD

MENU DECODER

NOODLES & WONTON

ก๋วยเตี๋ยวน้ำ	kũaytĩaw náam	rice noodle soup with vegetables & meat
ก๋วยเตี๋ยวแห้ง	kũaytĩaw hâeng	rice noodles with vegetables & meat
ราดหน้า	râat nâa	rice noodles with gravy
ก๋วยเตี๋ยวผัด ซีอิ๊ว	kũaytĩaw phàt sii-yíw	fried rice noodles with soy sauce
ผัดไทย	phàt thai	thin rice noodles fried with tofu, pork, vegetables, dried shrimp, egg & peanuts
บะหมี่น้ำ	bà-mìi náam	egg noodle soup with vegetables & meat
บะหมี่แห้ง	bà-mìi hâeng	egg noodles with vegetables & meat
เกี๊ยว	kíaw	wonton
เกี๊ยวกรอบ	kíaw kràwp	fried wonton
เกี๊ยวน้ำ	kíaw náam	wonton soup
บะหมี่เกี๊ยว	bà-mìi kíaw	wonton soup with egg noodles
ขนมจีบ	khanŏm jìip	Chinese dumplings

MENU DECODER

CURRIES

แกงเผ็ด	kaeng phèt	red Thai curry (usually very hot)
แกงมัสมั่น	kaeng mátsàmàn	rich & spicy Muslim-style curry (can be relatively mild or very hot)
แกงเขียวหวาน	kaeng khĭaw-wăan	green-sweet curry (medium hot)
แพนง	phánaeng	mild, savoury curry
แกงป่า	kaeng pàa	very hot curry without coconut extract (jungle curry)
แกงกะหรี่	kaeng kari	mild, Indian-style curry
แกงส้ม	kaeng sôm	hot & sour fish & vegetable ragout
แกงหน่อไม้	kaeng kài nàw mái	hot chicken curry with bamboo shoots
แกงปลาดุก	kaeng plaa dùk	hot catfish curry
แกงเป็ดย่าง	kaeng pèt yâang	roast duck curry (mild to hot)

FOOD

FOOD

MENU DECODER

STIR-FRIED DISHES

ปลาดุกผัดเผ็ด	plaa dùk phàt phèt	catfish fried in fresh chili paste & basil
ไก่ผัดเม็ดมะม่วง	kài phàt mét má-mûang	chicken with cashews
ไก่ผัดขิง	kài phàt khǐng	chicken with ginger
ไก่ผัดใบกระเพรา	kài phàt bai kà-phrao	chicken fried with holy basil and chillies
ไก่ผัดพริก	kài phàt phrík	chicken fried with chillies
ไก่ผัดเห็ด	kài phàt hèt	chicken with mushrooms
หมูเปรี้ยวหวาน	mǔu prîaw wǎan	sweet & sour pork
เนื้อผัดน้ำมันหอย	nǐua phàt náam-man hǎwy	beef in oyster sauce
ผัดผักรวม	phàt phàk ruam	stir-fried mixed vegetables
ผัดผักคะน้า	phàt phàk khánáa	stir-fried greens (similar to collard)
ผัดผักบุ้งไฟแดง	phàt phàk bûng fai daeng	morning glory vine fried in garlic & bean sauce

SEAFOOD

ปูนึ่ง	puu nêung	steamed crab
ก้ามปูนึ่ง	kâam puu nêung	steamed crab claws
หูฉลาม	hǔu chalǎam	shark fin soup

MENU DECODER

ปลาทอด	plaa thâwt	crisp-fried fish
กุ้งผัดพริกเผา	kûng phát phrík phǎo	prawns stir-fried with roasted chillies
กุ้งทอด	kûng thâwt	fried prawns
กุ้งชุบแป้งทอด	kûng chúp pâeng thâwt	batter-fried prawns
กุ้งเผา	kûng phǎo	grilled prawns
ปลานึ่ง	plaa nêung	steamed fish
ปลาเผา	plaa phǎo	grilled fish
ปลาเจี๋ยน	plaa jǐan	whole fish cooked in ginger & chillies
ปลาเปรี้ยวหวาน	plaa prîaw wǎan	sweet & sour fish
ห่อหมก	hàw mòk	ground fish curry mixed with curry paste & steamed in banana leaves
ปูอบวุ้นเส้น	puu òp wûn-sên	cellophane noodles baked with crab
ปลาหมึกผัดเผ็ด	plaa mèuk phát phèt	squid stired fried with chillies & basil
ปลาหมึกย่าง	plaa mèuk yâang	roast squid
หอยทอด	hǎwy thâwt	oysters fried in heavy egg batter
ปลาดุก	plaa dùk	catfish
ปลา	plaa	fish
ปลาไหล	plaa lǎi	freshwater eel
หอยแมลงภู่	hǎwy malaeng phùu	green mussel
หอยนางรม	hǎwy naang rom	oyster
ปลาหลด	plaa lòt	saltwater eel
หอยแครง	hǎwy kraeng	scallop

FOOD

FOOD

MENU DECODER

กุ้ง	kûng	shrimp
กุ้งมังกร	kûng mangkon	spiny lobster
ปลาหมึก	plaa mèuk	squid
ปลานิล	plaa nin	tilapia

NORTH-EAST

ลาบ	lâap	spicy salad of minced meat or fish with mint, lime juice, shallots & chillies
ลาบเนื้อ	lâap néua	with beef
ลาบหมู	lâap kài	with chicken
ลาบเป็ด	lâap pèt	with duck
ลาบปลา	lâap plaa	with fish
ส้มตำ	sôm-tam	green papaya salad
แบบลาว	bàep lao	'Lao-style sôm-tam', with fermented crab legs, no peanuts
แบบไทย	bàep thai	'Thai-style sôm-tam', with peanuts and dried shrimp
เนื้อน้ำตก	néua náam tòk	grilled beef salad (lit: waterfall salad)
ข้าวเหนียว	khâo nĭaw	sticky rice
ไก่ย่าง	kài yâang	grilled chicken

MENU DECODER

SOUTHERN THAILAND

โรตี	roh-tii	flatbread (roti)
โรตีกล้วย	roh-tii klûay	roti with bananas
โรตีแกง	roh-tii kaeng	roti with curry dip
โกปี๊	koh-píi	strong Hokkien-style coffee
ข้าวหมกไก่	khâo mòk kài	chicken briyani
ข้าวย่า	khâo yam	rice salad (with toasted coconut, dried shrimp, lime leaves)
แกงไตปลา	kaeng tai plaa	southern fish curry (very hot)
ขนมจีนน้ำยา	khanŏm jiin náam yaa	noodles with mild fish curry

NORTHERN THAILAND

ข้าวซอย	khâo sawy	Burmese-style chicken curry with wheat noodles
น้ำพริกหนุ่ม	náam phrík nùm	hot dipping sauce made with ground eggplant & chillies
น้ำพริกอ่อง	náam phrík àwng	hot dipping sauce made with ground pork & chilies
แคบหมู	khâep mǔu	fried pork rinds
แกงแค	kaeng khae	mild but bitter
แกง	kaeng	made with vegetables & herbs

FOOD

FOOD

MENU DECODER

SWEETS

สังขยา	sǎngkha-yǎa	Thai custard
สังขยามะพร้าว	sǎngkha-yǎa ma-phráo	coconut custard
ฝอยทอง	fǎwy thawng	sweet shredded egg yolk
หม้อแกง	mâw kaeng	egg custard
กล้วยบวดชี	klûay bùat chii	banana in coconut milk
กล้วยแขก	klûay khàek	Indian-style batter-fried banana
ลูกตาลเชื่อม	lûuk taan chêuam	palm kernels in sweet syrup
ตะโก้	ta-kôh	gelatin topped with coconut cream
ข้าวเหนียวแดง	khâo nǐaw daeng	sticky rice with coconut cream
ข้าวเหนียวมะม่วง	khâo nǐaw má-mûang	sticky rice in coconut cream with sliced ripe mango

DRINKS

น้ำต้ม	náam tôm	boiled water
ขวด	khùat	bottle
น้ำ	náam dèum khùat	bottled drinking water
ชาจีน	chaa jiin	Chinese tea
น้ำเย็น	náam yen	cold water
แก้ว	kâew	glass

MENU DECODER

กาแฟร้อน
  kaafae ráwn
  hot coffee with milk & sugar

ชาร้อน
  chaa ráwn
  hot Thai tea with milk & sugar

ชาดำร้อน
  chaa dam ráwn
  hot Thai tea with sugar

น้ำร้อน
  náam ráwn
  hot water

โอเลี้ยง
  oh-líang
  iced coffee with sugar, no milk

น้ำมะนาว
  náam manao
  iced lime juice with sugar (usually with salt too)

ชาเย็น
  chaa yen
  iced Thai tea with milk & sugar

ชาดำเย็น
  chaa dam yen
  iced Thai tea with sugar only

กาแฟถุง
  kaafae thǔng
  traditional filtered coffee with milk & sugar
(ภาคใต้เรียกโกปี๊)
  (ko-píi in southern Thailand)

FOOD

FOOD

MENU DECODER

น้ำชา	náam chaa	weak Chinese tea
น้ำส้ม	náam sôm	orange soda
น้ำแข็งเปล่า	náam khǎeng plào	plain ice
นมจืด	nom jèut	plain milk
น้ำเปล่า	náam plào	plain water
น้ำโซดา	náam soh-daa	soda water

ALCOHOL

เบียร์	bia	beer
เหล้า	lâo	distilled spirits
เบียร์สด	bia sòt	draught beer
เหล้ายาดอง	lâo yàa dong	herbal liquors
เหล้าเถื่อน	lâo theuan	jungle liquor (moonshine)
แม่โขง	mâe khǒng	Maekhong whisky
กลม	klom	750-ml bottle
แบน	baen	375-ml bottle
เหล้าขาว	lâo khǎo	white liquor (clear, brandless liquors)

VEGETABLES   ผัก

angle bean	thùa phuu	ถั่วพู
bitter melon	márá-jiin	มะระจีน
brinjal (round eggplant)	mákhēua pràw	มะเขือเปราะ
cabbage	phàk kà-làm (kà-làm plii)	ผักกะหล่ำ (กะหล่ำปลี)
cauliflower	dàwk kà-làm	ดอกกะหล่ำ
Chinese radish (daikon)	hūa chai thao	หัวไชเท้า
corn	khâo phôht	ข้าวโพด
cucumber	taeng kwaa	แตงกวา
eggplant	mákhēua yao	มะเขือยาว
garlic	kràtiam	กระเทียม
lettuce	phàk kàat	ผักกาด
long bean	thùa fák yao	ถั่วฝักยาว
okra (ladyfingers)	krà-jíap	กระเจี๊ยบ
onion (bulb)	hūa hāwm	หัวหอม
peanuts (groundnuts)	thùa lísōng	ถั่วลิสง
potato	man faràng	มันฝรั่ง
pumpkin	fak thawng	ฟักทอง
spring onions	tôn hāwm	ต้นหอม
taro	pheùak	เผือก
tomato	mákhēua thêt	มะเขือเทศ

FOOD

REGIONAL SPECIALTIES   อาหารเฉพาะภาค

Certain regional dishes can be found all over Thailand, though they are most popular in their place of origin.

North-East   อีสาน

Many of the dishes favoured in north-eastern Thailand are, like most north-easterners themselves, of Lao descent.

lâap	ลาบ	spicy salad of minced meat or fish with mint, lime juice, shallots & chillies
lâap nêua	ลาบเนื้อ	with beef
lâap kài	ลาบหมู	with chicken
lâap pèt	ลาบเป็ด	with duck
lâap plaa	ลาบปลา	with fish
sôm-tam	ส้มตำ	green papaya salad
bàep lao	แบบลาว	'Lao-style sôm-tam', with fermented crab legs, no peanuts
bàep thai	แบบไทย	'Thai-style sôm-tam', with peanuts and dried shrimp
néua náam tòk	เนื้อน้ำตก	grilled beef salad (lit: waterfall salad)
khâo nìaw	ข้าวเหนียว	sticky rice
kài yâang	ไก่ย่าง	grilled chicken

Southern Thailand   ใต้

Malay Muslim cooking exerts a strong influence on Southern Thai cuisine.

roh-tii	โรตี	flatbread (roti)
roh-tii klûay	โรตีกล้วย	roti with bananas
roh-tii kaeng	โรตีแกง	roti with curry dip
koh-píi	โกปี๊	strong Hokkien-style coffee
khâo mòk kài	ข้าวหมกไก่	chicken briyani
khâo yam	ข้าวยำ	rice salad (with toasted coconut, dried shrimp, lime leaves)

FOOD

| kaeng tai plaa | แกงไตปลา | southern fish curry (very hot) |
| khanōm jiin náam yaa | ขนมจีนน้ำยา | noodles with mild fish curry |

Northern Thailand   เหนือ

The cuisine of the north shows influences from Myanmar (Burma), northern Laos and Yunnan. Northern dishes aren't as popular throughout Thailand as foods from the south and north-east.

khâo sawy	ข้าวซอย	Burmese-style chicken curry with wheat noodles
náam phrík nùm	น้ำพริกหนุ่ม	hot dipping sauce made with ground eggplant & chillies
náam phrík àwng	น้ำพริกอ่อง	dipping sauce made with ground pork, chilies & tomatoes
khâep mūu	แคบหมู	fried pork rinds
kaeng khae kaeng	แก๊แค	mild but bitter made with vegetables & herbs

FOOD

CONDIMENTS, HERBS & SPICES
เครื่องปรุง, สมุนไพรเครื่องเทศ

Lime juice, lemon grass and fresh coriander leaf are added to give Thai food its characteristic tang. Náam plaa, a thin, clear fish sauce made from fermented anchovies, or kà-pì, fermented shrimp paste, provide the cuisine's main salty element.

Other common seasonings include laos or galanga root (khàa), three kinds of basil, tamarind juice (náam makhāam), ginger (khìng) and coconut extract (kàtí).

The main condiment on every Thai table is náam plaa phrík, a small dish of small, sliced hot chillies floating in fish sauce. For seafood this basic sauce is enhanced by the addition of lime juice and garlic. Grilled or fried chicken dishes are often accompanied by a sweet & sour sauce called náam jîm kài (chicken dipping sauce), made with garlic, vinegar, sugar, chillies and fish sauce. A spicy orange-red sauce called náam phrík síi raachaa (from Si Racha, of course) often comes with Thai omelettes and oyster dishes. It's made with tomatoes, garlic, salt, vinegar and chillies.

In noodle shops you'll usually find a rack of four condiments on the table. These hold ground red pepper (phrík pòn), ground peanuts (thùa pòn), vinegar with sliced chillies (náam sôm phrík) and sugar. Thai noodle-eaters improvise their own seasoning combination to balance the flavours of heat, oil (from the peanuts), sour and sweet. A bottle of fish sauce on the table offers added salt.

Granulated salt and ground black pepper are almost never present on a Thai table, although they may be used during the cooking. Soy sauce (náam síi-yú) can be requested, though this is normally used as a condiment for Chinese food only.

phrík thai	พริกไทย	black pepper
phrík	พริก	chilli
kà-tí	กะทิ	coconut extract
phàk chii	ผักชี	coriander (cilantro)
phrík phão	พริกเผา	crushed, roasted red chillies
náam jîm	น้ำจิ้ม	dipping sauces
kûng hâeng	กุ้งแห้ง	dried shrimp
náam plaa	น้ำปลา	fish sauce
náam plaa phrík	น้ำปลาพริก	fish sauce with chillies
khĭng	ขิง	ginger
bai krà-phrao	ใบกระเพรา	holy basil
náam mánao	น้ำมะนาว	lime juice

FOOD

ngaa	งา	sesame
kà-pì	กะปิ	shrimp paste
náam sii-yú	น้ำซีอิ๊ว	soy sauce
kleua	เกลือ	salt
náam phrík sǐi raachaa	ซ็อสพริกศรีราชา	Sri Racha sauce
náam-taan	น้ำตาล	sugar
bai hǒhráphaa	ใบโหระพา	sweet basil
makhǎam	มะขาม	tamarind
náam sôm	น้ำส้ม	vinegar
phrík náam sôm	พริกน้ำส้ม	vinegar with chillies

METHODS OF COOKING วิธีการปรุงอาหาร

òp	อบ	baked
tôm	ต้ม	boiled
sùk	สุก	cooked/ripe
kaeng	แกง	curried
thâwt	ทอด	fried in large pieces
phàt	ผัด	fried in small pieces/stir-fried
phàt phèt	ผัดเผ็ด	fried with chilli paste & sweet basil
phát kràthiam phrík thai	ผัดกระเทียมพริกไทย	fried with garlic and black pepper
phàt khǐng	ผัดขิง	fried with ginger
phǎo	เผา	grilled, barbecued or roasted (chillies, fish & shrimp only)
yâang	ย่าง	grilled, barbecued or roasted (everything else)
lûak	ลวก	parboiled
dìp	ดิบ	raw/unripe (fruits & vegetables)
nêung	นึ่ง	steamed (fish, rice only)

FOOD

FRUITS   ผลไม้

klûay	กล้วย	banana – over 20 varieties; available year-round
máphráo	มะพร้าว	coconut – grated for cooking when mature, it can be eaten with a spoon when young; juice is sweetest in young coconuts; year-round
náwy nàa	น้อยหน่า	custard-apple – July to October
thúrian	ทุเรียน	durian – held in high esteem by the Thais, but most Westerners dislike this fruit; several varieties and seasons, so keep trying
fa-ràng	ฝรั่ง	guava – year-round
kha-nŭn	ขนุน	jackfruit – similar in appearance to durian but much easier to take; year-round
má-nao	มะนาว	lime – year-round
lam yài	ลำไย	longan – 'dragon's eyes', small, brown, spherical, similar to rambutan; July to October
sôm	ส้ม	mandarin – year-round
má-mûang	มะม่วง	mango – several varieties & seasons
mang-khút	มังคุด	mangosteen – round, purple fruit with with juicy white flesh; April to September
málákaw	มะละกอ	papaya – year-round
sàp-pàrót	สัปปะรด	pineapple – year-round
sôm oh	ส้มโอ	pomelo – large citrus similar to grapefruit; year-round
máfai	มะไฟ	rambeh – small, reddish-brown, sweet, apricot-like; April to May
ngáw	เงาะ	rambutan – red, hairy-skinned fruit with grape-like interior; July to September

chom-phûu	ชมพู่	rose-apple – small, apple-like texture, very fragrant; April to July
lámút	ละมุด	sapodilla – small, brown, oval, sweet but pungent smelling; July to September
mákhǎam	มะขาม	tamarind – comes in sweet as well as tart varieties; year round
taeng moh	แตงโม	watermelon – year-round

WHAT?

When forming a question, avoid the normal English tonal patterns used to indicate a question. In Thai, question tags alone signify the interrogative. Resist the urge to alter the tone of the final word in the system to conform to the English question tones (which differ from country to country, but always interfere with Thai comprehension).

so say …   rót fai jà àwk kìi mohng?
              lit: train will leave what time)

not   rót fai jà àwk kìi mǒhng?

The one exception to this is the question word for 'where' (nǎi), which features a rising tone Thai, very much like the question tone used by some English speakers.

FOOD

SWEETS ของหวาน

Thai sweets are seldom sold in Thai restaurants. Instead they are purchased from small sweet shops or street vendors. Common ingredients are coconut and coconut extract, sticky rice, rice flour, palm and cane sugar, agar-agar (gelatin made from a type of seaweed), egg yolks and fruits of various kinds.

săngkha-yāa	สังขยา	Thai custard
săngkha-yāa ma-phráo	สังขยามะพร้าว	coconut custard
făwy thawng	ฝอยทอง	sweet shredded egg yolk
mâw kaeng	หม้อแกง	egg custard
klûay bùat chii	กล้วยบวดชี	banana in coconut milk
klûay khàek	กล้วยแขก	Indian-style batter-fried banana
lûuk taan chêuam	ลูกตาลเชื่อม	palm kernels in sweet syrup
ta-kôh	ตะโก้	gelatin topped with coconut cream
khâo nĭaw daeng	ข้าวเหนียวแดง	sticky rice with coconut cream
khâo nĭaw má-mûang	ข้าวเหนียวมะม่วง	sticky rice in coconut cream with sliced ripe mango

DRINKS เครื่องดื่ม

Juices & Shakes น้ำผลไม้ & น้ำปั่น

The incredible variety of fruits in Thailand means a corresponding availability of nutritious juices and shakes. The all-purpose term for fruit juice is náam phŏn-lá-mái. Put náam (water or juice) together with the name of any fruit and you can get anything from náam sôm (orange juice) to náam taeng moh (watermelon juice). When a blender or extractor is used, fruit juices may be called náam khán or 'squeezed juice', or example náam sàpparót khán is 'pineapple juice'. When mixed in a blender with ice the result is náam pon (lit: mixed juice) as in náam málákaw pon, a papaya smoothie or shake. Night markets will often have vendors specialising in juices and shakes.

Thais prefer to drink most fruit juices with a little salt mixed in. Unless a vendor is used to serving farangs, your fruit juice or shake will come slightly salted. If you prefer unsalted fruits juices, specify mâi sài kleua (without salt).

Sugar cane juice (náam âwy) is a Thai favourite and a very refreshing accompaniment to curry-and-rice plates. Many small restaurants or food stalls that don't offer any other juices will have a supply of freshly squeezed náam âwy on hand.

Coffee & Tea   กาแฟ & ชา

Traditionally, coffee in Thailand is locally grown (in hilly areas of northern and southern Thailand), roasted by wholesalers, ground by vendors and filtered just before serving. Some wholesalers add a bit of sugar to sweeten the bean. Thai-grown coffee may not be as full and rich-tasting as gourmet Sumatran, Jamaican or Kona beans, but when correctly brewed it's still considerably tastier than instant coffee.

Sometimes restaurants or vendors with the proper accoutrements for making traditional filtered coffee will keep a supply of instant just for farangs (or moneyed Thais, since instant always costs a few baht more per cup than filtered). To get real Thai coffee ask for kafae thǔng (lit: bag coffee), which refers to the traditional method of preparing a cup of coffee by filtering hot water through a bag-shaped cloth filter. The usual kafae thǔng is served mixed with sugar and sweetened condensed milk. If you don't want either, be sure to specify kafae dam (black coffee) followed with mâi sài náam-taan (without sugar). Kafae thǔng is often served in a glass instead of a ceramic cup. To pick a glass of hot coffee up, grasp it along the top rim.

FOOD

FOOD

Both Indian-style (black) and Chinese-style (green or semi-cured) teas are commonly served in Thailand. The latter predominates in Chinese restaurants and is the usual ingredient in náam chaa, the weak, often lukewarm tea-water traditionally served in Thai restaurants for free. The aluminium teapots seen on every table in the average restaurant are filled with náam chaa; ask for a plain glass (kâew plào) and you can drink as much as you like at no charge. For iced náam chaa ask for a glass of ice (usually 1B) and pour your own; for fresh, undiluted Chinese tea request chaa jiin. Black tea, both imported and Thai-grown, is usually available in the same restaurants or food stalls that serve real coffee. An order of chaa ráwn (hot tea) almost always results in a cup (or glass) of black tea with sugar and condensed milk. As with coffee you must specify on ordering whether you want black tea with or without milk and/or sugar. Thai tea derives its characteristic orange-red colour from ground tamarind seed added after the curing process.

Water   น้ำ

Water purified for drinking purposes is simply called náam dèum (drinking water), whether boiled or filtered. All water offered to customers in restaurants or to guests in an office or home will be purified, so one needn't fret about the safety of taking a sip. In restaurants you can ask for náam plào (plain water) which is always either boiled or taken from a purified source; it's served by the glass at no charge or you can order by the bottle. A bottle of carbonated water (soda) costs about the same as a bottle of plain purified water but the bottles are smaller. A glass of ice usually costs a baht or two.

No salt.	mâi sài kleua	ไม่ใส่เกลือ
No sugar.	mâi sài náam-taan	ไม่ใส่น้ำตาล
boiled water	náam tôm	น้ำต้ม
bottle	khùat	ขวด
bottled drinking water	náam dèum khùat	น้ำ
Chinese tea	chaa jiin	ชาจีน
cold water	náam yen	น้ำเย็น
glass	kâew	แก้ว
hot coffee with milk & sugar		
kaafae ráwn		กาแฟร้อน
hot Thai tea with milk & sugar		
chaa ráwn		ชาร้อน
hot Thai tea with sugar		
chaa dam ráwn		ชาดำร้อน
hot water		
náam ráwn		น้ำร้อน
iced coffee with sugar, no milk		
oh-líang		โอเลี้ยง
iced lime juice with sugar (usually with salt too)		
náam manao		น้ำมะนาว
iced Thai tea with milk & sugar		
chaa yen		ชาเย็น
iced Thai tea with sugar only		
chaa dam yen		ชาดำเย็น
traditional filtered coffee with milk & sugar		
(ko-píi in southern Thailand)		
kaafae thǔng		กาแฟถุง
		(ภาคใต้เรียกโกปี๊)
weak Chinese tea	náam chaa	น้ำชา
orange soda	náam sôm	น้ำส้ม
plain ice	náam khǎeng plào	น้ำแข็งเปล่า
plain milk	nom jèut	นมจืด
plain water	náam plào	น้ำเปล่า
soda water	náam soh-daa	น้ำโซดา

FOOD

Alcoholic   เครื่องดื่มที่มีแอลกอฮอล์

  is the most popular alcoholic drink in Thailand. Common Thai-made brands include Singha (pronounced sĭng), Amarit NB, Kloster and Carlsberg. Imported beers are also available in larger, tourist-oriented places like Bangkok, Chiang Mai, Hat Yai and Phuket.

    Rice whisky is also a big favourite in Thailand and somewhat more affordable than beer for the average Thai. It has a sharp, sweet taste not unlike rum, with an alcoholic content of 35%. There are several brands, including the infamous Maekhong label.

beer	bia	เบียร์
distilled spirits	lâo	เหล้า
draught beer	bia sòt	เบียร์สด
herbal liquors	lâo yàa dong	เหล้ายาดอง
jungle liquor (moonshine)	lâo theuan	เหล้าเถื่อน
Maekhong whisky	mâe khŏng	แม่โขง
750-ml bottle	klom	กลม
375-ml bottle	baen	แบน
white liquor	lâo khāo	เหล้าขาว
(clear, brandless liquors)		

FOOD

IN THE COUNTRY นอกเมือง

WEATHER อากาศ

What's the weather like?
  aakàat pen yang-ngai?   อากาศเป็นยังไง

The weather is nice today.
  wan-níi aakàat dii   วันนี้อากาศดี

The weather isn't good.
  aakàat mâi dii   อากาศไม่ดี

Is it going to rain?   fõn jà tók rẽu plào?   ฝนจะตกหรือเปล่า

(It's ...)

windy	lom phát	ลมพัด
not windy	lom mâi phát	ลมไม่พัด
very cold	não mâak	หนาวมาก
very hot	ráwn mâak	ร้อนมาก
raining hard	fõn tòk nàk	ฝนตกหนัก
flooding	náam tûam	น้ำท่วม

Useful Words & Phrases

cool season (Nov-Feb)	réuduu não	ฤดูหนาว
cool weather	aakàat yen	อากาศเย็น
fog	màwk	หมอก
hot season (Mar-May)	réuduu ráwn	ฤดูร้อน
hot weather	aakàat ráwn	อากาศร้อน
lightning	fáa lâep	ฟ้าแลป
monsoon	maw-rá-sũm	มรสุม
rainy season (Jun-Oct)	réuduu fõn	ฤดูฝน
weather	aakàat	อากาศ

GEOGRAPHY ภูมิประเทศ

Many town and village names in Thailand incorporate the following geographic or demographic features:

Ban/Baan (village)	bâan	บ้าน
Bang (place)	baang	บาง
Don (dry highland)	dawn	ดอน
Khok/Kok (knoll)	khôhk	โคก
Muang (city)	meuang	เมือง
Nakhon (large city)	nákhawn	นคร
Non (highland)	nohn	โนน
Nong (lake)	nǎwng	หนอง

Other Geographic Features

bay/gulf	ào	อ่าว
beach	chai-hàat	ชายหาด
cave	thâm	ถ้ำ
cliff	phǎa	ผา
coast	fàng tháleh	ฝั่งทะเล
coral	hǐn pàkaarang	หินปะการัง
countryside	chonabòt	ชนบท
creek	lam-thaan	ลำธาร
field	naa	นา
forest	pàa	ป่า
hill	noen	เนิน
mountain	phuu khǎo	ภูเขา
mountain peak	doi	ดอย
nature	thamachâat	ธรรมชาติ
ocean	ma-hǎasamùt	มหาสมุทร
river	mâe náam	แม่น้ำ
river rapids	kàeng	แก่ง
sea	thaleh	ทะเล
spring/well	bàw	บ่อ
stone	hǐn	หิน
stream	hûay	ห้วย
swamp	beung	บึง
trail/footpath	thaang doen	ทางเดิน
waterfall	náam tòk	น้ำตก

TREKKING

การเดินป่า

(I/we) would like to hire a guide.
  yàak jâang khon pen kai

อยากจ้างคนเป็นไกด์

How many hours per day will we walk?
  jà doen wan-lá kìi chûa-mohng?

จะเดินวันละกี่ชั่วโมง

How far is it from ... to ...?
  jàak ... thĕung ... klai thâo rai?

จาก...ถึง...ไกลเท่าไร

Where is the trail to ...?
  thaang doen pai ...
  yùu trong nǎi?

ทางเดินไป
อยู่ตรงไหน

Can (I/we) stay in this village?
  phák thîi mùu bâan níi dâi mǎi?

พักที่หมู่บ้านนี้ได้ไหม

Can (I/we) sleep here?
  nawn thîi níi dâi mǎi?

นอนที่นี่ได้ไหม

Is it a difficult walk?
  doen yâak mǎi?

เดินยากไหม

Who lives here?
  khrai yùu thîi níi?

ใครอยู่ที่นี่

Can (I/we) put a tent here?
  kaang tên thîi níi dâi mǎi?

กางเต็นท์ที่นี่ได้ไหม

Are there tents available for rent?
  mii tên hâi châo mǎi?

มีเต็นท์.ให้เช่าไหม

IN THE COUNTRY

DID YOU KNOW ...

Thais think that travelling alone on holiday is rather strange, and they have a very macabre rhyme to express how awful they find the prospect:
khon diaw hŭa hǎai,
sǎwng khon phêuan taai
'A person alone loses his head, two persons die friends.'

Is it safe?
  plàwt phai mãi?   ปลอดภัยไหม
Is drinking water available?
  mii náam dèum mãi?   มีน้ำดื่มไหม
Where is the park office?
  aw-fít khãwng   ที่ทำการ
  won-ùtayaan yùu thîi nãi?   วนอุทยาน

Does the price include ...?	raakhaa níi ruam... mãi?	ราคานี้รวม... หรือเปล่า
food	aahãan	อาหาร
transport	khõn-sòng	ขนส่ง

How many ...?	kìi ...?	กี่...
days	wan	วัน
hours	chûa-mohng	ชั่วโมง
kilometres	ki-loh-mêht	กิโลเมตร
metres	mêht	เมตร

Useful Words

blanket	phâa hòm	ผ้าห่ม
guide (person)	kai	ไกด์
hill tribe	chao khão	ชาวเขา
lodging	thîi phák	ที่พัก
medicine	yaa	ยา
mosquito(es)	yung	ยุง
mosquito coil	yaa kan yung	ยากันยุง
	(bàep jùt)	(แบบจุด)
opium	fìn	ฝิ่น
raft	phae	แพ
sleeping bag	thũng nawn	ถุงนอน
tent	tên	เต็นท์
tour/trek	thua	ทัวร์
village headman	phûu yài bâan	ผู้ใหญ่บ้าน
walk	doen	เดิน
water	náam	น้ำ

AT THE BEACH

Can we swim here?
  wâai náam thîi nîi dâi mãi?

Is it safe to swim here?
  wâai náam thîi nîi
  plàwt phai mãi?

What time is high/low tide?
  náam khêun/long kìi mohng?

ที่ชายหาด

ว่ายน้ำที่นี่ได้ไหม

ว่ายน้ำที่นี่
ปลอดภัยไหม

น้ำขึ้น/ลงกี่โมง

IN THE COUNTRY

coast	fàng thaleh	ฝั่งทะเล
fishing	tòk plaa	ตกปลา
reef	hĭn pàkaarang	หินปะการัง
rock	hĭn	หิน
sand	saai	ทราย
sea	tháleh	ทะเล
snorkelling	dam náam chái thâw hăai jai	ดำน้ำใช้ท่อหายใจ
sunblock	cream kan dàet	ครีมกันแดด
sunglasses	wâen taa kan dàet	แว่นตากันแดด
surf	soef; khlêun hŭa tàek	คลื่น
surfing	lên soef	เล่นโต้คลื่น
surfboard	soef-bawt (surfboard)	กระดานโต้คลื่น
swimming	kaan wâai náam	การว่ายน้ำ
towel	phâa chét tua	ผ้าเช็ดตัว
waterskiing	sàkii náam	สกีน้ำ
waves	khlêun	คลื่น
windsurfing	tham win-soef (windsurfing)	กระดานโต้คลื่น

Diving

การดำน้ำ

scuba diving
  dam náam
  ดำน้ำ

Are there good diving sites here?
  thăew níi mii thîi
  nâa dam náam măi?
  แถวนี้มีที่น่าดำน้ำไหม

Can we hire a diving boat/guide?
  jâang reua dam náam/
  kai dâi măi?
  จ้างเรือดำน้ำ/
  ไกด์ได้ไหม

We'd like to hire diving equipment.
  yàak jà châo
  khrêuang dam náam
  อยากจะเช่า
  เครื่องดำน้ำ

I'm interested in exploring wrecks.
  phŏm/dì-chăn sŏn jai thîaw
  tàek reua yùu tâi náam
  ผม/ดิฉันสนใจเรือ
  รือแตกอยู่ใต้น้ำ

ANIMALS

สัตว์

ant	mót	มด
banteng (type of wild cattle)	wua dae	วัว
barking deer	ii-kêhng	อีเก้ง
bear	mǐi	หมี
bee	phêung	ผึ้ง
bird	nók	นก
butterfly	phǐi sêua	ผีเสื้อ
centipede	tàkhàap	ตะขาบ
cockroach	malaeng sàap	แมลงสาบ
cow	wua	วัว
civet	chámót	ชะมด
clouded leopard	sěua laai mêhk	เสือลายเมฆ
crocodile	jaw-rákhêh	จรเข้
deer	kwaang	กวาง
dog	mǎa	หมา
dolphin	plaa lohmaa	ปลาโลมา
duck	pèt	เป็ด
elephant	cháang	ช้าง
fish	plaa	ปลา
fishing cat	sěua plaa	เสือปลา
fly	malaeng wan	แมลงวัน
frog	kòp	กบ
gaur	kràthing	กระทิง
gecko	túk-kae	ตุ๊กแก
gibbon	chánii	ชะนี
horse	máa	ม้า
monitor lizard	hào cháang	เห่าช้าง
leaf monkey	khàang	ค่าง
leopard	sěua dao	เสือดาว
Malayan sun bear	mǐi mǎa	หมีหมา
monkey	ling	ลิง
pangolin	lin (nîm)	ลิ่น(นิ่ม)
rabbit	kràtài	กระต่าย

IN THE COUNTRY

IN THE COUNTRY

rhinoceros	râet	แรด
scorpion	malaeng pàwng	แมลงป่อง
shellfish (clams, oysters, etc)	hǎwy	หอย
shrimp, lobster	kûng	กุ้ง
snake	nguu	งู
snake (venomous)	nguu phít	งูพิษ
tapir	sǒm sèt	สมเสร็จ
tiger	sěua	เสือ
turtle	tào	เต่า
water buffalo	khwaai	ควาย
water fowl	nók náam	นกน้ำ
wild animals	sàt pàa	สัตว์ป่า
wild buffalo	khwaai pàa	ควายป่า
young animal/offspring	lûuk	ลูก

FLORA & FAUNA   รุกขชาติ & สัตว์ป่า

agriculture	kàsìt-kam	กสิกรรม
bamboo	tôn phài	ต้นไผ่
coconut palm	tôn má-phráo	ต้นมะพร้าว
corn	khâo phôht	ข้าวโพด
crops	phêut phǒn	พืชผล
dipterocarp	yaang	ยาง
flower	dàwk mái	ดอกไม้
grass/herb	yâa	หญ้า
to harvest	kèp kìaw	เก็บเกี่ยว
to irrigate/irrigation	thót náam	ต้นน้ำ
leaf	bai mái	ใบไม้
pine	tôn sǒn	ต้นสน
planting/sowing	plùuk	ปลูก
rice field	naa/thûng khâo	นา/ทุ่งข้าว
sugar cane	âwy	อ้อย
teak	tôn sàk	ต้นสัก
tobacco	yaa sùup	ยาสูบ
tree	tôn mái	ต้นไม้

สุขภาพ

I need a ...	phõm/dì-chãn tâwng-kaan ...	ผม/ดิฉัน ต้องการ...
doctor	mãw	หมอ
dentist	mãw fan	หมอฟัน
hospital	rohng phayaabaan	โรงพยาบาล
chemist (pharmacist)	phesàtchakawn	เภสัชกร

I'm not well.
phõm/dì-chãn mâi sabai — ผม/ดิฉันไม่สบาย

My friend is sick.
phêuan mâi sabai — เพื่อนไม่สบาย

I need a doctor who speaks English.
tâwng-kaan mãw thîi phûut
phaa-sãa angkrìt dâi — ต้องการหมอที่พูด
ภาษาอังกฤษได้

It hurts there.	jèp thîi nîi	เจ็บที่นี่
I feel nauseous.	khlêun hĩan	คลื่นเหียน

Ive been vomiting.
phõm/dì-chãn
ûak lãai khráng láew — ผม/ดิฉัน
อ้วกหลายครั้งแล้ว

I feel better/worse.
rúu-sèuk sabaai khêun/yâelong — รู้สึกสบายขึ้น/แย่ลง

I'm tired.
phõm/dì-chãn nèuay — ผม/ดิฉันเหนื่อย

(I have)...		
a cold	pen wàt	เป็นหวัด
a fever	pen khâi	เป็นไข้
diarrhoea	tháwng doen	ท้องเดิน
a sore throat	jèp khâw	เจ็บคอ
vomited several times	aajian lãai khráng	อาเจียนหลายครั้ง

(My) stomach aches.	pùat tháwng	ปวดท้อง
It hurts here.	pùat thîi-nii	ปวดที่นี่
(I) can't sleep.	nawn mâi làp	นอนไม่หลับ
(My) head aches	pùat sǐi-sà	ปวดศรีษะ
There's pain in my chest.	jèp nâa òk	เจ็บหน้าอก
(My) back hurts.	pùat lǎng	ปวดหลัง
I've been like this for two weeks.	pen bàep-níi sǎwng aathít láew	เป็นแบบนี้ สองอาทิตย์แล้ว
Is it serious?	pen mâak mǎi?	เป็นมากไหม

AILMENTS

โรค

AIDS	rôhk éht	โรค AIDS
an allergy	aakaan pháe	อาการแพ้
anaemia	rôhk lo hìt jaang	โรคโลหิตจาง
asthma	rôhk hèut	โรคหืด
cancer	mareng	มะเร็ง
cholera	ahìwaa	อหิวาต์
a cold	pen wàt	เป็นหวัด
constipation	tháwng pùuk	ท้องผูก
cough	ai	ไอ
cramps	tàkhriu	ตะคริว
cystitis	tòk khǎo	ตกขาว
dengue fever	khâi sâa	ไข้ส่า
diarrhoea	tháwng doen	ท้องเดิน
diabetes	rôhk bao wǎan	โรคเบาหวาน
dysentery	rôhk bìt	โรคบิด
a fever	pen khâi	เป็นไข้
gastroenteritis	rôhk kràpháw àk-sèhp	โรคกระเพาะ อักเสบ

headache	pùat sǐi-sà	ปวดศรีษะ
a heart condition	rôhk hǔa jai	โรคหัวใจ
indigestion	aahǎan mâi yâwy	อาหารไม่ย่อย
an infection	mii chéua rôhk	มีเชื้อโรค
influenza	khâi wàt yài	ไข้หวัดใหญ่
lice	hǎo	เหา
malaria	khâi jàp sàn (maalaaria)	ไข้จับสั่น
a pain	jèp	เจ็บ
pneumonia	rôhk pàwt àk sèhp	โรคปอดอักเสบ
rabies	rôhk klua náam	โรคกลัวน้ำ
a sore throat	jèp khaw	เจ็บคอ
sprain	khlét	เคล็ด
stomachache	pùat tháwng	ปวดท้อง
toothache	pùat fan	ปวดฟัน
a urinary infection	rôhk thaang doen pàtsǎawá	โรคทางเดินปัสสาวะ
veneral disease	kaamá rôhk	กามโรค
worms	phayâat	พยาธิ

THEY MAY SAY ...

bâa	crazy/mad
baa bâa baw baw	crazy (slang)
bâa náam lǎi	talkative ('flowing water crazy')
bâa sombàat	money-obsessed
kêun	clever (slang, literally 'gizzard')
phlaan pen mǎa bâa	'fidgety as a mad dog'
pràsàat	neurotic
ting táwng	slightly crazy (slang)

USEFUL PHRASES

This is my usual medicine.
 níi yaa thîi phǒm/dì-chǎn
 kiin pràjam

นี่ยาที่ผม/ดิฉัน
กินประจำ

I have been vaccinated.
 phǒm/dì-chǎn
 chìit wák-siin láew

ผม/ดิฉัน
ฉีดวัคซีนแล้ว

I don't want a blood transfusion.
 phǒm/dì-chǎn
 mâi yàak thàai loh-hìt

ผม/ดิฉัน
ไม่อยากถ่ายโลหิต

Can I have a receipt for my insurance?
 khǎw bai sèht ráp ngoen
 sǎm-ràp pràkan dâi mǎi

ขอใบเสร็จรับเงิน
สำหรับประกันได้ไหม

WOMEN'S HEALTH   สุขภาพของผู้หญิง

I'd like to see a female doctor.
 dì-chǎn yàak hǎa
 mǎw thîi pen phûu yǐng

ดิฉันอยากหาหมอ
ที่เป็นผู้หญิ

I'm pregnant.
 dì-chǎn mii khan

ดิฉันมีครรภ์

I think I'm pregnant.
 khít wâa mii khan

คิดว่ามีครรภ์

I'm on the pill.
 dì-chǎn kin yaa
 khum kamnòet

ดิฉันกินยา
คุมกำเนิด

I haven't had my period for ... weeks.
 mâi mii prájam deuan ...
 aathít láew

ไม่มีประจำเดือน...
อาทิตย์

I'd like to get the morning-after pill.
 yàak dâi yaa khum
 kam-noet chûa khrao

อยากได้ยาคุม
กำเนิดชั่วคราว

I'd like to use contraception (condoms).
 yàak chái wíthii khum kamnòet
 (thǔng yaang anaamai)

อยากใช้วิธีคุมกำเนิด
(ถุงยางอนามัย)

abortion	kaan tham tháeng	การทำแท้ง
cystic fibrosis	sin néua àwk	ซีส,เนื้องอก
cystitis	tòk khǎo	ตกขาว

diaphragm	kàbang lom	กระบังลม
IUD	hùang khum kamnòet	ห่วงคุมกำเนิด
mamogram	x-ray nâa òk	เอ็กซเรย์หน้าอก
	(maemohgram)	
menstruation	mii pràjam deuan	มีประจำเดือน
miscarriage	khlâwt lûuk	คลอดลูก
	kàwn kamnòt	ก่อนกำหนด
pap smear	trùat phai nai	ตรวจภายใน
period pain	bùat pràjam deuan	ปวดประจำเดือน
the Pill	yaa khum kam-nòet	ยาคุมกำเนิด
pregnant	mii khan/mii tháwng	มีครรภ์/
		มีท้อง

premenstrual tension		
ngùt ngìt kàwn		หงุดหงิดก่อน
mii pràjam deuan		มีประจำเดือน
thrush		
tòk khāo		ตกขาว
ultrasound		
ultrasound		อัตราซาวน์

SPECIAL HEALTH NEEDS
ความต้องการรักษาพิเศษ

I'm ...	phōm/dì-chán ...	ผม/ดิฉัน...
diabetic	pen rôhk bao wān	เป็นโรคเบาหวาน
asthmatic	pen hèut	เป็นหืด
anaemic	pen rôhk lo hìt jaang	เป็นโรคโลหิตจาง

I'm allergic to ...	phōm/dì-chán pháe ...	ผม/ดิฉันแพ้ยา...
antibiotics	yaa patichiiwana	ปฏิชีวนะ
aspirin	yaa aet-sa-phai-rin	ยาแอสไพริน
bees	phêung	ผึ้ง
codeine	codeine	โคดีน
dairy products	sìng tii tham dûay nom	สิ่งที่ทำจากนม
penicillin	penicillin	เพนนิซิลิน
pollen	keh sāwn dàwk mái	เกสรดอกไม้

HEALTH

I have a skin allergy.
    rôhk phum phaé phíu nãng   โรคภูมิแพ้ผิวหนัง
I've had my vaccinations.
    phõm/dì-chãn chìt wák-siin láew   ผม/ดิฉันฉีดวัคซีนแล้ว
I have my own syringe.
    phõm/dì-chãn mii làwt chìt yaa   ผม/ดิฉันมีหลอดฉีดยา
I'm on medication for ...
    kamlang kin yaa sãm-ràp …   กำลังกินยาสำหรับ...
I need a new pair of glasses.
    tâwngkaan wâen taa mài   ต้องการแว่นตาใหม่

addiction	tìt yaa	ติดยา
bite	kàt	กัด
blood test	trùat loh-hìt	ตรวจโลหิต
contraceptive (condom)	thũng yaang anaamai	ถุงยางอนามัย
injection	chìt yaa	ฉีดยา
injury	bàat jèp	บาดเจ็บ
vitamins	wítaa-min	วิตามิน
wound	bàat phlãe	บาดแผล

ALTERNATIVE TREATMENTS
แนวทางการรักษา

acupuncture	mãw fãng khẽm	หมอฝังเข็ม
herbalist		
khon khãai khrêuang yaa;		คนขายเครื่องยา;
mãw sàmun phrai		หมอสมุนไพร
homeopathy		
kaan sãang phum khúum kan		การสร้างภูมิคุ้มกัน
massage	nûat	นวด
meditation		
wípàtsànãa/samãathí		วิปัสนา/สมาธิ
naturopathy		
kaan rák saa dûay wii tii		การรักษาด้วยวิธี
thaang thamachâat		ทางธรรมชาติ
reflexology	kaan kòt jùt	การกดจุด
yoga	yoh-khá	โยคะ

PARTS OF THE BODY
ส่วนต่าง ๆ ของร่างกาย

ankle	khâa tháo	ข้อเท้า
appendix	sâi tìng	ไส้ติ่ง
arm	khǎen	แขน
back	lǎng	หลัง
bladder	kràpháw pàtsǎawá	กระเพาะปัสสาวะ
blood	loh-hìt; lêuat	โลหิต;เลือด
bone	kràdùuk	กระดูก
breast	tâo nom	เต้านม
chest	òk	อก
ear(s)	hǔu	หู
eye(s)	taa	ตา
finger(s)	níu meu	นิ้วมือ
foot/feet	tháo	เท้า
hand(s)	meu	มือ
head	sǐi-sà (hǔa)	ศรีษะ
heart	hǔa jai	หัวใจ
kidney	tai	ไต
knee	khào	เข่า
leg	khǎa	ขา
liver	tàp	ตับ
lungs	pàwt	ปอด
mouth	pàak	ปาก
muscle	klâam néua	กล้ามเนื้อ
nose	jà-mùuk	จมูก
penis	awai-yáwá phêht chaai	อวัยวะเพศชาย
shoulders	lài	ไหล่
skin	phǐu	ผิว
stomach	tháwng (kràpháw)	ท้อง(กระเพาะ)
teeth	fan	ฟัน
throat	khaw	คอ
toes	níu tháo	นิ้วเท้า

YOU MAY HEAR ...

pen à-rai?
เป็นอะไร   What's the matter?

jèp mǎi?
เจ็บไหม   Do you feel any pain?

jèp thîi nǎi?
เจ็บที่ไหน   Where does it hurt?

mii pràjam deuan mǎi?
มีประจำเดือนไหม   Are you menstruating?

mii khâi mǎi?
มีไข้ไหม   Do you have a
                               temperature?

pen bàep níi naan thâo rai?
เป็นแบบนี้นานเท่าไร   How long have you
                               been like this?

mêua-kàwn pen bàep -níi mǎi?
เมื่อก่อนเป็นแบบนี้ไหม   Have you had this before?

kamlang kiin yaa mǎi?
ก็กินยาอยู่ไหม   Are you on medication?

pòkàtì sùup bùrìi mǎi?
ปกติสูบบุหรี่ไหม   Do you smoke?

pòkàtì kin lâo mǎi?
ปกติกินเหล้าไหม   Do you drink?

pòkàtì chái yaa sèhp tìt mǎi?
ปกติใช้ยาเสพติดไหม   Do you take drugs?

pháe à-rai mǎi?
แพ้อะไรไหม   Are you allergic to anything?

khun thǎwng rêu plào?
คุณท้องหรือเปล่า   Are you pregnant?

AT THE CHEMIST

ร้านขายยา

I need something for ...
  phŏm/dì-chăn
  tâwng-kaan yaa săm-ràp ...

ผม/ดิฉัน
ต้องการยาสำหรับ...

Do I need a prescription for ...?
  tâwng-kaan bai
  sàng yaa săm-ràp ...?

ต้องการใบ
สั่งยาสำหรับ...

How many times a day?
  wan-lá kìi khráng?

วันละกี่ครั้ง

Four times a day.
  wan-lá sìi khráng

วันละ4ครั้ง

How much per tablet/pill?
  mét-láa thâo rai?

เม็ดละเท่าไร

antibiotics	yaa kâe aàk sèhp	ยาแก้อักเสบ
antiseptic	yaa kâa sèhp	ยาฆ่าเชื้อ
aspirin	yaa aet-sa-phai-rin	ยาแอสไพริน
bandage	phâa phan phlǎe	ผ้าพันแผล
Band-aid (plaster)	phalaastoe	พลาสเตอร์
condom	thŭng yaang	ถุงยาง
	anaamai	อนามัย
contraceptives	thîi khum	ที่คุมกำเนิด
	kamnòet	
cotton balls	sǎmlii kâwn	สำลีก้อน
cough medicine	yaa kâe ai	ยาแก้ไอ
gauze	phâa káwt	ผ้าก๊อซ
injection	chìit yaa	ฉีดยา
insulin	yaa kâe rôhk	ยาแก้โรคเ
	bao wǎan	บาหวาน
laxatives	yaa rábaai	ยาระบาย
morphine	maw-fiin	มอร์ฟิน
painkiller	yaa kâe pùat	ยาแก้ปวด
pill/tablet	mét	เม็ด
sleeping medication	yaa nawn làp	ยานอนหลับ
vitamin	wí-taamin	วิตามิน

HEALTH

AT THE DENTIST   ร้านหมอฟัน

I have a toothache.	bùat fãn	ปวดฟัน
I have a hole.	mii rûa	มีรู
I've lost a filling.	fan thîi ùt wái lùt	ฟันที่อุดไว้หลุด
I've broken my tooth.	fan hàk	ฟันหัก
My gums hurt.	ngèuak jèp	เหงือกเจ็บ
I don't want it extracted.	mâi yàak thǎwn fan	ไม่อยากถอนฟัน
Please give me	ka-rúnaa	กรุณาให้ยาสลบ
an anaesthetic.	hâi yaa sa-lòp	
Ouch!	ûay!	อู้ย

USEFUL WORDS

accident	ù-bàt-tì-hèht	อุบัติเหตุ
addict	khon tìt yaa	คนติดยา
allergic (to)	phae	แพ้
ambulance	rót phayaabaan	รถพยาบาล
blood	lêuat	เลือด
bone	kràdùuk	กระดูก
faint	pen lom	เป็นลม
hospital	rohng phayaabaan	โรงพยาบาล
ill	pùay	ป่วย
injection	kaan-chìit yaa	การฉีดยา
itch	khan	คัน
mentally ill	bâa	บ้า
nurse	naang phayaabaan	นางพยาบาล
pain	khwaam jèp-pùat	ความเจ็บปวด
patient (n)	phûu pùay	ผู้ป่วย
pharmacy	ráan khǎai yaa	ร้านขายยา

DISABLED TRAVELLERS
นักท่องเที่ยวที่เป็นคนพิการ

I'm disabled/handicapped.
phŏm/dì-chăn pen khon phí-kaan   ผม/ดิฉันเป็นคนพิการ

I need assistance.
phŏm/dì-chăn
tâwngkaan khwaam chûay lĕua   ผม/ดิฉัน
ต้องการความช่วยเหลือ

What services do you have for disabled people?
mii bawrikaan àrai bâang   มีบริการอะไรบ้าง
săm-ràp khon phí-kaan?   สำหรับคนพิการ

Is there wheelchair access?
mii thaang săm-ràp   มีทางสำหรับ
rót khĕn măi?   รถเข็นไหม

I'm hard of hearing. Speak more loudly, please.
hŭu nŭak, kawrú-naa   หูหนวก,กรุณา
phûut dang nâwy   พูดดังหน่อย

I have a hearing aid.
phŏm/dì-chăn sài   ผม/ดิฉันใส่เ
khrêuang chûau fang   ครื่องช่วยฟั

Are guide dogs permitted?
ao măa nam thaang   เอาหมานำทาง
maa dûay dâi măi?   มาด้วยได้ไหมbraille

braille library
hâwng samùt àk săwn braille   ห้องสมุดอักษรเบรล

disabled person   khon phí-kaan   คนพิการ
guide dog   măa nam thaang   หมานำทาง
wheelchair   rót khĕn   รถเข็น

GAY TRAVELLERS   นักท่องเที่ยวที่เป็นเกย์
Thai culture is very tolerant of homosexuality, both male and
female. The nation has no laws that discriminate against
homosexuals and there is a fairly prominent gay/lesbian scene

SPECIFIC NEEDS

around the country. Hence there is no gay movement as such in Thailand since there's no antigay establishment to move against. Whether speaking of dress or mannerism, lesbians and gays are generally accepted without comment.

Is there a (predominantly) gay street/district?

mii thanŏn/khèt năi
cha-pháw khon keh mǎi?

มีถนน/เขตไหนเ
ฉพาะเกย์ไหม

Where can I buy some gay/lesbian magazines?

mii năng sěu keh/lesbian
khǎai thîi nǎi?

มีหนังสือเกย์/เลสเบียน
ขายที่ไหน

| butch | thawm | ทอม |
| femme | dǐi | ดี้ |

TRAVELLING WITH THE FAMILY
การเดินทางเป็นครอบครัว

Do you have a child minding service?

mii bawri-kaan
duu láe dèk mǎi?

มีบริการดูแลเด็กไหม

Where can I find a (English-speaking) babysitter?

hǎa khon duu láe
dèk dâi thîi nǎi?

หาคนดูแลเด็กได้ที่ไหน

Can you put an (extra) bed/cot in the room?

khǎw tiang ìik tiang
nai hâwng dâi mǎi?

ขอเตียงอีกเตียงในห้องได้ไหม

Is it suitable for children?

máw-sǎm-ràp dèk mǎi?

เหมาะสำหรับเด็กไหม

Are there any activities for children?

mii à-rai sǎm-ràp dèk mǎi?

มีอะไรสำหรับเด็กไหม

Is there a family discount?

mii sùan lót sǎm-ràp
khrâwp khrua mǎi?

มีส่วนลดสำหรับครอบครัวไหม

LOOKING FOR A JOB   หางานทำ

Do I need a work permit?

tâwng-kaan bai anúyâat
tham ngaan mǎi?

ต้องการใบอนุญาต
ทำงานไหม

I've had experience.	mii pràsòpa-kaan	มีประสบการณ์
What is the wage?	khâa jâang thâo rai?	ค่าจ้างเท่าไร
Do I have to pay tax?		
tâwng sĭa phaa-sĭi mǎi?		ต้องเสียภาษีไหม

I can start ...	phŏm\dì-chán	ผม/ดิฉัน
	rôem thamngaan dâi ...	เริ่มทำงานได้...
today	wan-níi	วันนี้
tomorrow	phrûng níi	พรุ่งนี้
next week	aathít nâa	อาทิตย์หน้า

Useful Words

employee	lûuk jâang	ลูกจ้าง
employer	naai jâang	นายจ้าง
full-time	tem wan	เต็มวัน
job	ngaan	งาน
occupation/trade	aa-chîip	อาชีพ
part-time	mâi châi tem wan	ไม่ใช่เต็มวัน
resume/cv	reh-suu-meh	เรซูเม่
traineeship	kaan àprom	การอบรม
work experience	pràsòpa-kaan	ประสบการ
	thaam ngaan	ณ์การทำงาน

ON BUSINESS — มาเพื่อธุรกิจ

We're attending a ...	maa phêua ...	มาเพื่อ...
conference	pràchum sǎmmánaa	ประชุมสัมมนา
meeting	pràchum	ประชุม
trade fair	ngaan sadaeng	งานแสดง
	sĭn kháa	สินค้า

I'm doing a course.	kamlang àprom	กำลังอบรม
I have an appointment with ...		
mii nát kàp ...		มีนัดกับ...
Here's my business card.		
níi naam bàt khǎwng		นี่นามบัตรของ
phŏm/dì-chán		ผม/ดิฉัน
I need an interpreter.	tâwng-kaan lâam	ต้องการล่าม

SPECIFIC NEEDS

I need to use a computer.
    tâwng chái computer   ต้องใช้คอมพิวเตอร์
I need to send a fax/an email.
    yàak sòng fax/email   อยากส่งแฟกซ์/อีเมล์

Useful Words

cellular/ mobile phone	thohrásàp meu thěu	โทรศัพท์มือถือ
client	lûuk kháa	ลูกค้า
colleague	phûu rûam ngaan	ผู้ร่วมงาน
distributor	phûu jam-nàai	ผู้จำหน่าย
email	ii-meh	อีเมล์
exhibition	kaan sa-dàeng; níthátsakaan	การแสดง; นิทรรศการ
manager	phûu jàt kaan	ผู้จัดการ
profit	pràyòht	ประโยชน์
proposal	khâw sa-nōe	ข้อเสนอ

ON TOUR   มาท่องเที่ยว

We're part of   pen krúp/   เป็นกรุ๊ป/
a group.   wong dontrii   วงดนตรี
We're on tour.   tham thua   ทำทัวร์

I'm with the ...   maa kàp ...   มากับ
    band   wong dontrii   วงดนตรี
    team   kha-ná phûu lên   คณะผู้เล่น
    crew   phûak lûuk meu   พวกลูกมือ

Please speak with our manager.
    choen phûut kàp   เชิญพูดกับ
    phûu jàt kaan   ผู้จัดการ
We've lost our equipment.
    ùpàkawn hāai   อุปกรณ์หาย

We sent equipment   sòng ùpàkawn   ส่งอุปกรณ์
on this ...   dohy...   โดย...
    flight   khrêuang bin   เครื่องบิน
    train   khàbuan rót fai   ขบวนรถไฟ
    bus   rót bàt   รถบัส

SPECIFIC NEEDS

DID YOU KNOW ...

When Thais want to describe an event that's not likely to happen even in the distant future, they may say cháat nâa bàai bàai, 'in the late afternoon of the next life'.

We're taking a break of ... days.
yùt phák … wan
หยุดพัก...วัน

We're playing on ...
jà lên wan thîi …
จะเล่นวันที่...

FILM & TV CREWS
กองถ่ายภาพยนตร์ & ทีวี

We're on location.
yùu thîi sathǎanthîi thàai tham
อยู่ที่สถานถ่ายทำ

We're filming!
kamlang thàai!
กำลังถ่าย

May we film here?
thàai phâapháyon
thîi nîi dâi mǎi?
ถ่ายภาพยนตร์
ที่นี่ได้ไหม

We're making a ...	thàai ...	ถ่าย...
film	phâapháyon	ภาพยนตร์
documentary	bòt phâapháyon	บทภาพยนตร์
TV series	tàwn thii-wii	ตอนทีวี
camera (film)	klâwng phâaphayon	กล้องภาพยนตร์
camera (video)	klâwng thàai	กล้องถ่าย
	wii-dii-oh	วีดีโอ
makeup	châang taeng nâa	ช่างแต่งหน้า

I'm a/an …	pen …	เป็น...
director	phûu kam kàp	ผู้กำกับ
editor	châang tàt tàw	ช่างตัดต่อ
producer	phûu sâang	ผู้สร้าง
	phâaphayon	ภาพยนตร์

PILGRIMAGE & RELIGION
การนมัสการ & ศาสนา

What's your religion?	khun náp thēu sàatsànāa àrai?	คุณนับถือ ศาสนาอะไร

My religion is …	phŏm/dì-chān náp thēu …	ผม/ดิฉันนับถือ...
Islam	sàatsànāa ìt-salaam	ศาสนาอิสลาม
Buddhism	sàatsànāa phút	ศาสนาพุทธ
Christianity	sàatsànāa khrít	ศาสนาคริสต์
Judaism	lát-thí yiw	ลัทธิยิว
Hinduism	sàatsànāa hinduu	ลัทธิฮินดู

I'm (Catholic), but not practising.
phŏm\dì-chān kòet pen
(khae-tho-lik) tàe mâi náp thēu
ผม/ดิฉันเกิดเป็น
(แคทอลิก) แต่ไม่นับถือ

I think I believe in God.
khít wâa chêua thēu phrá jâo
คิดว่าเชื่อถือพระเจ้า

I believe in destiny/fate.
chêua thēu kam
เชื่อถือกรรม

I'm interested in astrology.
phŏm/dì-chān
sŏn jai hŏhraasàat
ผม/ดิฉัน
สนใจโหราศาสตร์

I'm interested in philosophy.
phŏm/dì-chān
sŏn jai pràtcha-yaa
ผม/ดิฉัน
สนใจปรัชญา

I'm an atheist.
   phŏm/dii-chăn
   mâi chêua thĕu phrá jâo

Can I attend this ceremony?
   taam phíthii níi dâi măi?

Can I pray here?
   sùat mon thîi níi dâi măi?

ผม/ดิฉัน
ไม่เชื่อถือพระเจ้า

ทำพิธีนี้ได้ไหม

สวดมนต์ที่นี่ได้ไหม

SPECIFIC NEEDS

Where can I pray/worship?
sùat mon/wâi   สวดมนต์/ไหว้
phrá dâi thîi nǎi?   พระได้ที่ไหน

church	bòt khrít	โบสถ์คริสต์
funeral	ngaan sòp	งานศพ
god	phrá jâo	พระเจ้า
monastery	wát	วัด
monk	phrá sŏng; nák bùat	พระสงฆ์/นักบวช
prayer	kaan sùat mon	การสวดมนต์
relic	thâat	ธาตุ
sabbath	wan phrá	วันพระ
shrine	sǎan	ศาล
temple	wát	วัด

TRACING ROOTS & HISTORY
ร่องรอย & ประวัติศาสตร์

(I think) my ancestors came from this area.
(khít wâa) bàp-bùrút khǎwng   (คิดว่า) บรรพบุรุษของ
phŏm/dì-chán maa jàak   ผม/ดิฉันมาจาก
bawriwehn níi   บริเวณนี้

I'm looking for my relatives.
phŏm/dì-chán hǎa yâat   ผม/ดิฉันหาญาติ

I have/had a relative who lives around here.
mii yâat yùu thǎew níi   มีญาติอยู่แถวนี้

Is there anyone here by the name of ...?
thîi níi mii khrai chêu …?   ที่นี่มีใครชื่อ...

I'd like to go to the cemetery/burial ground.
yàak pai sùsǎan   อยากไปสุสาน

I think he fought/died near here.
khít wâa khǎo sǐa klâi thîi níi   คิดว่าเขาเสียใกล้ที่นี่

My (father) died here during the Indochina War.
(phâw) sǐa thîi níi rá-wàang   (พ่อ) เสียที่นี่ระหว่าง
sŏngkhraam indoh-jiin   สงครามอินโดจีน

VISITING A WÁT   เยี่ยมชมวัด

Virtually every village in Thailand has at least one wát (from the
Pali-Sanskrit avasatha or 'dwelling for pupils and ascetics'), while
in towns and cities they're quite numerous. In rural Thailand, the
wát often serves as a combination religious centre, grammar school,
health clinic, herbal sauna, community centre, astrology house,
transient guesthouse, funeral home and geriatric ward, with monks
and nuns serving as staff for one or more of these functions.

The typical wát is also a focus for much festival activity and is
thus an important social centre for Thais. Especially lively are the
ngaan wát or 'temple fairs'. These take place regularly on certain
auspicious dates (the advent and end of the Rains Retreat; the
anniversary of the Buddha's birth, enlightenment and death; the
anniversary of the first Dhamma lecture etc) and usually feature
music, feasting, outdoor cinema and occasional fireworks.

If you visit a wát, be sure to dress appropriately – no shorts,
short skirts or – sleeveless tops. Shoes must be removed before
entering any buildings.

How long have you been a monk/nun?
  bùat pen phrá/mâe   บวชเป็นพระ/แม่
  chii kìi phansãa láew?   ชีกี่พรรษาแล้ว
(Four) rainy seasons (years)
  (sìi) phansãa (pii)   (สี่) พรรษา(ปี)
May I watch the ceremony?
  duu phíthii dâi mãi?   ดูพิธีได้ไหม
May I practise meditation here?
  pàtìbàt wípàtsánãa   ปฏิบัติวิปัสสนา
  thîi nîi dâi mãi?   ที่นี่ได้ไหม
Is there a meditation teacher here?
  thîi nîi mii khruu   ที่นี่มีครู
  sãwn wípàtsànãa mãi?   สอนวิปัสสนาไหม
Can I stay overnight here?
  phák thîi nîi dâi mãi?   พักที่นี่ได้ไหม
Very peaceful.
  sà-ngòp mâak   สงบมาก

SPECIFIC NEEDS

Buildings/Structures อาคาร/การก่อสร้าง

bell tower	hǎw rákhang	หอระฆัง
bone/ash reliquaries	thâat kràdùuk	ธาตุกระดูก
Buddha image	phrá phútthá-rûup	พระพุทธรูป
drum tower	hǎw klawng	หอกลอง
herbal sauna	hâwng òp yaa	ห้องอบยา
monastic quarters	kùti	กุฏิ
open-sided pavilion	sǎalaa	ศาลา
ordination chapel	bòt	โบสถ์
stupa/chedi	jehdii	เจดีย์
tripitaka (Buddhist scriptures) library	hǎw trai	หอไตร
vihara (building where important Buddha images are housed)	wihǎan	วิหาร

People ผู้คน

abbot	jâo aawâat	เจ้าอาวาส
deputy abbot	ráwng jâo aawâat	รองเจ้าอาวาส
fully ordained monk	phíkkhù/phra sǒng	ภิกษุ
novice monk	sǎamánaen	สามเณร
nun	mâe chii	แม่ชี

Activities กิจกรรม

blessing ceremony	phíthii mongkhon	พิธีมงคล
ceremony	phíthii	พิธี
chanting	sùat mon	สวดมนต์
festival	ngaan/thêhtsàkaan	งาน/เทศกาล
folk magic	sǎiyásàat	ไสยศาสตร์
funeral	ngaan sòp	งานศพ
massage	nûat	นวด
merit-making	tham bun	ทำบุญ
meditation	samathí/wípàtsànǎa	สมาธิ/วิปัสสนา
morning alms round	bintàbàat	บิณฑบาตร
scripture study	pawriyàat tham	ปริยัติธรรม
temple fair	ngaan wát	งานวัด

TIME, DATES & FESTIVALS
เวลา, วัน เทศกาล

TELLING THE TIME
การบอกเวลา

What's the time?	kìi mohng láew?	กี่โมงแล้ว
The time is ...	... mohng láew	...โมงแล้ว

There are three ways of expressing time in Thailand: 'official' (râatchakaan) time, based on the 24-hour clock; the common 12-hour system; and the traditional six-hour system.

Official (24-Hour) Time
เวลาอย่างเป็นทางการ (24 ชั่วโมง)
This is used by government agencies, in official documents and at bus and railway stations.

9 am (0900)	kâo naalikaa	เก้านาฬิกา
midday (1200)	sìp-sǎwng naalikaa	สิบสอง นาฬิกา
1 pm (1300)	sìp-sǎam naalikaa	สิบสามนาฬิกา
midnight	yîi-sìp-sìi naalikaa	ยี่สิบสี่นาฬิกา

The Twelve-Hour Clock   เวลาแบบ 12 ชั่วโมง
The 12-hour system divides the day into four sections (tawn): morning (cháo), afternoon (bàai), evening (yen) and night (khâm).

6 am to midday	tawn cháo	ตอนเช้า
midday to 4 pm	tawn bàai	ตอนบ่าย
4 to 6 pm	tawn yen	ตอนเย็น
6 to 11 pm	tawn khâm	ตอนค่ำ

After 11 pm time is referred to as klaang kheun. The 12-hour system is commonly used during the daylight hours.

9 am	kâo mohng cháo	เก้าโมงเช้า
midday	thîang	เที่ยง
1 pm	bai mohng	บ่ายโมง

3 pm	bai sǎam mohng	ป่ายสามโมง
6 pm	hòk mohng yen	หกโมงเย็น
midnight	thîang kheun	เที่ยงคืน

The Six-Hour Clock   เวลาแบบ 6 ชั่วโมง

From dusk to dawn, most Thais use the traditional six-hour system. In this system, times are expressed in the same way as with the 12-hour clock until 6 pm; from 7 pm to midnight the speaker uses thûm, counting from one to six; after midnight, it's back to one again with the hours referred to as tii (beats).

7 pm (1 thûm)	neùng thûm	หนึ่งทุ่ม
8 pm (2 thûm)	sǎwng thûm	สอ์งทุ่ม
midnight	hòk thûm	หกทุ่ม
1 am (1 tii)	tii neùng	ตีหนึ่ง
3 am (3 tii)	tii sǎam	ตีสาม
6 am (daylight system again)	hòk mohng cháo	หกโมงเช้า

Both tii and thûm derive from the custom of keeping night watches from 7 pm until dawn. Many residential neighbourhoods in Thailand, both in Bangkok and up-country, still hire yaam or night watchmen (often Indians) who roam the neighbourhood with iron bars or sticks, beating the time every hour. If the neighbourhood's inhabitants don't hear the comforting clanks or clacks throughout the night they become alarmed.

DAYS OF THE WEEK   วันในสัปดาห์

Sunday	wan aathít	วันอาทิตย์
Monday	wan jan	วันจันทร์
Tuesday	wan angkhaan	วันอังคาร
Wednesday	wan phút	วันพุธ
Thursday	wan phréuhàt	วันพฤหัสฯ
Friday	wan sùk	วันศุกร์
Saturday	wan sǎo	วันเสาร์

MONTHS   เดือน

All months with 31 days end in -khom while months with 30
end in -yon. (February has its own idosyncratic ending, -phan).
In everyday speech, Thais often leave off the suffixes, so that deuan
mókaraa-khom, for example, becomes deuan mókaraa.

January	deuan mókaraa-khom	เดือนมกราคม
February	deuan kumphaa-phan	เดือนกุมภาพันธ์
March	deuan miinaa-khom	เดือนมีนาคม
April	deuan mehsǎa-yon	เดือนเมษายน
May	deuan phréutàphaa-khom	เดือนพฤษภาคม
June	deuan míthùnaa-yon	เดือนมิถุนายน
July	deuan kàrakàdaa-khom	เดือนกรกฎาคม
August	deuan sǐnghǎa-khom	เดือนสิงหาคม
September	deuan kanyaa-yon	เดือนกันยายน
October	deuan tùlaa-khom	เดือนตุลาคม
November	deuan phréutsàjìkaa-yon	เดือนพฤศจิกายน
December	deuan thanáwaa-khom	เดือนธันวาคม

SEASONS   ฤดู

hot season (Mar–May)	réuduu ráwn	ฤดูร้อน
rainy season (Jun–Oct)	réuduu fǒn	ฤดูฝน
cool season (Nov–Feb)	réuduu nǎo	ฤดูหนาว

DATES   วันที่

The official year in Thailand is reckoned from 543 BC, the
beginning of the Buddhist Era (abbreviated BE in English) or
phútthá-sàk-àràat (abbreviated phaw sǎw) in Thai. Hence
2000 AD is the same as 2543 BE.

Most educated Thais are also familiar with the Gregorian (khrít
sàk-àràat) calendar.

2542 (BE)
  (phaw sǎw) sǎwng phan
  hâa ráwy sìi-sìp sǎwng
1999 (AD)
  (khaw sǎw) nèung phan
  kâo ráwy kâo-sìp-kâo

(พ.ศ.) สองพัน
ห้าร้อยสี่สิบสอง

(ค.ศ.) หนึ่งพัน
เก้าร้อยเก้าสิบเก้า

TIMES, DATES & FESTIVALS

Days of the month are numbered according to the familiar western solar calendar.

date	wan thîi	วันที่
What date (is it)?	wan thîi thâo-rai?	วันที่เท่าไร
The thirteenth of January.		วันที่สิบสามเดือน
wan thîi sìp-sǎam deuan		นมกราคม
mókaraa-khom		

Present ปัจจุบัน

today	wan níi	วันนี้
this evening	yen níi	เย็นนี้
tonight	kheun níi	คืนนี้
this morning	cháo níi	เช้านี้
this afternoon	bàai níi	บ่ายนี้
this month	deuan níi	เดือนนี้
all day long	talàwt wan	ตลอดวัน

Past อดีต

yesterday	mêua waan níi	เมื่อวานนี้
the day before yesterday	mêua waan seun	เมื่อวานซืน
last week	aathít kàwn	อาทิตย์ก่อน
two weeks ago	sǎwng aathít kàwn	อาทิตย์ก่อน
three months ago	sǎam deuan thîi láew	สามเดือนที่แล้ว
four years ago	sìi pii maa láew	สี่ปีมาแล้ว

Future อนาคต

tomorrow	phrûng níi	พรุ่งนี้
the day after tomorrow	má-ruen níi	มะรืนนี้
next week	aathít nâa	อาทิตย์หน้า
next month	deuan nâa	เดือนหน้า
two more months	ìik sǎwng deuan	อีกสองเดือน

During the Day ระหว่างวัน

dawn	rûng cháo	รุ่งเช้า
morning	cháo	เช้า
noon	thîang	เที่ยง
afternoon	bàai	บ่าย
evening	yen	เย็น

early	cháo	เช้า
daytime	klaang wan	กลางวัน
night	kheun	คืน
midnight	thîang kheun	เที่ยงคืน
sunrise	wehlaa phrá aathít	เวลาพระอาทิ
	khêun; rûng	ตย์ขึ้น;รุ้
sunset	wehlaa phrá	เวลาพระ
	aathít tòk	อาทิตย์ตก

FESTIVALS & HOLIDAYS
เทศกาล & วันหยุดประจำชาติ

Exact dates for festivals may vary from year to year, either because of the lunar calendar which isn't quite in sync with the Gregorian calendar or because local authorities decide to change festival dates. The TAT publishes an up-to-date *Major Events & Festivals Calendar* each year, which is useful for anyone planning to attend a particular event.

On dates noted as public holidays, all government offices and banks will be closed.

February   เดือนกุมภาพันธ์

Magha Puja   mâakkhà buchaa   มาฆบูชา
  held on the full moon of the third lunar month to commemorate the preaching of the Buddha to 1250 enlightened monks who came to hear him 'without prior summons'. A public holiday throughout the country culminating in a candle-lit walk around the main chapel at every wat.

Late February to early March
ปลายเดือนกุมภาพันธ์ถึงต้นมีนาคม

Chinese New Year   trùt jiin   ตรุษจีน
  Chinese populations all over Thailand celebrate their lunar new year (the date shifts from year to year) with a week of housecleaning, lion dances and fireworks. The most impressive festivities take place in the Chinese-dominated province capital of Nakhon Sawan.

TIMES, DATES & FESTIVALS

6 April   6 เมษายน
Chakri Day   wan jàk-rii   วันจักรี
a public holiday commemorating the founder of the Chakri
Dynasty, Rama I

13 to 15 April   13 ถึง 15 เมษายน
Songkran Festival thêhtsàkaan sǒngkraan   เทศกาลสงกรานต์
Thailand's lunar new year celebration. Buddha images are
'bathed', monks and elders receive the respect of younger Thais
by the sprinkling of water over their hands, and a lot of water
is tossed about for fun. Songkran generally gives everyone a
chance to release their frustrations and literally cool off during
the peak of the hot season. Hide out in your room or expect
to be soaked; the latter is a lot more fun.

May (Full Moon)
พฤษภาคม   (วันพระจันทร์เต็มดวง)

Visakha Puja   wísǎakhà buuchaa   วิสาขบูชา

a public holiday which falls on the 15th day of the waxing
moon in the sixth lunar month. This is considered the date of
the Buddha's birth, enlightenment and parinibbana, or passing
away. Activities are centred around the wat, with candle-lit
processions, much chanting and sermonising.

5 May
5 พฤษภาคม

Coronation Day   wan chàt mongkhon   วันฉัตรมงคล

public holiday. The king and queen preside at a ceremony at
Wat Phra Kaew in Bangkok, commemorating their 1946
coronation.

Second Week of May
5 พฤษภาคม

Royal Ploughing Ceremony
phí-thii râek   พิธีแรกนาขวัญ
naa khwǎn

to kick off the official rice-planting season, the king participates
in this ancient Brahman ritual at Sanam Luang (the large field
across from Wat Phra Kaew) in Bangkok. Thousands of Thais
gather to watch, and traffic in this part of the city reaches a
standstill. The Thai name of the event means 'Ceremony to
Change the Spirit/Soul of the Fields'.

Rocket Festival   bun bâwng fai   บุญบั้งไฟ

all over the north-east, villagers craft large skyrockets of bamboo
which they then fire into the sky to bring rain for rice fields.
This festival is best celebrated in the town of Yasothon, but is
also good in Ubon and Nong Khai.

July
กรกฎาคม

Asanha Puja   asǎanhà buchaa   อาสาฬหบูชา

full moon is a must for this public holiday which commemorates
the first sermon preached by the Buddha

Rains Retreat Opening
    khâo phansăa   เข้าพรรษา
    a public holiday and the beginning of Buddhist 'lent', this is
    the traditional time of year for young men to enter the
    monkhood for the rainy season and for all monks to station
    themselves in a single monastery for the three months. It's a
    good time to observe a Buddhist ordination.
Candle Festival   ngaan hàe thian   งานแห่เทียน
    Khao Phansaa is celebrated in the north-east by carving huge
    candles and parading them on floats in the streets. This festival
    is best celebrated in Ubon.

12 August   12 สิงหาคม
Queen's Birthday
    wan chalŏem phrá chaná phansăa   วันเฉลิมพระชนมพรรษา
    sŏmdèt phrá răachínii (wan mâe)   สมเด็จพระราชินี(วันแม่)
    public holiday. Ratchadamnoen Ave and the Grand Palace are
    festooned with coloured lights. Celebrated as 'Mother's Day'.

Late September to Early October
ปลายกันยายนถึงต้นตุลาคม
Vegetarian Festival   thêhtsàkaan kin jeh   เทศกาลกินเจ
    a nine-day celebration in Trang and Phuket during which
    devout Chinese Buddhists eat only vegetarian food. There are
    also various ceremonies at Chinese temples and merit-making
    processions that bring to mind Hindu Thaipusam in their
    exhibitions of self-mortification. Smaller towns in the south
    such as Krabi and Phang-Nga also celebrate the veggie fest on
    a smaller scale.

Mid-October to mid-November
กลางตุลาคมถึงกลางพฤศจิกายน
Annual Forest Robes Offering
    thâwt kàthin   ทอดกฐิน
    a one-month period at the end of the Buddhist rains retreat
    (phansăa) during which new monastic robes and requisites are
    offered to the Sangha. Several provincial capitals hold longboat
    races on nearby rivers.

23 October   23 ตุลาคม

Chulalongkorn Day

  wan pìyá mahăarâat   วันปิยะมหาราช

  a public holiday in commemoration of King Chulalongkorn
  (Rama V)

November

พฤศจิกายน

Loi Krathong   lawy kràthong   ลอยกระทง

  on the proper full-moon night, small lotus-shaped baskets or
  boats made of banana leaves containing flowers, incense,
  candles and a coin are floated on Thai rivers, lakes and canals.
  This is a peculiarly Thai festival that probably originated in
  Sukhothai and is best celebrated in the north. In Chiang Mai,
  where the festival is called Yi Peng, residents also launch hot-air
  paper balloons into the sky. At the Sukhothai Historical Park
  there is an impressive sound and light show.

5 December   5 ธันวาคม

King's Birthday

  wan chaloem khăwng nai lŭang

  วันเฉลิมของในหลวง

  this is a public holiday which is celebrated with some fervour
  in Bangkok. As with the Queen's birthday, it features lots of
  lights along Ratchadamnoen Ave. Some people erect temporary
  shrines to the King outside their homes or businesses.

10 December   10 ธันวาคม

Constitution Day   wan rát-thamanuun   วันรัฐธรรมนูญ

  public holiday

31 December to 1 January 31

ธันวาคม ถึง 1 มกราคม

New Year's Day   wan pii mài   วันปีใหม่

  a rather recent public holiday in deference to the western
  calendar

USEFUL WORDS & PHRASES

TIMES, DATES & FESTIVALS

always	samōe	เสมอ
annual	rai pii	รายปี
before	kàwn	ก่อน
century	sàtàwát	ศตวรรษ
closed	pìt	ปิด
date	wan thîi	วันที่
every day	thúk wan	ทุกวัน
forever	talàwt kaan	ตลอดกาล
holiday	wan yùt	วันหยุด
late	sāai (cháa)	สาย(ช้า)
now	tawn níi	ตอนนี้
nowadays	samāai níi	สมัยนี้
open	pòet	เปิด
period (era)	samāi	สมัย
period (interval)	ráyá wehlaa	ระยะเวลา
sometimes	baang thii	บางที
time	wehlaa	เวลา
in time	than wehlaa	ทันเวลา
on time	trong wehlaa	ตรงเวลา
until	jon thēung	จนถึง
when (conjunction)	mêua	เมื่อ
When?	mêua-rai?	เมื่อไร
whenever	mêua-rai kâw-dâi	เมื่อไรก็ได้
minute(s)	naa-thii	นาที
hour(s)	chûa-mohng	ชั่วโมง
half a month	khrêung deuan	ครึ่งเดือน
a month and a half	deuan khrêung	เดือนครึ่ง
year	pii	ปี
weekend	sāo-aathít	เสาร์อาทิตย์

NUMBERS & AMOUNTS
ตัวเลข & จำนวน

See the Grammar section, page 36, for important information on how to use classifiers or counters with Thai numbers.

CARDINAL NUMBERS   เลขนับจำนวน

0	sǔun	ศูนย์
1	nèung	หนึ่ง
2	sǎwng	สอง
3	sǎam	สาม
4	sìi	สี่
5	hâa	ห้า
6	hòk	หก
7	jèt	เจ็ด
8	pàet	แปด
9	kâo	เก้า
10	sìp	สิบ
11	sìp-èt	สิบเอ็ด
12	sìp-sǎwng	สิบสอง
13	sìp-sǎam	สิบสาม
14	sìp-sìi	สิบสี่
...-teen	sìp ...	สิบ...
20	yîi-sìp	สิบ
21	yîi-sìp-èt	ยี่สิบเอ็ด
22	yîi-sìp-sǎwng	ยี่สิบสอง
23	yîi-sìp-sǎam	ยี่สิบสาม
30	sǎam-sìp	สามสิบ
40	sìi-sìp	สี่สิบ
50	hâa-sìp	ห้าสิบ
60	hòk-sìp	หกสิบ
70	jèt-sìp	เจ็ดสิบ

80	pàet-sìp	แปดสิบ
90	kâo-sìp	เก้าสิบ
100	ráwy	ร้อย
200	sǎwng ráwy	สองร้อย
300	sǎam ráwy	สามร้อย
1000	phan	พัน
10,000	mèun	หมื่น
100,000	sǎen	แสน
one million	láan	ล้าน
one billion	phan láan	พันล้าน

ORDINAL NUMBERS
เลขนับตำแหน่ง

These are formed by adding thîi before the cardinal numbers.

first	thîi nèung	ที่หนึ่ง
second	thîi sǎwng	ที่สอง
thirty-first	thîi sǎam-sìp-èt	ที่สามสิบเอ็ด

FRACTIONS   เศษส่วน

Fractions (sèht-sùan) are formed by inserting sèht before the
upper integer of the fraction, sùan before the lower integer.
In everyday speech, if the upper integer is one, the sèht phrase
may be omitted. 'Half' has its own term, khrêung.

1/4	(sèht nèung) sùan sìi	เศษหนึ่งส่วนสี่
1/8	(sèht nèung) sùan bàet	เศษหนึ่งส่วนแปด
3/8	sèht sǎam sùan bàet	เศษสามส่วนแปด
1/2	khrêung	ครึ่ง

NUMBERS

COUNTERS REMINDER!

In Thai, whenever you specify a particular number of any noun you must use a classifier. First you name the thing, then the number, and finally the appropriate classifier. So five oranges is sôm hâa lûuk 'orange five fruit'.

If you don't know (or forget) the appropriate classifier, an may be used for almost any small object. Alternatively, Thais sometimes repeat the noun rather than not use a classifier at all.

animals, furniture, clothing	tua
books, candles	lêm
children, young animals, fruit, balls	lûuk
eggs	fawng
glasses (of water, tea, etc)	kâew
houses	lăng
letters, newspapers (flat sheets)	chàbàap
monks, Buddha images	rûup
pairs of items (people, things)	khûu
people	khon
pieces, slices (cakes, cloth)	chín
pills, seeds, small gems	mét
plates (food)	jaan
rolls (toilet paper, film)	múan
round hollow objects	bai
royal persons, stupas	ong
sets of things	chút
stamps, planets, stars	duang
small objects, miscellaneous things	an
trains (whole)	khabuan
vehicles (bikes, cars, train carriages)	khan

NUMBERS

USEFUL WORDS

count	náp	นับ
couple	khûu	คู่
decimal point	jùt	จุด
dozen	lōh	โหล
equal (adj)	thâo kan	เท่ากัน
equal to	thâo kàp	เท่ากับ
half	khrêung	ครึ่ง
large	yài	ใหญ่
least	náwy thîi-sùt	น้อยที่สุด
little/few	náwy	น้อย
many	mâak	มาก
minus	lóp	ลบ
most	mâak thîi-sùt	มากที่สุด
much	mâak	มาก
number (amount)	jam-nuan	จำนวน
number (numeral)	lêhk	เลข
plus	bùak	บวก
small (size)	lék	เล็ก
too (much) ...	... koen pai	...เกินไป
weight	náam-nàk	น้ำหนัก

HILL TRIBES

Almost everyone in Thailand speaks Thai. However, there are several extremely interesting and frequently visited groups in the north of the country who have their own languages and speak Thai much less well. These groups are sometimes called 'hill tribes' in Thailand. The same groups, speaking the same languages, also live nearby in Myanmar (Burma), Laos, southwestern China and parts of northern Vietnam. In Thailand the hill tribes have a population of nearly 800,000 or under 2% of the total; most arrived there in the last century or two from China via Laos or Myanmar.

This chapter introduces the languages of five of the largest such groups. The first three are Lahu, Akha and Lisu, three closely related languages which are more distantly connected with Burmese. The other two languages here are Mong and Mien, formerly known as Meo and Yao. These two languages are fairly close to each other but quite different from the languages around them. Some Mong in Thailand pronounce their own name as Hmong. These five groups account for nearly half the total hill tribe population in Thailand and a much higher proportion in the north of the country. Overall, there are about 15 million people worldwide who speak these five languages, including over 300,000 in Thailand and five million elsewhere who speak exactly the dialects given here; most of the other 10 million would understand them because they are the major dialects of each language.

The other main hill tribe of Thailand is the Karen; divided into two main groups, Sgaw in the north and Pho along the western border. Most of the many Karen in Thailand are long-established residents and speak Thai fairly well.

Lahu, Akha and Lisu, along with Karen, Burmese and several hundred other languages along both sides of the Himalaya, form the Tibeto-Burman subgroup of the Sino-Tibetan language family. The relationship with Tibetan is a fairly distant one, and that with Chinese (the Sino part of Sino-Tibetan) even more so. Apart from Karen and Chinese, all these languages are similar in structure; for example, they end the sentence with the verb, not its object.

In the past 20 years many Westerners have gone on 'hill tribe treks' in northern Thailand. Just about all of them have to rely on a Thai guide – who most probably won't speak any minority language – for slow and inadequate communication with the locals. There are also a few guides who are members of these groups, and you may want to find one of these. With this chapter you can begin to speak directly, and the resulting surprise and joy of these people must almost be seen to be believed. Almost all foreigners who speak these languages are missionaries, so you may be assumed to be one; people in some non-Christian villages may therefore be a bit wary at first.

There are many good books on the hill tribes of Thailand. A particularly useful and beautifully illustrated one, available in several languages, is *Peoples of the Golden Triangle* by Paul & Elaine Lewis (Thames & Hudson, London, 1984) and widely available in Thailand. *Proto-Loloish* by David Bradley (Curzon Press, London, 1979) provides a summary of the distribution, culture and linguistic history of the Lahu, Akha, Lisu and related groups, and is available from the author or from the publisher.

THE LANGUAGES

Each of the five languages introduced here is written with the Roman alphabet; examples are given in these writing systems, which some hill tribe people in Thailand can read and which represent the sounds quite accurately. Among the Lahu Christians you often find literate speakers, but less frequently elsewhere. There's another Lisu writing system using capital letters, right side up and upside down, which isn't shown here. Unfortunately each writing system has its own rules, so no general pattern for pronunciation can be given. However, a number of features are present in all these languages, and can be summarised here.

All five languages are tonal, like Thai, Chinese and most other languages of South-East and East Asia; that is, the pitch of the voice must be controlled, as the same combination of consonant and vowel means different things under different pitches. Lahu and Akha indicate these tones with small diacritics after the vowel of each syllable; Lisu, Mong and Mien use a consonant after each vowel to signify the tone. Speaking a tonal language is not like singing – you don't need to get exactly the same pitch every time; just control the pitch in a relative way. This is done when saying 'Yes.' versus 'Yes?' or 'Yes!' in English, but in English it carries over the whole sentence, not just one word; here each syllable must be controlled for pitch.

The five languages make a contrast of aspiration for sounds such as 'p', 't' and 'k'. This contrast is automatic and when used in English doesn't make a difference to meaning, but must be maintained in these languages or the wrong word will result. In English the 'p', 't' and 'k' preceded by an 's' as in 'spar', 'star' and 'scar' have no puff of air after the consonant; these are called unaspirated. The 'p', 't' and 'k' in 'par', 'tar' and 'car' have a strong puff of air after the consonant; these are called aspirated. You can most easily feel the puff of air by putting your hand in front of your mouth when you say these words. To get used to controlling this difference, you can start by saying a slight 's' sound before the unaspirated consonants, then gradually leaving it off but not releasing the puff of air afterwards; the aspirated sounds present no difficulty for English speakers. Some other European languages use primarily unaspirated sounds, so speakers of these may need to emphasise the pushing out of air for them.

Each language has relatively simple syllable structure, with few sequences of consonants before the vowel and only one, or in some cases, no consonant, possible after it; and every syllable has a tone.

Most of the five languages use some vowels that are unlike those of most European languages; these include sounds like 'u' and 'o' but made with the lips spread at the edges rather than rounded. You can try looking in a mirror and controlling the lips to get the idea: make a rounded 'u' or 'o', then keep saying it but spread the lips by smiling. These spread and rounded sounds are different vowels, and must be kept apart. So too must the spread and rounded sounds like German 'i' and 'ü', 'e' and 'ö' or the similar French 'i' and 'u', 'e' and 'eu', which are also distinct sounds in some of these languages.

Furthermore, in most of the vowels there is no tongue movement during the sound; in English 'a' and 'o' glide off into 'i' and 'u' sounds, and 'u' starts with a 'y' sound, but these movements are not found in the hill tribe languages – just as they are absent from many European languages such as French, Italian, and so on.

Like Thai, Chinese and other surrounding languages, all these languages have grammatical features in common. For example, all adjectives function like verbs, so there's no need for a verb like 'to be' in addition to the adjective in a sentence like 'He is tall'. Another example is that every number must be accompanied by a classifier. The noun being counted determines which classifier, so for example 'one person' comes out as 'person one human-classifier' in Lahu, Akha and Lisu; and as 'one human-classifier person' in Mong and Mien.

In some instances question marks aren't used with the hill tribe languages – this is either because the question is presented in the form of a statement, or to indicate that there's no rise in intonation at the end of the sentence. In general, responses to questions involve simply repeating the verb used, with a negative word before it if the reply is negative.

None of these languages has endings on words to mark gender, case, tense or other categories often attached to words in European languages; instead, the corresponding meanings are expressed, if at all, by separate words.

LAHU

The Lahu are a group of over 800,000 people; the approximately 90,000 Lahu in Thailand represent five main subgroups of this complex ethnic group: Black Lahu (La˘hu_na^); Red Lahu (La˘hu_nyi); White Lahu (La˘hu_ hpu); Shehleh (La˘hu_sheh˘ leh-), and Yellow Lahu (La˘hu_shi).

Tones

The most complex thing about the sounds of Lahu is the tones; there are seven. Actually many Lahu have trouble keeping two of these seven (low falling and low level) apart, and the Shehleh have collapsed two others (high falling and low falling) completely in their speech; but they are absolutely essential to speaking and understanding Lahu. Tones mainly involve the pitch of the voice; it's not quite like singing, but you must control the pitch for each syllable.

The tones are:

high falling	indicated by a raised ˘ after the vowel
mid level	indicated by the absence of any mark
low falling	indicated by a lowered ˏ after the vowel
low level	indicated by an underline _ after the vowel
high rising	indicated by ¯ after the vowel
high short	indicated by ^ after the vowel
low short	indicated by lowered ˏ after the vowel

For example:

ca˘	eat
ca	look for
caˏ shi_	rice grain
ca_	feed
ca¯	join
ca^	a strip
caˏ	push

Don't ignore these tones, as they make a difference to the meaning, as in Thai and most other languages of the area. The tones of Yellow Lahu are quite different, but as noted above most Yellow Lahu in Thailand can understand and speak Black Lahu. When you see a tone mark in the phrases, try to use the correct pitch. Remember to attempt the right pitch for each syllable, instead of rising at the end of a question sentence or falling at the end of a statement sentence as in English. The two short tones are cut off by a catch at the end, rather like that in the middle of the expression of imminent danger, 'oh-oh!', or the Cockney replacement for 't' at the end of a word like 'fat'. The other five tones are longer, and in some cases have more pitch movement during the syllable: rising or falling as the case may be.

Greetings & Civilities

How are you? (lit: is life easy?)	Cheh˘ sha la˘?
Fine. (lit: life is easy)	Cheh˘ sha la˘.
Where are (you) going?	Hk'aw_ k'ai le?
(I'm) going to ...	... k'ai ve.
the Lahu village	la˘ hu_ hk'a^
wash [oneself, not clothes]	i˘ka^ heh˘
the Akha village	taw_ kaw hk'a^
home	a˘hk'aw
Where have you come from?	Hk'aw_ ka∧ la˯ le?
I've come ...	... la˯ ve.
for a visit	ca gui˘
from the North Thai village	kaw˘law˘ hk'a^ka∧
Have (you) eaten (rice)?	(Aw_) ca˘ peu˯ o˯ la˘?
(I've) eaten (rice).	(Aw_) ca˘ peu˯ o˯ .
(I) haven't eaten (rice).	(Aw_) ma˘ ca˘ she_?
Come inside the house!	A˘hk'aw la˯!
[you should take off your shoes before entering]	

Sit down inside the house!   A–hk'aw mui!

Drink (some) tea!   La‿g'ui‿daw‿.
Drink (some) water!   I˜ ka^ daw‿!

Very good!   Da∧ ja˜!

Thank you.   Aw‿ bon ui_ja˜!
   (lit: blessing is very big – this phrase is mainly used by
   Christians)

You're welcome.   Te∧chi˜ ma˜ he^!
   (lit: it's nothing)

HILL TRIBES

SOME USEFUL WORDS

to sell	hawn˜ve
to buy	vui. ve
to meet	maw. da∧ve
to give	pi˜ve
to sing	k'a mui. ve
to be happy	ha leh. ve
to take	yu. ve
to be sad	daw˜ha‿ve
to remember	daw˜naw˜ve
forget	leun˜ve
to have a conversation	na‿u˜ te da∧ve
quickly	ha^ha^
slowly	a yeh˜yeh˜
country/nation	mvuh˜mi.
town	meun˜
market	tcuh
silver	hpu
gold	shi
this	chi ve
that	o˜ve

Goodbye.	K'aw⁻eh∧ ve.
(lit: (I'm) going back)	
[said by person who is leaving]	
Goodbye!	A yeh⁻ k'ai meh‿.
(lit: please go slowly)	
[said by person who is staying]	

Small Talk

What is your name?	Naw‿ aw‿ meh a‿ hto∧ ma meh ve le?
Where do you live?	Naw‿ cheh⁻ kui‿ hk'a‿ lo cheh⁻ ve le?
My name is ...	... meh ve.
I live at ...	Nga‿ ... mvuh⁻mi‿ lo cheh⁻ve.
Have you got a ...?	Naw‿ ... caw‿ la˅?
(lit: are they alive?)	
wife	mi˅ma
husband	haw⁻ hk'a^pa‿
brothers and sisters	aw‿ vi⁻ aw‿ nyi
mother and father	aw‿ pa aw‿ e
sons and daughters	ya˅pa_ya˅mi˅

AT THE TABLE

Please eat until you're full.	Aw_ ca˅ bvuh^ meh_!
Drink whisky!	Tzuh‿ daw‿!
I can't eat chillies.	A⁻ hpe∧ ca⁻ma⁻hpeh∧.
Have you got salt?	A⁻ leh∧ caw‿ la˅?
It's very delicious!	Meh_ ja˅ ve.

HILL TRIBES

How many brothers and sisters do you have?	Aw‿vi‾ aw‿ nyi hk'a‿ nyi‾ g'a‿ caw‿ le?
How many children do you have?	Ya‿pa‿ya‾mi‾ hk'a‿ nyi‾g'a‿ caw‿ le?
(I have) only one (person).	Te‾g'a‿ ti‾ caw‿.
(I have) four (people).	Awn‿g'a‿ caw‿.

Accommodation & Meals

May I sleep in your house?	Naw‿ a‾hk'aw zuh ‿hpeh ‿ tu‿ la‾?
Where shall I put my things down?	Nga‿ maw‾ hk'a‿ lo teh ta‿tu‿ le?
If I stay one night, how much is it?	Te‾ha‾ha‾k'o aw‿hpfuh‾ hk'a‿ ma yu‿ le?
One night is 20 baht.	Te‾ha‾ nyi‿chi ba ‿.

Do you have (a) ...?	... caw‿ la‾?
blanket	a‾bo ‿
flashlight (torch)	da^ mi‿
lamp	kaw^f ai‾
mat	gu‾ye^
mattress	hpa‿ teh
mosquito net	hpa‿ ka‿
pillow	u‾geh‾

How much is ...?	... hk'a‿ ma le?
one	te‾ ma‿
one animal	te‾ hkeh
one kg	te‾ ki‾lo‾

HILL TRIBES

Can (you) give me ...?	... pi˘ la˘ tu‿ la˘?
a banana	a˜paw˘k'u
a bowl	hkeh˘
chopsticks	a˜cu ka
a teacup	la‿ hkeh
fruit	i˜shi‿
hot water	g'ui‿ haw
a (small) knife	a˜ hte∧ (eh˜)
a spoon	lu˘k'u

Will (you) make me ...?	... te la˘ tu‿ la˘?
beans	naw^shi‿
curry	aw‿chi˘
pork curry	va∧sha‿aw‿chi˘
chicken curry	g'a^sha‿aw‿chi˘
eggplant	ma˜hkui˜shi‿
jackfruit	nu˜feu˜k'o‿shi‿
pumpkin	hpui˜mui˜shi‿
(cooked) rice	aw‿
taro	peh˜shi‿
vegetables	g'aw˜naw g'aw˘ca˜

Can I buy ...?	... vui‿hpeh∧tu‿la˘?
batteries (flashlight)	da^ mi‿shi‿
a chicken	g'a∧te˜hkeh
egg(s)	g'a^ u
fish	nga˜
(some) meat	aw‿sha‿
pork	va∧sha‿
soap	sa‿bu‿

AKHA

The Akha numbered about 600,000 in 1998, of which there are 55,000 in Thailand Most Akha in Thailand live in Chiang Rai province. This group calls itself Akha (with both syllables spoken on a low tone). The Thai groups in South-East Asia call them Kaw or Ekaw (Igor), a name the Akha do not like.

The Akha will realise that you cannot speak their language flawlessly, but there are certain taboo terms to steer clear of. For example, the words for: twins, hail, flowers and certain other expressions having to do with taboo items in the Akha culture. Also, do *not* ask a man or woman the name of their spouse. This is very rude in Akha, and she or he will not be able to tell you – at least this is true among the non-Christian Akha. Almost anything having to do with death is best left unsaid – unless you hear the Akha say it. It is also very important to refer to the Akha as A˅ka˅ (both low tones, the second syllable aspirated), and not as Kaw or Ekaw.

Remember too that those following the 'Akha Way' (A˅ ka˅ zah˅ taw˅ -eu) will be outraged if you do anything to hurt their sacred objects and places. Not only will they be outraged – they could also fine you. The fine would probably pay for the things they would need to repurify the object or area.

Your sensitivity to their language and culture will be greatly appreciated by them, and make your stay more enjoyable.

Greetings & Civilities

Where are you going?	Naw˅a˅ ga˅ i ˅te?
(I) have come here.	Heu ga˅ la˅ma.
(I) have come to your place.	Naw˅ jaw ˅ga˅ la˅-eu˅ ma.
(I'm) not going anywhere.	Ti˅ ga˅ -i˅ma˅ i˅.
(I'm) going to the mountain field.	Ya˅ngeh i˅ma.
(I'm) going to get firewood.	Mi˅ dza˅ k'eh^-i ˅ma.
(I'm) going to get water.	I˅ cu˄ k'aw˄-i ˅ ma.
(I'm) going to town.	Meu˅-ah ˅i ˅ma.

To make it more polite, de can be added to all of the positive sentences.

(I) bow my head in greeting (to you).	Uˬ duˬ tahˬ ma.
(I) bow my head in greeting (to you too).	Uˬ duˬtahˬ ma de.
Thank (you). (lit: great blessing/value – this is often said to a person who is staying behind)	Guiˬlahˬhuiˬmiˇ-a de.
Thank (you) very much indeed!	Guiˬlahˬhuiˬdui dui ma.
Never mind. [used both in answer to the 'thanks', and as we would use 'never mind' in English]	Tiˬjeˬ-iˬmaˬngeuˇ.
Are you well? (lit: living easily?)	Jawˇ saˇdo^ miˇ-a loˇ?
I'm well.	Jawˇsaˇdo^miˇ-a.
I'm not well.	Jawˇsaˇmaˬ do^nya.
(I) have come (up) for a visit.	Dawˬdeh g'a laˇ-euˬma.
Please come (to) sit in the house.	Iˇkahˇnuiˇlaˇ -awˬde.
Please drink some tea.	Lawˇbawˬ dawˇ-awˬde.
Please drink some water.	Iˇcuˬdawˇ-awˬde.
Please eat some fruit.	Aˇsiˬdzaˬ-awˬde.
Thanks. [with the idea that there will be blessing/value involved]	Guiˬ lahˬ huiˬtehˬ-a.
(I) am returning (down) now.	G'oˬ-i ˇma de.
(I) am returning (up) now. [said by those leaving]	G'oˬ leˇ ma de.

Go slowly back down.	Aw law^law^-eh˅ g'o˄ -i˅ de.
Go slowly back up.	Aw law^law^-eh˅ g'o˄ le˅ de.
[said by those remaining behind]	

Small Talk

What is your name?	Naw˅ -eu˅ tsaw˅ myah a˅ jo^-eh˅ ku˅ te?
My name is ...	Nga˅ -eu˅ tsaw˅ myah˅ -a˅, ... leh˅ ku˅ -eu meh.
My name is Li Nah˅. [a boy's name]	Li Nah˅ leh˅ ku˅ -eu meh.
My name is Mi˅Nah˅. [a girl's name]	Mi˅ Nah˅ leh˅ ku˅ -eu meh.
What village do (you) live in?	A˅ geu pu -ah˅ jaw˅ te?
What are (you) looking for?	A˅ je˅ po^-eu cah te?
Is (your) field good?	Ya˅ yaw mui˅ nga lo˅?
(It) is good.	Yaw mui˅ nga.
Not all that good.	Teu na^ na^ -eh˅ ma˅ mui˅ -a.
Not all that good.	Ti˅ paw^-i˅ ma˅ mui˅ -a.
(There are) many rocks.	K'a˅ lo yaw mya˅ meh.
Is that so (OK)?	Ngeu˅ ma lo˅?
[when speaking of oneself, otherwise it will be: Ngeu˅meh lo.]	
It is so.	Ngeu˅ ma.
It is not so.	Ma˅ ngeu˅.
Have (you) planted rice (yet)?	Ceh˅ ka ta˅ ma˅ lo˅?
(I) haven't planted rice yet.	Ceh˅ ma˅ ya ka-a˅ si˅.
(I) have planted rice.	Ceh˅ ka ji˅ ma˅.

Note: For most animate objects jawˇ is used, for inanimate objects jaˆ is used.

How many children do you have?	Nawˇ zaᵥ aˇ myaˆ g'aᵥ jawˇ e?
I have two boys and two girls.	Ngaᵥ aᵥli nyiᵥ g'aᵥ aᵥbuˇ nyiᵥ g'aᵥ jawˇ ma.
I have no children yet.	Ngaˇ zaᵥ tiᵥg'aᵥ-iᵥ maᵥ jawˇ le siᵥ.
Is your father present (alive)?	Nawᵥ da jawˇ meh lo?
My father is present (alive).	Ngaᵥ da jawˇ meh.

AT THE TABLE

Have (you) eaten rice yet?	Hawᵥ dzaᵥ g'aᵥ maᵥ loˇ?
(I) have eaten.	Dzaᵥ g'aᵥ maᵥ.
(I) have eaten morning rice.	Shawᵥ hawᵥ dzaᵥ g'aᵥ maᵥ.
(I) have eaten noon rice.	G'ahˇ hawᵥ dzaᵥ g'aᵥ maᵥ.
(I) have not eaten evening rice yet.	Ciˆ hawᵥ maᵥ dzaᵥ-aᵥ siᵥ.
Are you hungry?	Nawˇ hawᵥ mehˆ nya loˇ?
I am hungry.	Ngaˆ-ahˇ hawᵥmehˆ nya.
(I) am not hungry yet.	Maᵥmehˆ nya siᵥ.
I am not hungry yet.	Ngaᵥ-ahˇ hawᵥ maᵥ mehˆ nya siᵥ.
Are you thirsty?	Iˇ cuˆ mehˆ miˇ-a loˇ?
I am thirsty.	Ngaᵥ-ahˇ iˇcuˆ mehˆ nya.
(I) am not thirsty yet.	Maᵥ mehˆ nya siᵥ.
(I) want to drink water.	Iˇ cuˆ dawˇ mawˆ miˇ-a.

Do (you) have a father?	A∨ da baw ma lo∨?
(I) have a father.	A∨ da baw ma.
Do (you) have a mother?	A∨ ma baw ma lo∨?
I do not have a mother since she has died.	A∨ ma shi∨-eu, mi∨ neh ma∨ baw-a.
How old are (you)?	A∨ k'o∧ a∨ mya∧ k'o∧ k'aw∧ la∨ -eu∨te?
(I) am over 20 years old.	A∨ k'o∧ nyi∨ tse∨ dzeh∨ -i∨ma∨.

Accommodation & Meals

Do (you) want to stay overnight?	Ya∧ maw∧ mi∨-a lo∨?
(I) want to stay overnight.	Ya∧ maw∧ mi∨-a.
(I) cannot stay overnight.	Ma∨ ya∧ nya-a.
Thank you very much. [polite]	Gui∨ lah∨ hui∨ ma de.
I want to stay one or two nights.	Ti∨ mi∨ nyi∨ mi∨ ya∧ maw∧ mi∨-a de.
How much (money) do (you) want?	A∨ poe∨ a∨ mya∧ geu∧ ma∧ nya?
Fifty baht should be enough.	Nga∨ tse∨ ba∧ lo∧ du∨.
(I) want to ask (beg) 60 baht.	Ko∧ tse∨ ba∧ sha∧ maw∧ mi∨- a.
Do (you) want rice liquor?	Ji∨ ba∨ daw∨ maw∧ mi∨-a lo∨?
I do not want to drink rice liquor.	Nga∨ ji∨ ba∨ ma∨ daw∨ maw∧ nya.
Do you want to smoke ('drink') opium?	Naw∨ ya pi∨ daw∨ maw∧ mi∨- a lo∨?
(I) don't want to smoke (it).	Ma∨ daw∨ maw∧ nya.
Do (you) want to drink tea?	Law∨ baw∨ daw∨ maw∧ mi∨- a lo∨?
(I) want to drink tea please.	Law∨ baw∨ daw∨ maw∧ mi∨ - a de.

HILL TRIBES

What do you want to eat?	Naw˅ a˅ je˅ dza˅maw∧ nya?
(I) do not (have it).	Ma˅ ja^.
(I) do not have any more.	Ma˅ pa˅ ja^.
(lit: I had them and they are gone)	
(I) have. [polite]	Ja^ ma de.
(I) would like to eat chicken.	Ya ci^ sha˅ ji˅ dza˅ maw∧ mi˅-a de.

Do you have (a) ...?	... ja^ ma lo˅?
banana	nga beh^
beans	a˅nui^
blanket	a˅bui
bowl	k'm˅ ma˅
chicken eggs	ya u^
chicken [meat]	ya ci^ sha˅ ji˅
chilli	la^ pi˅
chopsticks	ju da˅
fruit	a˅si˅
knife	mi ceh˅
mat	gaw˅ pu
mushroom	a˅hm˅
pillow	u˅ g'm˅
(cooked) rice	haw˅
pork	a˅ za∧ sha˅ ji˅
pumpkin	ma˅deh
spoon	ku˅ tsa∧
stool	nui˅gaw˅
taro	mah˅
vegetables	g'aw˅pa∧
water	i˅cu∧

LISU

The Lisu are a group of some 950,000 people, of which about 35,000 live in Thailand. Almost all of those in Thailand have come from the southernmost Lisu areas in China over the past 50 years, and speak a dialect of Lisu heavily influenced by Yunnanese Chinese. This dialect is different from the 'standard' Lisu used in China and Myanmar.

There are substantial dialect differences within Lisu; the forms given here are those used in Thailand. In the writing system shown here, the values of the letters differ from those of the other four languages in this book, but mainly correspond to the Chinese pinyin system

Tones

Lisu has six tones, two of which involve constriction of the voice and four of which do not. The writing shows five of these tones with a consonant following the vowel. For example, the following are six different words in Lisu:

see	mo
old	mot
to aim/millstone	mol
tattoo	moq
high	mox
weed/to weed	mor

No consonant after the vowel indicates the mid tone. The following t indicates a low tone and following l shows a high tone. The q represents a rising tone, x is for a mid tone said with a creaky sound, and r represents a low, short tone with a creaky sound or cut off with a glottal stop.

Greetings & Civilities

What is it?   Ali nga?

The above is the usual greeting; the following are three possible answers:

(I) am very busy now.   Tei zil mit atkel cat niaq nga.
(lit: this time work very busy able be)

(I) don't have much to do.   Alshit lil mat yi niaq.
(lit: what all not do able)

(I) don't have much on.   Atdor nat niaq nga.
(lit: this side able be)

Where are you going?   Nu ala jjei nga?
(lit: you where go be)

I am going to the village.   Ngua zeilzi jjei nga.
(lit: I village go be)

I am going to wash myself.   Ngua ggoddeit cit jjei.
(lit: I body wash go)

I am going home.   Ngua hin kut jjei.
(lit: I home to go)

Where have you come from?   Nu al lal jox la nga?
(lit: you where out-of come be)

Where is your home/house?   Nu hin ala ddaq-a?

I have come from the market.   Ngua ga-i zir jox la.

I have come for a visit.   Ngua chual la.

Have you eaten?   Nu zza zzat mat zzat?

I have eaten.   Ngua zza zzat o.

I have not eaten yet.   Ngua zza mat zzat sir.

HILL TRIBES

Come inside the house.	Hiku a nat la.
Sit down.	Niq dal jaq-a.
Drink tea.	Catyi ddo.
Drink water.	Ajjaix ddo.
Thank you.	Xual mu wa; Atkel bboxmu
or Dut zoil.	
Good, very good!	Nga, nga qar!
(I) want to go.	Lat jjei ddor wa.
[said by person who is about to leave]	
Until later.	Nat sir.
[said by person staying or person going]	
Go slowly.	Assa assa jjei.
[said by person staying]	

Small Talk

What is your name?	Nu imi ali nga?
My name is ...	Ngua mi ... nga.
Where do you come from?	Nu agua jo la nga?
I come from ...	Ngua ... gua jo la nga.
Thailand	Ta-i met
Myanmar	Lot mieit met
China	Het met

WHICH LANGUAGE

I don't understand.	Ngua na naq mat meir.
Please say that again.	Ame tit to bbaix.
Can you speak ...?	Nu ... tei gul mat gul?
Chinese	Het ngot
Thai	Tai ngot
Burmese	Lot mieit ngot
English	Ang kix ngot

HILL TRIBES

Do you have a wife?	Nu ssatme hua ggu wai?
Do you have a husband?	Nu ssatggu hiaq wai?
I am not married yet.	Ngua hi mat hua heit.
How many brothers and sisters do you have?	Nu kolko cil cil nixssat nixmax amia yo niaq?
Do you have children?	Nu ssatnei niaq mat niaq?
I don't have any.	Mat jjuaq.

I have ...	Ngut ... niaq nga.
two children	ssatnei nit yo
one older brother	kolko tit yo
three older sisters	jiljil sa yo
four younger brothers	nixssat li yo
five younger sisters	nixmax nguat yo

Accommodation & Meals

May I sleep in your house?	Ngua nu hinkut a eirdal dda mat dda?
Can I stay in your house? one night?	Ngua nu hi tit metkel nat mat dda?
(You) may.	Dda nga.
How much is a car to the market?	Tei gua jo ga-i zirgua chi tait lox ge pet amia nga?
A car is ... 20 baht	Lox ge pet ... nici bbar
Where shall I put my things?	Ngua ex ma agua nat bbaix?
Put it there.	Ta ge dal.

YOU'RE WELCOME

The phrase Olli tat bbaix! – You're welcome! – has a literal meaning of 'Don't say that!'.

Do you have (a) ...?	Nu ... jjuaq mat jjuaq?
blanket	yiq bbe
flashlight (torch)	ma ta
lamp	lail wa
mat	tat por; siqzir
mattress	pal gol
mosquito net	zal pot
pillow	wol gor lo
soap	cat biax

Can you lend me ...?	Nu ngua dail ... tit ma ngol la dda ma dda?

MONG

The Mong – who are known as Miao in Chinese, as Meo in Vietnamese, and as Maew in Thai and Lao – are a group of nearly ten million people who originated in southwestern China but have been migrating southwestwards for a millenium or more under pressure from the expanding Chinese. All those outside China and over a million of those in Yunnan and parts of western Guizhou in China speak dialects quite similar to the one given here.

Of the Mong in Thailand the majority belong to the subgroup known as Green Mong (Moob Ntsuab). The other subgroup represented is the White Hmong (Hmood Dawb). Although these are the names that the Mong themselves prefer, they are also known collectively as Miao (from Chinese) or Meo (from Thai and Lao). Furthermore, the Green Mong (Moob Ntsuab) are called 'Blue Meo' by the Thai. The word ntsuab could be translated as either 'green' or '(dark) blue', but the Mong think of blue as the colour of sickness and death; green is the colour of life, and so is obviously the preferred translation. Green Mong are also rather derogatorily nicknamed 'Striped Hmong' (Hmoob Leej) by the White Hmong, because of the horizontal stripes on the women's skirts.

HILL TRIBES

Tones

Every word in Green Mong has its own tone. If you put the wrong vowel or consonant in a word, you will either make a word which means something different, or a nonsense word; the same applies if you use the wrong tone.

Tones in Mong are symbolised by a consonant symbol at the end of the syllable. This doesn't mean that the tone is something which is said after the vowel; the symbol actually tells you how the vowel is said.

The tone symbols and their pronunciations are as follows:

unmarked	mid, level pitch
b	high, level pitch (think of the English word 'balance' to help you remember)
j	starts high and falls in pitch (think of 'jump')
g	starts not so high and falls with a breathy sigh (think of 'gasp')
v	starts with mid pitch and rises (think of 'vaporise')
m	very low and short, with a tiny creak at the end (think of 'mutter')
s	starts quite low and falls even a bit lower (think of 'slide'). It's very hard to distinguish this tone from the mid level tone, but listen for the slight fall, as if the speaker is finishing off a sentence rather than leaving it in mid-air

AT THE TABLE

Eat up, everybody!	Sawv-dlawg noj!
Drink whisky!	Haus cawv!
I can't eat chillies.	Kuv noj hov-txob tsis tau.
Have you got salt?	Koj puas muaj ntsev.
It's very tasty.	Qaab qaab kawg.

There is another tone letter, d, which appears very occasionally in words which usually have tone m, for example nam, 'mother'; nad!, 'Hey, Mum!' It's pronounced like v mid rising. For example:

scratch the ground	raub
a hammer	rauj
to be affected/hurt	raug
six	rau
light a fire	rauv
to dip in liquid/wet	raus
kidney	raum

The two 'high' tones – b (high level) and j (high falling) – sometimes influence the pronunciation of the following tones: j, s, and m change to g: v changes to mid level; mid level changes to s. This is especially common in compound nouns, for example nqaij is 'meat' plus npua; 'pig' is nqaij-npuas, ('pork'), or in combinations involving numbers (eg rau caum, '60' but tsib caug, '50'). However, there are plenty of exceptions to the rule, where tone change doesn't occur when you'd expect it (eg cuaj caum, '90'), and your Mong will be perfectly understandable if you don't make any tone changes. Just be prepared to hear them.

Greetings & Civilities

Hello.	Nyob zoo.
(lit: live well!)	
How are you?	Koj nyob le caag?
(lit: how are you doing?)	
How are you?	Koj puas noj qaab nyob zoo?
I'm fine.	Kuv noj qaab nyob zoo.

HILL TRIBES

WHICH LANGUAGE?

I don't understand.	Kuv tsis to-taub.
Do you speak ...?	Koj has lug ... puas tau?
English	Aas-kiv
Thai	Thaib
Chinese	Suav
Burmese	Maab
French	Faab-kis

Where are you going?	Koj moog qhov-twg?
I'm going ...	Kuv moog ...
up to the White Mong village	peg zog Moob Dlawb
down to the river valley	nrag haav dlej
to buy vegetables	yuav zaub
home	tsev

Where have you come from?	Koj moog dlaab-tsi lug?
(lit: which place did you go to and come back from?)	
I have come from ...	Kuv moog ... lug.
over at the Yao village	tim zog Cu
I'm just coming to visit you all.	Kuv tuaj saib mej xwb.

Welcome. (lit: you've come!)	Koj tuaj los.
I've arrived.	Kuv tuaj os.
[standard response on entering a village]	

Sit down! (on a chair)	Nyob (ntawm rooj) os.
Have a drink!	Haus dlej.
(lit: drink some water!)	

Have you eaten (rice)?	Koj puas tau noj (mov)?
I've finished eating.	Noj taag lawm os.
I haven't eaten yet.	Tseem tsis tau noj.
Thank you (very much).	Ua tsaug (ntau ntau).
You're welcome.	Tsis ua le caag.
I'll be going back (home).	Kuv yuav rov qaab moog (tsev).
(Go, and) come again!	Moog ho tuaj nawb!
Goodbye.	Sib ntsib dlua.
(lit: we'll meet again.)	

Small Talk

What is your name?	Koj lub npe hu le caag?
My name is ...	Kuv lub npe hu ua ...
Where do you live?	Koj nyob qhov-twg?
I live in ...	Kuv nyob huv ...
Have you got ...?	Koj puas muaj ...?
a wife	tug quas-puj
a husband	tug quas-yawg
brothers and sisters	kwv-tij viv-ncaug
mother and father	nam hab txiv
(ie are they alive?)	
children	miv-nyuas

Accommodation & Meals

May I sleep in your house?	Kuv thov su huv koj tsev puas tau?
If I stay one night, how much is it?	Yog kuv pw ib mo, pis-tsawg nyaj?
One night is 20 baht.	Ib mo yog neeg-nkaum Nbaj nyaj.
Where shall I put my things?	Kuv tso kuv cov khoom rua qhov-twg?

HILL TRIBES

Do you have a (lit: one) ...?	Koj puas muaj ib ...?
blanket	dlaim choj
flashlight (torch)	lub teeb nyem
lamp	lub teeb
mattress	dlaim tswm-zooj
mosquito net	lub vij-tsam (kauv yoov)
pillow	lub hauv-ncoo
woven mat	dlaim lev

Are you willing to make ...	Koj puas kaam ua ... rau kuv
for me to eat?	noj?
beans	taum
beef	nqaj-nyug
buffalo meat	nqaj-twm
chicken	nqaj-qab
corn	pob-kws
eggplant	lws-ntev
jackfruit	txiv-plaab-nyug
pork	nqaj-npuas
pumpkin	taub-dlaag
(cooked) rice	mov
taro	qos-tsw-haa
vegetables	zaub

I would like to eat ...	Kuv xaav noj ...
banana	txiv-tsawb
fruit	txiv
mango	txiv-txhais

I would like to get ...	Kuv xaav tau ...
a (small) bowl	ib lub ntim
a pair of chopsticks	ib txwg rawg
a (tea) cup	ib lub khob
hot water	dlej kub
a knife	ib raab rag
a spoon	ib raab dlav

MIEN

The Mien are an ethnic group known to the Thai, the Lao and the Chinese as Yao, and to the Vietnamese as Dao (pronounced *Zao*). Under the name of Yao they have figured for centuries in Chinese official records, and in modern times, in Western anthropological and travel literature. Mien means 'people', and in a narrower sense it means 'Mien people' as opposed to everybody else. To specify the narrower sense of 'Mien people' they add Iu in front, yielding a full name Iu Mien. Iu is pronounced 'EE-oo'.

The Mien language is fairly closely related to the language of the Mong. Mien culture has been much influenced by Chinese culture. Perhaps 50% of the ordinary vocabulary of the Mien language is of Chinese origin, and the proportion of Chinese words in the Mien ritual language may be 90%.

The total population of Mien speakers is about 2 million, including about 45,000 in Thailand. The Mien in Thailand are concentrated in the extreme north, mainly Chiang Rai, Phayao and Nan provinces, with a few villages scattered further south. Some of the most easily accessible villages north-west of Chiang Rai are Mien; you may pass a Mien village on the way to a Lahu, Akha or Lisu village at a higher altitude, as the Mien often attempt to get some valley land which can be irrigated.

AT THE TABLE

Please eat until you're full!	Nyanc beuv hnaangx oc!
Drink whisky!	Hopv diuv oc!
I can't eat chillies.	Yie nyanc maiv duqv fanh-ziu.
Have you got salt?	Meih maaih nzaauv nyae?
It's very delicious.	Naic kuv haic ni aa!

HILL TRIBES

Tones

Every syllable in Mien has a fixed pitch or melody known as its tone. A syllable must be said with the right tone before it can be recognised as having a meaning. Tones are indicated in the spelling system by a silent consonant at the end of the syllable: either h, v, z, x or c, and a sixth tone indicated by the absence of any of these five consonants. For example, maaih means 'to have'; maaiz means 'to buy'; maaic means 'to sell'. These tones have the following sounds:

unmarked	medium-high level
-v	high rising-falling
-h	mid falling
-x	medium-low rising
-z	low rising-falling
-c	low level

Greetings & Civilities

How are you?	Meih yiem longx nyae?
(lit: are you well?)	
Fine.	Longx nyae.
Where are you going?	Meih mingh haiv hdau?
I'm returning home.	Yie nzuonx uov biauv.
I'm going to ...	Yie mingh ...
the Mien village	Mienh nyei laangz
wash myself	nzaaaux sin
the Akha village	Janh-aa-khaa nyei laangz

HILL TRIBES

Where have you come from?	Mei yiem haix daaih?
I've come for a visit.	Yie daaih nziaauc.
I've come from the Northern Thai village.	Yie yiem Janh-kor-lorkv nyei laangz daaih.
Have you eaten (rice)?	Meih mv gaengh nyanc hnaangx saa?
(I) have eaten already.	Nyanc liuz aq.
(I) have not eaten yet.	Mv kaengh nyanc oc.
Come inside the house!	Bieqc biauv oc!
Drink (some) tea!	Hopv kaax zaah!
Drink (some) water!	Hopv uom oc!
Thank you.	Laengz zingh.
Very good.	Longx haic ni aa.
You're welcome. (lit: it's nothing)	Mv penx haiv nyungc lorq.
Goodbye. (lit: go visit us) [said by person who is leaving]	Mingh nziaauc oc!
Goodbye. [said by person who is staying]	Mingh longz oc.
Please come again!	Dih hnoi aengz daaih nziaauc oc!

Small Talk

Where do you live?	Meih yiem haiv ndau?
I live in ... the USA Australia	Yie yiem ... A-mev-riv-kaa deih-bung Australia deih-bung
What is your name?	Meih heuc haiv nyungc?
My name is ...	Yie heuc ...

HILL TRIBES

Have you got ...?	Meih maaih ...?
a wife	auv mic aq
a husband	nqox mic aq
brothers and sisters	muah-doic nyae
Are your parents still alive?	Meih nyei domh-mienh corc yiem nyae?
How many brothers and sisters have you got?	Meih maaih mbuqc-ziex muaz?
How many children have you got?	Meih maaih mbuqc ziexdauh fuqc-jueiv?

Accommodation & Meals

May I sleep in your house?	Yie tov bueix meih nyei biauv duqv nyae?
If I stay one night, how much is it?	Se gorngv yie yiem yietc muonz norq, mbuqcziexorqv?
One night is 20 baht.	Yietc muonz nyic-ziepc mbaatv.
Where shall I put my things down?	Yie nyei gaqc-naiv an haiv ndau?
Will you cook me some ...?	Tov meih zouv deix ... bun yie oc?
rice	hnaangx
pork	dungh-orv

HILL TRIBES

Will you cook me some ...?

    chicken
    vegetables
    pumpkin
    eggplant
    beans
    eggs

Tov meih zouv deix ... bun
yie oc?
    jaeh-orv
    laih-maeng
    fuqc-nyomv
    jiah
    dopc
    jaux

Do you have (a) ...?
    blanket
    flashlight (torch)
    lamp
    mat
    mattress
    mosquito net
    pillow

Meih maaih ... nyae?
    suanqx
    dienx tongh
    dang
    ziqc
    suangh-timh-hoz
    mungh-dangx
    nzuom-dauh

Can I buy ...?
    a chicken
    eggs
    fish
    (flashlight) batteries
    meat
    pork
    soap

Yie maaiz ... duqv nyae?
    jae
    jaux
    biaux
    dienx tongh ndie
    orv
    tungh-orv
    sabu

Can you give me ...?

    some fruit
    some bananas
    some mangoes
    a bowl
    a pair of chopsticks
    a spoon

Tov meih bun ... yie duqv
nyae?
    deix biouv
    deix normh-ziuh-biouv
    deix mamong biouv
    norm nzormc
    sung zouc
    norm ken

HILL TRIBES

Can you give me ...?

Tov meih bun ... yie duqv nyae?

    a (small) knife
    some hot water

    zung nzuqc-dorn
    diex uomh-jorm

Do you smoke tobacco?

Meih buov inh-mbiaatc nyae?

ฉุกเฉิน

General

ทั่วไป

Could you help me please?
  khun chûay chǎn dâi mǎi?

คุณช่วยฉันได้ไหม

Help!	chûay dûay!	ช่วยด้วย
Stop!	yùt!	หยุด
Go away!	bai sí!	ไปซิ
Thief!	khamōhy!	ขโมย
Fire!	fai mâi!	ไฟไหม้
It's an emergency!	chùk chōen!	ฉุกเฉิน
Watch out!	ráwang!	ระวัง
I'm lost.	chǎn lǒng thaang	ฉันหลงทาง

There's been an accident!
  mii úbátìhet!

มีอุบัติเหตุ

Call the police!
  chûay rîak tam-rùat dûay!

ช่วยเรียกตำรวจด้วย

I'll get the police.
  chǎn jà rîak tam-rùat

ฉันจะเรียกตำรวจ

Where are the toilets?
  hâwng sûam yùu thîi nǎi?

ห้องส้วมอยู่ที่ไหน

Police

ตำรวจ

Where is the police station?
  sathǎanii tam-rùat yùu thîi nǎi?

สถานีตำรวจอยู่ที่ไหน

I've been raped.
  chǎn thùuk khòm khěun

ฉันถูกข่มขืน

I've been assaulted.
  phǒm/dì-chǎn
  thùuk tham ráai râang kaai

ผม/ดิฉัน
ถูกทำร้ายร่างกาย

I've been robbed.
  chǎn thùuk kha-mōhy

ฉันถูกขโมย

My ... was stolen.
  kha-mōhy ... khǎwng chǎn

ขโมย...ของฉัน

I've lost my ...	...hǎai láew.	ˋ...หายแล้ว
Bags	kràpao	กระเป๋า
money	ngoen	เงิน
travellers cheques	chék doen thaang	เช็คเดินทาง
passport	nǎng sěu doen thaang	หนังสือเดินทาง

Could I please use the telephone?
chái thohrásàp dâi mǎi? — ขอโทรศัพท์ได้ไหม

I wish to contact my embassy/consulate.
yàak tìt tàw kàp — อยากติดต่อกับ
sathǎan-thûut khǎwng chán — สถานทูตของฉัน

I speak (English).
chán phûut phaa-sǎa (angkrìt) — ฉันพูดภาษาอังกฤษ

I have health insurance.
chán mii pràkan sùkhàphâap — ฉันมีประกันสุขภาพ

I understand.   chán khâo jai — ฉันเข้าใจ
I don't understand.   chán mâi khâo jai — ฉันไม่เข้าใจ

I didn't realise I was doing anything wrong.
chán mâi rúu dâi tham a-rai phìt — ฉันไม่รู้ได้ทำอะไรผิด

I didn't do it.   chán mâi dâi tham — ฉันไม่ได้ทำ

I'm sorry, I apologise.
sǐa jai khǎw thôht, — ขอโทษ,เสียใจ

Can I call someone?
khǎw thohrásàp dâi mǎi? — ขอโทรศัพท์ได้ไหม

Can I have a lawyer who speaks English?
khǎw rîak thanaaikhwaam — ขอเรียกทนายความ
thîi phûut phaa-sǎa — ที่พูดภาษา
angkrìt dâi mǎi? — อังกฤษได้ไหม

Is there a fine we can pay to clear this?
jai khâa pràp dâi mǎi? — จ่ายค่าปรับได้ไหม

Can we pay an on-the-spot fine?
jai khâa pràp thîi nîi dâi mǎi? — จ่ายค่าปรับที่นี่ได้ไหม

I understand.
phǒm/dì-chán khâo jai — ผม/คิฉันเข้าใจ

I don't understand.
phǒm/dì-chán mâi khâo jai — ผม/คิฉันไม่เข้าใจ

I know my rights.

   phǒm/dì-chǎn rúu wâa   ผม/ดิฉันรู้ว่า

   phǒm/dì-chǎn mii sìt   ผม/ดิฉันมีสิทธิ์

arrested	thùuk jàp	ถูกจับ
cell	hâwng khǎng	ห้องขัง
embassy/consulate	sathǎan thûut/	สถานทูต/
	kongsǔun	กงสุล
fine (payment)	khâa pràp	ค่าปรับ
guilty	mii khwaam phìt	มีความผิด
lawyer	thanaaikhwaam	ทนายความ
not guilty	mâi mii	ไม่มีความผิด
	khwaam phìt	
police officer	jâo nâa thîi	เจ้าหน้าที่ตำรวจ
	tam-rùat	
police station	sathǎan-nii	สถานีตำรวจ
	tam-rùat	
prison	khúk	คุก
trial	kaan phíttjàránaa	การพิจารณาคดี
	khádii	

What am I accused of?

   phǒm/dì-chǎn tham phìt àrai?   ผม/ดิฉันทำผิดอะไร

You will be charged with …

   khun tham phìt khâw hǎa …   คุณทำผิดข้อหา..

She/He will be charged with ...

   khǎo tham phìt khâw hǎa …   เขาทำผิดข้อหา..

assault

   tham rái râang kaai   ทำร้ายร่างกาย..

disturbing the peace

   tham-lai khwaam sà-ngòp   ทำลายความสงบ

possession (of illegal substances)

   mii khǎwng phìt kòt-mǎai   มีของผิดกฎหมาย

working with no permit

   tham ngaan dawy mâi   ทำงานโดยไม่

   dâi ráp anúyâat   ได้รับอนุญาต

illegal entry	bùk-rúk	บุกรุก
murder	khâatàkam	ฆาตกรรม
no visa	mâi mii wii-sâa	ไม่มีวีซ่า
overstaying your visa	yùu koen kam-nòt	อยู่เกินกำหนด
rape	khóm khěun	ข่มขืน
robbery/theft	khàmōhy	ขโมย
traffic violation	tham phìt kòt jaraa-jawn	ทำผิดกฎจราจร

Health   เกี่ยวกับสุขภาพ

Call a doctor!
chûay taam măw hâi dûay!   ช่วยตามหมอให้ด้วย

Call an ambulance!
chûay rîak rót
phayaabaan dûay!   ช่วยเรียกรถ
                                                            พยาบาลด้วย

I am ill.   chăn bùay   ฉันป่วย

**My blood group is
(A,B,O,AB) positive/negative.**
lêuat phŏm/dì-chăn krúp   เลือดผม/ดิฉันกรุ๊ป
... bùak/lóp   ...บวก/ลบ

My friend is ill.
phêuan mâi sabaai   เพื่อนไม่สบาย

I have medical insurance.
mii pràkan sùkhàphâap   มีประกันสุขภาพ

A

able (be able to)	dâi	ได้
I can (not) go. pai (mâi) dâi		ไป(ไม่) ได้
aboard	khêun láew	ขึ้นแล้ว
abortion	kaan tháeng	การแท้ง
above	nĕua	เหนือ
abroad	tàang pràthêht	ต่างประเทศ
to accept	yawm ráp	ยอมรับ
accident	ùbàtihèht	อุบัติเหตุ
accommodation	thîi phák	ที่พัก
account (bill)	bin	บิล
across	khâam	ข้าม
adaptor	khrêuang plaeng fai	เครื่องแปลงไฟ
addict	khon tìt	คนติด
addiction	kaan tìt	การติด
address	thîi yùu	ที่อยู่
administration	kaan bawríhăan ngaan	การบริหารงาน
admire (people)	yók yâwng	ยกย่อง
admission (fee)	khâa phàan pràtuu	ค่าผ่านประตู
to admit	khâo	เข้า
adult	phûu yài	ผู้ใหญ่
advice	kham náe nam	คำแนะนำ
to advise	náe nam	แนะนำ
aeroplane	khrêuang bin	เครื่องบิน
afraid	klua	กลัว
after	lăng jàak	หลังจาก
afternoon	tawn bàai	ตอนบ่าย
again	ìik thii	อีกที
against	kháan	ค้าน
age	aayú	อายุ
to agree	tòk-long	ตกลง

I (don't) agree.
   phŏm/dì-chăn (mâi) hĕn dûay   ผม/ดิฉัน(ไม่)เห็นด้วย

agriculture	kasèt-kam	เกษตรกรรม
aid	khwaam chûay lĕua	ความช่วยเหลือ
AIDS	rôhk eht	โรคเอดส์
air	aakàat	อากาศ
air-conditioned	pràp aakàat	ปรับอากาศ
airline	săai kaan bin	สายการบิน
airmail	thaang aakàat	ทางอากาศ
alarm clock	naalikaa plùk	นาฬิกาปลุก
all	tháng mòt	ทั้งหมด
allow	anúyâat hâi	อนุญาตให้
It's (not) allowed.	(mâi) anúyâat hâi	(ไม่)อนุญาตให้
almost	kèuap	เกือบ
alone	khon diaw	คนเดียว
already	láew	แล้ว
also	dûay	ด้วย
always	samŏe	เสมอ
amazing	nâa thêung	น่าทึ่ง
ambassador	thûut	ทูต
among	ráwaang	ระหว่าง
ancient	boraan	โบราณ
and	láe	และ
angry	kròht	โกรธ
animals	sàt	สัตว์
annual	pràjam pii	ประจำปี
to answer	tàwp	ตอบ
antibiotics	yaa bàtì chii-wáná (aenthibai-awthìk)	ยาปฏิชีวนะ
antinuclear	tàw tâan nuukhlia	ต่อต้านนิวเคลียร์
antique	khăwng boraan	ของโบราณ
antiseptic	yaa khâa chéua	ยาฆ่าเชื้อ
any	bâang	บ้าง
anything	á-rai kaw dâi	อะไรก็ได้

anytime	mêua-rai kaw dâi	เมื่อไรก็ได้
anywhere	thîi nǎai kaw dâi	ที่ไหนก็ได้
appointment (time)	wehlaa nát	เวลานัค
approximately	rao rao, pramaan	ราวราว,ประมาณ
archaeological	thaang boraanákhádii	ทางโบราณคดี
argue	tôh yáeng	โต้แย้ง
argument	kaan tôh yáeng	การโต้แย้ง
arrive	thěung	ถึง
art	sìlápà	ศิลปะ
art gallery	hâwng sàdaeng sìlápà	การแสดงศิลปะ
artist	sìlápin	ศิลปิน
artwork	ngaan sìlápà	งานศิลปะ
ashtray	thîi khìa bù-rìi	ที่เขี่ยบุหรี
ask	thǎam	ถาม
asleep	kamlang jàlàp	กำลังจะหลับ
aspirin	yaa aèt-saphairin	ยาแอสไพริน
at	thîi	ที่
atmosphere	banyaakàat	บรรยากาศ
aunt/uncle		
(father's younger sister/ brother)		
	aa	อา
(mother's younger sister/brother)		
	náa	น้า
aunt (older sister of either parent)		
	pâa	ป้า
automatic	àtànoh-máti	อัตโนมัติ
automatic teller (ATM)		เครื่องบริการเงินด่วน
autumn	reúduu bai mái rûang	ฤดูใบไม้ร่วง
avenue	thanǒn	ถนน
awful	yâe	แย่

B

baby	dèk àwn	เด็ก
babysitter	khon líang dèk	คนเลี้ยงเด็ก
back (body)	lăng	หลัง
at the back (behind)	kháang lăng	ข้างหลัง
backpack	pêh sàphai lăng	เป้สะพายหลัง
bad	mâi dii	ไม่ดี
bag	thŭng	ถุง
baggage	sămphaará	สัมภาระ
ball	lûuk bawn	ลูกบอล
band (music)	wong dontrii	วงดนตรี
bandage	phalaasatoe	พลาสเตอร์
bank	thanaakhaan	ธนาคาร
bar	baa	บาร์
to barbecue	yâang	ย่าง
bathe	àap náam	อาบน้ำ
bathing suit	chút wâai náam	ชุดว่ายน้ำ
bath	aang àap náam	อ่างอาบน้ำ
bathroom	hâwng náam	ห้องน้ำ
battery	bàet-toe-rii	แบตเตอรี่
beach	chaai-hàat	ชายหาด
beautiful	sŭay	สวย
because	phráw wâa	เพราะว่า
bed	tiang nawn	เตียงนอน
before	kàwn	ก่อน
beggar	khon kǎw thaan	คนขอทาน
begin	rôem	เริ่ม
beginner	khon phôeng rôem	คนเพิ่งเริ่ม
behind	lăng	หลัง
below	lâang	ล่าง
bent/crooked	khót	คด
beside	yùu khâang	อยู่ข้าง
best	dii thîi-sùt	ดีที่สุด
better	dii kwàa	ดีกว่า

D
I
C
T
I
O
N
A
R
y

English	Transliteration	Thai
between	rá-wàang	ระหว่าง
bicycle	rót jàkrayaan	รถจักรยาน
big	yài	ใหญ่
bill (account)	bin	บิล
biodegradable	yôwy sàlǎi dâi	ย่อยสลายดี
biography	pràwàt bùkhon	ประวัติบุคคล
bird	nók	นก
birth certificate	sùutibàt /bài kòet	สูติบัตร/ใบเกิด
birthday	wan kòet	วันเกิด
bite	kàt	กัด
bitter	khom	ขม
black	sěi dam	สีดำ
to blame	thôht	โทษ
blanket	phâa hòm	ผ้าห่ม
bless	hâi phawn	ให้พร
blind	taa bàwt	ตาบอด
boat	reua	เรือ
blood	lêuat/loh-hìt	เลือด/โลหิต
to board (train, bus)	khêun	ขึ้น
to board (boat, ship)	long	ลง
body	ráang kaai	ร่างกาย
boil	tôm	ต้ม
boiled water	náam tôm	น้ำต้ม
bone	kràdùuk	กระดูก
a book	nǎng sěu	หนังสือ
to book	jawng	จอง
bookshop	ráan khǎai nǎng sěu	ร้านขายหนังสือ
border	chaai daen	ชายแดน
bored	bèua	เบื่อ
to borrow	khǎw yeum	ขอยืม
boss	hǔa nâa	หัวหน้า
both	tháng sǎwng	ทั้งสอง
bottle	khùat	ขวด
bottle opener	thîi pòet khùat	ที่เปิดขวด

box	klàwng	กล่อง
boy	dèk chaai	เด็กชาย
boyfriend	faen	แฟน
bracelet	sâwy khâw meu	สร้อยข้อมือ
brave	klâa	กล้า
bread	khanŏm bang	ขนมปัง
break	tàek	แตก
broken	tàek láew	แตกแล้ว
breakfast	aahàan cháo	อาหารเช้า
to breathe	hăai jai	หายใจ
bribe	sĭn bon	สินบน
to bribe	tìt sĭn bon	ติดสินบน
bridge	saphaan	สะพาน
bright (light)	sawàang	สว่าง
to bring	ao maa	เอามา
broken	tàek láew	แตกแล้ว
building	tèuk	ตึก
to burn	mâi	ไหม้
bus	rót meh	รถเมล์
bus station	sathăa-nii khŏn sòng	สถานีขนส่ง
bus stop	pâai rót meh	ป้ายรถเมล์
business	thúrákit	ธุรกิจ
business person	nák thúrákit	นักธุรกิจ
busy	mâi wâang	ไม่ว่าง
but	tàe	แต่
buttons	kràdeum; pùm	กระดุม,ปุ่ม
to buy	séu	ซื้อ
by	dohy	โดย

C

café	ráan kaafae	ร้านกาแฟ
camera	klâwng thàai rûup	กล้องถ่ายรูป
camp	khâai phák raem	ค่ายพักแรม

C

to camp	yùu khâai phák raem	อยู่ค่ายพักแรม
can (to be able)	dâi	ได้

I/We can do it.
rao tham (mâi) dâi   เราทำ(ไม่)ได้

a can	kràpǎwng	กระป๋อง
can opener	thîi pòet kràpǎwng	ที่เปิดกระป๋อง
to cancel	yók lôek	ยกเลิก
candle	thian	เทียน
capitalism	látthí naai thun	ลัทธินายทุน
car	rót yon	รถยนต์
cards (playing)	phâi	ไพ่
care (take care of)	duu lae	ดูแล
careful	rámát ráwang	ระมัดระวัง
carry	bàek (nam pai)	แบก(น้ำหนัก)
cashier	phûu ráp jàai ngoen	ผู้รับจ่ายเงิน
cemetery	sùsǎan	สุสาน
certain	nâe nawn	แน่นอน
chance	oh-kàat	โอกาส
chair	kâo-îi	เก้าอี้
change (coins)	ngoen plìik	เงินปลีก
to change (buses, trains etc)	plìan rót	เปลี่ยนรถ
cheap	thùuk	ถูก
cheque (bill)	ngoen	เก็บเงิน
to check-in (hotel)	khâo phák	เข้าพัก
chemist (pharmacy)	ráan khǎai yaa	ร้านขายยา
child	dèk	เด็ก
choose	lêuak	เลือก
cigarettes	bùrii	บุหรี่
cigarette papers	kràdàat muan bùrii	กระดาษมวนบุหรี่
cinema (place)	rohng nǎng;	โรงหนัง;
	rohng phâaphávon	โรงภาพยนตร์
cinema (film)	nǎng; phâaphávon	หนัง; ภาพยนตร์

D
I
C
T
I
O
N
A
R
Y

circus	kaan sàdaeng	การแสดง
	lákhawn sàt	ละครสัตว์
citizenship	sǎn-châat	สัญชาติ
city	meuang	เมือง
city centre	sǔun meuang	กลางเมือง
clean	sa-àat	สะอาด

This room isn't clean.
hâwng níi mâi sa-àat   ห้องที่นี่ไม่สะอาด

to climb	khêun	ปีน
clock	nawliikaa	นาฬิกา
to close	pìt	ปิด
closed	pìt láew	ปิดแล้ว
close (adj)	klâi	ใกล้
clothing	sêua phâa	เสื้อผ้า
coast	chaai fàng	ชายฝั่ง
coat	sêua khôht	เสื้อโค้ท
cold (weather)	nǎo	หนาว

It's cold.
aakàat nǎo   อากาศหนาว

a cold	rôhk wàt	โรคหวัด
to have a cold	pen wàt	เป็นหวัด
colleague	phûu rûam ngaan	ผู้ร่วมงาน
come	maa	มา
comfortable	sabaai	สบาย
communism	látthí khawm-miw-nít	ลัทธิคอมมิวนิสต์
company	bawrisàt	บริษัท
compass	khěm thít	เข็มทิศ
complex (adj)	yûng yâak sáp-sáwn	ยุ่งยากซับซ้อน
computer games	kehm khawmpiwtoe	เกมส์คอมพิวเตอร์
condom	thǔng yaang anaamai	ถุงยางอนามัย
to confirm (a booking)	yin yan	ยืนยัน

ENGLISH – THAI

C

Congratulations!	yin dii!	ยินดี
conservative	hŭa boraan	หัวโบราณ
to be constipated	tháwng phùk	ท้องผูก
constipation	tháwng phùk	ท้องผูก
construction work	ngaan kaw-sâang	งานก่อสร้าง
consulate	kongsŭun	กงสุล
contact lens	lehn kantàek	เลนส์กันแตก
contagious	tìt tàw kan dâi	ติดต่อกันได้
contraceptive	khrêuang khum kam-nòet	เครื่องคุมกำเนิด
contract	sănyaa	สัญญา
conversation	kaan sŏnthánaa	การสนทนา
to cook	prung aahăan	ปรุงอาหาร
cooperative	rûam meu kan	ร่วมมือกัน
corner	mum	มุม
corruption	kaan ráp sēn bon	การรับสินบน
to cost	raakhaa	ราคา

It costs a lot.
phaeng mâak   แพงมาก

cotton	fâai/sămlii	ฝ้าย/สำลี
country	prathêht	ประเทศ
countryside	chonátbòt	ชนบท
cough	ai	ไอ
to count	náp	นับ
court (legal)	săan	ศาล
court (tennis)	sànăam tennít	สนามเทนนิส
cramp	tàkhriw	ตะคริว
crazy	bâa	บ้า
credit card	bàt khrehdìt	บัตรเครดิต
crop	pháw	เพาะ
cross (angry)	moh/hōh	โมโห
cross-country trail	thaang doen	ทางเดิน

DICTIONARY

crowded	nâen	แน่น
cry	ráwng hâi	ร้องไห้
customs (officials)	dàan	ด่าน
to cut	tàt	ตัด
to cycle	thìip rót jàkrayaan	ถีบรถจักรยาน
cycling	kaan thìip rót jàkrayaan	การถีบรถจักรยาน

D

daily	pràjam wan	ประจำวัน
damp	chún	ฉุน
dance	tên ram	เต้นรำ
dangerous	antàraai	อันตราย
dark	mêut	มืด
date (time)	wan thîi	วันที่
daughter	lûuk sǎo	ลูกสาว
dawn	rûng cháo	รุ่งเช้า
day	wan	วัน
day after tomorrow	máreun	มะรืน
day before yesterday	wan seun	วานซืน
in (six) days	ìik (hòk) wan	อีกหกวัน
dead	taai láew; sǐa laew	ตายแล้ว;เสียแล้ว
deaf	hǔu nùak	หูหนวก
death	khwaam taai	ความตาย
to decide	dàt sǐn jai	ตัดสินใจ
decision	kaan dàt sǐn jai	การตัดสินใจ
deep	léuk	ลึก
deer	kwaang	กวาง
deforestation	kaan tàt mái	
	tham-laay pàa	การตัดไม้ทำลายป่า
degree (academic)	parinyaa	ปริญญา
degree (temperature)	ong-sǎa	องศา
delay	phìt kamnòt wehlaa	ผิดกำหนดเวลา

delicious	aràwy	อร่อย
delirious	phóe	เพ้อ
democracy	pràchaathípawtai	ประชาธิปไตย
demonstration (protest)	kaan pràthúang	การประท้วง
to deny	pàtisèht	ปฏิเสธ
to depart	àwk	ออก
departure	kaan àwk	การออก
desert	tháleh saai	ทะเลทราย
to design	àwk bàep	ออกแบบ
destination	jùt mãai	จุดหมาย
to destroy	tham-laai	ทำลาย
detail	raai lá-ìat	รายละเอียด
development	kaan phátthanaa	การพัฒนา
dictatorship	aam-nâat phadèht-kaan	อำนาจเผด็จการ
dictionary	phót-jànaanúkrom	พจนานุกรม
to die	taai; sĩa	ตาย;เสีย
different	tàek tàang	แตกต่าง
difficult	yâak	ยาก
dinner	aahãan yen	อาหารเย็น
direct	trong-trong	ตรงๆ
dirt	din	ดิน
dirty	sòk-kàpròk	สกปรก
disabled	pen khon phí-kaan	เป็นคนพิการ
disadvantage	khâw sĩa priap	ข้อได้เปรียบ
discount	lót raakhaa	ลดราคา
discover	khón phóp	ค้นพบ
discrimination	kaan bàeng-yâek kitjàkaan	การแบ่งแยกกิจการ
disinfectant	yaa khâa chéua rôhk	ยาฆ่าเชื้อโรค
distant	klai	ไกล
distributor	phûu jamnaai	ผู้จำหน่าย
diving	dam náam	ดำน้ำ
diving equipment	ùpakawn dam náam	อุปกรณ์ดำน้ำ

dizzy	wian hŭa	เวียนหัว
to do	tham	ทำ

What are you doing?
tham à-rai? — ทำอะไร

I didn't do it.
phŏm/dì-chán mâi dâai tham. — ผม/ดิฉันไม่ได้ทำ

doctor	măw	หมอ
a documentary	bòt phâaphayon	เอกสาร
dog	măa	หมา
dole	sàwàtdikaan	สวัสดิการ
doll	túkkàdaa	ตุ๊กตา
door	pràtuu	ประตู
dope (drugs)	yàa sèhp tìt	ยาเสพติด
double	khûu	คู่
down	long	ลง
downstairs	khâang lâang	ข้างล่าง
to dream	făn	ฝัน
dried	hâeng	แห้ง
a drink	khrêuang dèum	เครื่องดื่ม
to drink	dèum	ดื่ม
drinkable (water)	dèum dâi	ดื่มได้
to drive	khàp rót	ขับรถ
driver's licence	bai khàp khìi	ใบขับขี่
drugs	yaa	ยา
drug addiction	kaan tìt yaa	การติดยา
drug dealer	phûu jamnài	ผู้จำหน่ายยาเสพติด
	yaa sèhp tìt	
drunk (inebriated)	mao	เมา
dry	hâeng	แห้ง
during	ráwàang thîi	ระหว่าง
dust	fùn	ฝุ่น

E

each	thúk	ทุก
early	cháo	เช้า
earn	hǎa ngoen	หาเงิน
Earth	lôhk	โลก
earthquake	phàen din wǎi	แผ่นดินไหว
easy	ngâai	ง่าย
to eat	thaan (pol)	ทาน
	kin (inf)	กิน

Have you eaten yet?
 thaan khâo láew rêu yang?   ทานข้าวแล้วหรือยัง

I've eaten already.
 thaan láew   ทานแล้ว

economical	pràyàt	ประหยัด
economy	sèhtàkit	เศรษฐกิจ
education	kaan sèuk-sǎa	การศึกษา
elder	phûu mii aayú maak	ผู้มีอายุมากกว่า
election	kaan lêuak tâng	การเลือกตั้ง
electricity	fai fáa	ไฟฟ้า
embarrassment	khwaam àp aai khǎai nâa	ความอับอายขายหน้า
embassy	sathǎan thûut	สถานทูต
employer	naai jâang	นายจ้าง
empty	wâang plào	ว่างเปล่า
end	sùt	สุด
energy	phloeng ngaan	พลังงาน
English	phaasǎa angkrìt	ภาษาอังกฤษ
to enjoy (oneself)	sanùk sanǎan	สนุกสนาน
enough	phaw	พอ
enter	khâo	เข้า
entrance	thaang khâo	ทางออก
environment	sìng wâet láwm	สิ่งแวดล้อม
equal	thâo kan	เท่ากัน

F

evening	tawn yen	ตอนเย็น
event	hèht-kaan	เหตุการณ์
every	thúk	ทุก
every day	thúk wan	ทุกวัน
everyone	thúk khon	ทุกคน
everything	thúk yàng	ทุกอย่าง
to exchange	lâek plian	แลกเปลี่ยน
exhausted	nèuay	เหนอย
exile	nehn thêht	เนรเทศ
expensive	phaeng	แพง
experience	pràsòpàkaan	ประสบการณ์
to export	sòng àwk nâwk pràthêht	ส่งออกนอกประเทศ

F

false	mâi jiing	ไม่จริง
family	khrâwp khrua	ครอบครัว
fan	phát lom	พัดลม
far	klai	ไกล

How far is ...?
  ... klai thâo rai? ...ไกลเท่าไร

farm	thûng naa	ทุ่งนา
fast (rapid)	rehw	เร็ว
fat	ûan	อ้วน
fault	khwaam phìt	ความผิด
fear	khwaam klua	ความกลัว
fee	khâa	ค่า
to feel	rúu-sèuk	รู้สึก
feeling	khwaam rúu-sèuk	ความรู้สึก
female	phûu yĕng	ผู้หญิง
ferry	reua dohysāan	เรือโดยสาร
festival	thêht sa kaan	เทศกาล
fever	khâi	ไข้

F

few	náwy	น้อย
fiancé	khûu mán	คู่หมั้น
a fight	kaan tàw sùu	การต่อสู้
film (movie)	nǎng	หนัง
film (roll of)	fim	ฟิล์ม
to find	phóp	พบ
fine (penalty)	khâa pràp	ค่าปรับ
fire	fai	ไฟ
firewood	feun	ฟืน
first	râek	แรก
flag	thong	ธง
flashlight (torch)	fai chǎai	ไฟฉาย
flight	thîaw bin	เที่ยวบิน
flood	náam thûam	น้ำท่วม
floor	pheun	พื้น
follow	taam	ตาม
food	aahǎan	อาหาร
for	sǎm-ràp	สำหรับ
foreign	tàang pràthêht	ต่างประเทศ
forever	talàwt kaan	ตลอดกาล
to forget	leum	ลืม
to forgive	yók thôht	ยกโทษ
formal	pen thaang kaan	เป็นทางการ
fragile	tàek ngâai	แตกง่าย
free (of charge)	frii (mâi khít ngoen)	ฟรี(ไม่คิดเงิน)
free (not bound)	ìtsàrà	อิสระ
freeze	sâe khǎeng	แช่แข็ง
fresh (not stale)	sòt	สด
fried	thâwt	ทอด
friend	phêuan	เพื่อน
friendly	pen kan aeng (thaan phêuan)	เป็นกันเอง
from	jàak	จาก
fruit	phǒn-lámái	ผลไม้

DICTIONARY

full	tem	เต็ม
fun	sanùk	สนุก
funny	talòk	ตลก

G

game	kehm lên	เกมส์เล่น
garbage	kha-yà	ขยะ
garden	sŭan	สวน
gas (natural)	káet	แก๊ส
gas cartridge/cylinder	thăng káet	ถังแก๊ส
gate	pràtuu	ประตู
generous	jai kwâang	ใจกว้าง
girl	dèk phûu yǐng	เด็กผู้หญิง
girlfriend	faen	แฟน
give	hâi	ให้
glass	kâew	แก้ว
glasses (spectacles)	wâen taa	แว่นตา
to go	pai	ไป

I want to go to ...

	phŏm/dii-chǎn yàa ...	ผม/ดิฉัน...
god	phrá jâo	พระเจ้า
gold	thawng	ทอง
good	dii	ดี
government	ráthábaan	รัฐบาล
greedy	tàklà	ตะกละ
grow	plùuk	ปลูก
to guess	dao	เดา
a guide	kai	ไกด์
guidebook	khûu meu thâwng thîaw	คู่มือท่องเที่ยว
guilty	mii khwaam phìt	มีความผิด
guitar	kii-taa	กีตาร์

H

half	khrêung	ครึ่ง
handbag	kràpǎo thěu	กระเป๋าถือ
handicrafts	ngaan fǐi-meu	งานฝีมือ
	(hàttakam)	(หัตถกรรม)
handsome	rûup law	รูปหล่อ
happy	mii khwaam sùk	มีความสุข
hard	khǎeng	แข็ง
to hate	klìat	เกลียด
have	mii	มี
health	sùkhàphâap	สุขภาพ
hear	dâi yin	ได้ยิน
heat	khwaam ráwn	ความร้อน
heavy	nàk	หนัก
hello (greetings)	sawàt-dii	สวัสดี
	(khráp/khâ)	(ครับ/ค่ะ)
to help	chûay	ช่วย
here	thîi nǐi	ที่นี่
high	sǔung	สูง
hill	noen	เนิน
to hire	jâang	จ้าง
holiday	wan yùt	วันหยุด
holy	sàksìt	ศักดิ์สิทธิ์
home	bâan	บ้าน
homeland	bâan meuang	บ้านเมือง
homesick	khít thěung bâan	คิดถึงบ้าน
homosexual	khon rák rûam phêht	คนรักร่วมเพศ
honest	sêu sàt	ซื่อสัตย์
hope	wǎng	หวัง
hospitality	khwaam òhp	ความโอบอ้อมอารี
	âwm aarii	
hot (spicy)	phèt	เผ็ด
hot (weather)	ráwn	ร้อน
hotel	rohng raem	โรงแรม

house	bâan (reuan)	บ้าน(เรือน)
housework	ngaan bâan	งานบ้าน
how	yàang-rai	อย่างไร

How much?
thâo rai? เท่าไร

How much to ...?
pai ... thâo rai? ไป...เท่าไร

human	mánút	มนุษย์
hungry	hǐw	หิว
to hurry	rîip	รีบ
hurt	jèp	เจ็บ
husband	sǎa mii	สามี
hypnotism	kaan sàkòt jìt	การสะกดจิต

I

ice	náam khǎeng	น้ำแข็ง
idea	khwaam khít	ความคิด
identification (card)	bàt pràjam tua	บัตรประจำตัว
if	thâa	ถ้า
ill	pùay	ป่วย
illegal	phìt kòt-mǎai	ผิดกฎหมาย
imagination	jintànaakaan	จินตนาการ
imitation	khǎwng thiam	ของเทียม
immediately	than thii than dai	ทันทีทันใด
to import	nam khâo maa	นำเข้ามา
	jàak tàang pràthêht	จากต่างประเทศ

It's (not) important
(mâi) sǎmkhan (ไม่)'สำคัญ

impossible	pen pai mâi dâi	เป็นไปไม่ได้
imprisonment	kaan khǎng khúk	การขังคุก
in	nai	ใน
included	ruam tháng	รวมทั้ง

English	Transliteration	Thai
inconvenient	mâi sadùak	ไม่สะดวก
indoors	khâang nai	ข้างใน
industry	ùtsăahàkam	อุตสาหกรรม
infection	kaan tìt chíua	การติดเชื้อ
infectious	tìt tàw kan	ติดต่อกัน
informal	lam lawng	ลำลอง
information	khâw khwaam	ข้อความ
injection	chìit yaa	ฉีดยา
injury	kaan bàat jèp	การบาดเจ็บ
insect repellant	yaa kan malaeng	ยากันแมลง
inside	khâang nai	ข้างใน
instant	than thii	ทันที
insurance	pràkan	ประกัน
to insure	thaam pràkan	ทำประกัน
intelligent	chalàat	ฉลาด
interested	sŏn jai	สนใจ
interesting	nâa sŏn jai	น่าสนใจ
international	naanaachâat	นานาชาติ
to invite	chuan	เชิญ
itch	khan	คัน

J

jail	khúk	คุก
jazz	don-trii jaét	ดนตรีแจ๊ส
jeans	kaang kehng yiin	กางเกงยีนส์
jewellery	phêht-phlawy	เพชรพลอย
job	ngaan	งาน
joke	rêuang talò	เรื่องตลก
justice	khwaam yúttitham	ความยุติธรรม

K

key	lûuk kun-jae	ลูกกุญแจ
kill	khâa	ฆ่า

kind (type)	chanít	ชนิด
king	naai lŭang	ในหลวง
kiss	juup	จูบ
to know (a person)	rúujàk	รู้จัก
to know (something)	rúu	รู้
to know (how to do something)	pen	เป็น

L

lake	beung (thaleh sàap)	บึง
land	phàen din; tii din	แผ่นดิน;ที่ดิน
landslide	phàen din thalòm	แผ่นดินถล่ม
language	phaasăa	ภาษา
last (adj)	sùt-tháai	สุดท้าย
last week	aathít kàwn	อาทิตย์ก่อน

What time does the last vehicle leave?
khan sùt-tháai jà àwk kii mohng? คันสุดท้ายจะออกกี่โมง

late	săai (cháa)	สาย(ช้า)
laugh	hŭa ráw	หัวเราะ
laundry	bawrikaan sák	บริการซักรีดเสื้อผ้า
	rîit sêua phâa	
law	kòt-măai	กฎหมาย
lawyer	thanai-khwaam	ทนายความ
lazy	khîi kìat	ขี้เกียจ
learn	rian	เรียน
left	sáai	ซ้าย
left-wing	kaan meuang fàai sáai	การเมืองฝ่ายซ้าย
legal	thùuk kòt-măai	ถูกกฎหมาย
less	náwy kwàa	น้อยกว่า
letter	jòt-măai	จดหมาย
liar	phûu koh-hòk	พูดโกหก
lice	hăo	เหา

life	chiiwít	ชีวิต
lift (elevator)	lif	ลิฟท์
light	fai	ไฟ
lighter	sáek fai	แสงไฟ
like (similar)	mĕuan	เหมือน
to like	châwp	ชอบ
line	naew (sên)	แนว(เส้น)
listen	fang	ฟัง
little	lék (náwy)	เล็ก(น้อย)
to live	yùu thîi	อยู่ที่
a lock	kun-jae	กุญแจ
long	yao	ยาว
long ago	naan láew	นานแล้ว
to look for	hăa	หา
to lose	tham hăai	ทำหาย
lost	lŏng thaang	หลงทาง
loud	dang	ดัง
love	rák	รัก
lucky	chôhk dii	โชคดี
lunch	aahăan thîang	อาหารเที่ยง

M

machine	khrêuang	เครื่อง
mad (crazy)	bâa	บ้า
made (be made of)	tham dûay	ทำด้วย
majority	sùan yài	ส่วนใหญ่
make	tham	ทำ
many	mâak	มาก
map	phăen thîi	แผนที่
market	talàat	ตลาด
marriage	kaan tàeng-ngaan	การแต่งงาน
marry	tàeng-ngaan	แต่งงาน
matches	mái khìit fai	ไม้ขีดไฟ

maybe	àat jà	อาจจะ
meet	phóp	พบ
menu	raai-kaan aahãan	รายการอาหาร
message	khâw khwaam	ข้อความ
mind	jìt-jai	จิตใจ
minute	naathii	นาที
to miss (family etc)	khít thẽung	คิดถึง
mistake	khâw phìt phlâat	ข้อผิดพลาด
to mix	phasõm	ผสม
modern	than samãi	ทันสมัย
money	ngoen	เงิน
monument	anú-sãa-wárii	อนุสาวรีย์
more	iik	อีก
morning	tawn cháo	ตอนเช้า
mountain	phuu khão	ภูเขา
movie	nãng	หนัง
museum	phíphítháphan	พิพิธภัณฑ์
music	don-trii	คนตรี

N

| name | chêu | ชื่อ |

What is your name?
| khun chêu arai? | คุณชื่ออะไร |

My name is ...
| phõm chêu ... (m) | ผมชื่อ… |
| dìi-chán chêu ... (f) | ดิฉันชื่อ… |

national park	won-ùtháyaan hàeng châat	
		วนอุทยานแห่งชาติ
nature	thamachâat	ธรรมชาติ
near	klâi	ใกล้
necessary	jam pen	จำเป็น
never	mâi khoei	ไม่เคย

new	mài	ใหม่
news	khào	ข่าว
newspaper	năng sẽu phim	หนังสือพิมพ์
next	nâa	หน้า
next week	aathít nâa	อาทิตย์หน้า
nice	dii	ดี
night	tawn kham	ตอนค่ำ
noise	sẽang dang	เสียงดัง
none	mâi mii loei	ไม่มีเลย
nothing	mâi mii a-rai	ไม่มีอะไร
not yet	yang	ยัง
now	dĩaw níi	ตอนนี้
nuclear energy	phlang ngaan pàrámaanuu	พลังงานปรมาณู

O

obvious	praakòt chát (hẽn ngâai)	ปรากฏชัด(เห็นง่าย)
occupation (job)	aachíip	อาชีพ
ocean	mahãa samùt	มหาสมุทร
offend	kràtham phìt	กระทำผิด
to offer	sanõe	เสนอ
office	awfít	สำนักงาน
officer	jâo nâa thîi	เจ้าหน้าที่
often	bàwy-bàwy	บ่อยๆ
oil	náam-man	น้ำมัน
old (things)	kào	เก่า
on	bon	บน
once	khráng nèung	ครั้งหนึ่ง
one	nèung	หนึ่ง
only	thâo-nán	เท่านั้น
open	pòet	เปิด

to open	pòet	เปิด
opinion	khwaam khít hĕn	ความคิดเห็น
opportunity	oh-kàat	โอกาส
opposite	trong khâam	ตรงข้าม
or	rĕu	หรือ
to order	sàng	สั่ง
ordinary	thamadaa	ธรรมดา
organisation	ong-kaan	องค์การ
organise	jàt	จัด
original	doem	เดิม
other	èun	อื่น
out	nâwk	นอก
outside	phaai nâwk	ภายนอก
over (finished)	jòp (sèht)	จบ(เสร็จ)
overboard	tòk náam	ตกน้ำ
overseas	meuang nâwk	เมืองนอก
to owe	pen nîi	เป็นหนี้
owner	jâo khǎwng	เจ้าหนี้

P

package	hàw	หัว
pack of cigarettes	bùrìi sawng	บุหรี่ซอง
packet	sawng	ซอง,หีบ,ห่อ
padlock	kun-jae	กุญแจ
painful	jèp	เจ็บ
pair	khûu	คู่
paper	kràdàat	กระดาษ
parcel	phátsàdù	พัสดุ
park	suan	สวน
parliament	rátsaphaa	รัฐสภา
part	sùan	ส่วน
to participate	mii sùan rûam	มีส่วนร่วม
participation	kaan mii sùan rûam	การมีส่วนร่วม

party	ngaan paatîi	งานปาร์ตี้
passenger	phûu dohy-sâan	ผู้โดยสาร
passport	nǎng-sěu doen thaang	หนังสือเดินทาง
past	adìit	อดีต
path	thaang doen	ทางเดิน
to pay	jàai	จ่าย
peace	sǎntiphâap	สันติภาพ
people	khon	คน
perfect	sǒm-khuan	สมควร
permanent	thǎa-wawn	ถาวร
permission	anúyâat	อนุญาต
permit	bai anúyâat	ใบอนุญาต
persecution	kaan khòm hěhng	การข่มเหง
person	khon	คน
personal	pen sùan tua	เป็นส่วนตัว
personality	bùkhálìk	บุคลิก
pharmacy (chemist)	ráan khǎai yaa	ร้านขายยา
photograph	rûup (phâap)	รูป(ภาพ)
to photograph	thàai rûup	ถ่ายรูป
piece	chín	ชิ้น
place	thîi	ที่
plant	phan mái	พรรณไม้
to play	lên	เล่น
plenty	mâak	มาก
to point	chíi	ชี้
police	tam-rùat	ตำรวจ
politics	kaan meuang	การเมือง
pollution	sàphâap wâet láwm pen phít	สภาพแวดล้อมเป็นพิษ
pool (swimming)	sà wâai náam	สระว่ายน้ำ
poor	yâak jon	ยากจน
positive	nâe nawn	แน่นอน
postcard	praisanii bàt	ไปรษณียบัตร

pottery/ceramics	khrêuang pân din phǎo/khrêuang thûay chaam	เครื่องปั้นดิน เผา/เครื่อง ถ้วยชาม
poverty	khwaam yâak jon	ความยากจน
power	amnâat	อำนาจ
practical	mii pràyòht	มีประโยชน์
prayer	bòt sùat mon	บทสวดมนต์
prefer	níyom	นิยม
pregnant	mii khan (mii tháwng)	มีครรภ์(มีท้อง)
prepare	triam	เตรียม
present (time)	pàt-jùban	ปัจจุบัน
present (gift)	khǎwng khwǎn	ของขวัญ
president	pràthaan	ประธาน
pretty	sǔay	สวย
prevent	pâwg kan	ป้องกัน
price	raakhaa	ราคา

Can you lower the price?

lót raakhaa dâi mǎi? ลดราคาได้ไหม

priest	phrá	พระ
prime minister	naaiyók ráthámontrii	นายกรัฐมนตรี
prison	khúk	คุก
prisoner	nák thôht	นักโทษ
private	sùan tua	ส่วนตัว
probably	khong jà	คงจะ
problem	panhǎa	ปัญหา
process	witthii kaan	วิธีการ
procession	khabûan	ขบวนการ
to produce	phlit	ผลิต
professional	mii aachiip	มีอาชีพ
profit	pràyòht	ประโยชน์
promise	sǎnyaa	สัญญา
prostitute	sôh-pheh-nii	โสเภณี

ENGLISH – THAI

protect	pâwg kan	ป้องกัน
protest	kaan pràthúang	การประท้วง
to protest	pràthúang	ประท้วง
province	jang-wàt	จังหวัด
public	sǎathaa-ráná	สาธารณะ
pull	deung	ดึง
push	phlàk	ผลัก

Q

quality	khunáphâap	คุณภาพ
a question	kham thǎam	คำถาม
quick	rehw	เร็ว
quiet	ngîap	เงียบ

R

race (contest)	khàeng	แข่ง
racist	khít kan bàeng yâek phǐw	คิดการแบ่งแยกผิว
radio	witháyú	วิทยุ
railway	thaang rót fai	ทางรถไฟ
rain	fǒn	ฝน
raining	fǒn tòk	ฝนตก
rape	kaan khòm khěun	การข่มขืน
to rape	khòm khěun	ข่มขืน
rare	hǎa yâak	หายาก
raw	dìp	ดิบ
ready	phráwm láew	พร้อมแล้ว
reason	hèht-phǒn	เหตุผล
receipt	bai sèht ráp ngoen	ใบเสร็จรับเงิน
recently	mêua rehw rehw níi	เมื่อเร็วๆนี้
to recommend	náe nam	แนะนำ

255

refugee	phûu òpháyóp	ผู้อพยพ
refund	kheun ngoen	คืนเงิน
refuse	pàtisèht	ปฏิเสธ
region	phâak	ภาค
regulation	kòt-kehn	กฎเกณฑ์
relation	khwaam sǎmphan	ความสัมพันธ์
relationship	khwaam kìaw-phan kan	ความเกี่ยวพันกัน
relax	phák phàwn	พักผ่อน
religion	sàatsànǎa	ศาสนา
remember	jam dâi	จำได้
remote	hàang klai	ห่างไกล
rent	khâa châo	ค่าเช่า
to rent	châo	เช่า
representative	phûu thaen	ผู้แทน
republic	sǎathaa-ránárát	สาธารณรัฐ
reservation	kaan jawng	การจอง
to reserve	jawng	จอง
respect	khao róp	เคารพ
responsibility	khwaam ráp phìt châwp	ความรับผิดชอบ
to rest	yùt phák	หยุดพัก
restaurant	ráan aahǎan	ร้านอาหาร
to return	klap	กลับ
revolution	kaan pàtiwát	การปฏิวัติ
rich	ruay	รวย
right (not left)	khwǎa	ขวา
right (not wrong)	thùuk tâwng	ถูกต้อง
right-wing	kaan meuang faai khwǎa	การเมืองฝ่ายขวา
risk	sìang	เสี่ยง
road	thanǒn	ถนน
robber	khàmohy	ขโมย
robbery	kaan khàmohy	การขโมย
roof	lǎng-khaa	หลังคา
room	hâwng	ห้อง

rope	chêuak	เชือก
round	klom	กลม
rubbish	kha-yà	ขยะ
rule	kòt	กฎ

S

sad	sâo jai	เศร้าใจ
safe (for valuables)	tûu sehf	ตู้เซฟ
safe	plàwt phai	ปลอดภัย
safety	khwaam plàwt phai	ความปลอดภัย
salty	khem	เค็ม
same	mĕuan kan	เหมือนกัน
save	kèp wái	เก็บไว้
scenery	thiw thát	ทิวทัศน์
seasick	mao khlêun	เมาคลื่น
secret	láp	ลับ
selfish	hĕn kàe tua	เห็นแก่ตัว
sell	khăai	ขาย
send	sòng	ส่ง
serious	ao jing ao jang	เอาจริงเอาจัง
several	lăai	หลาย
sexist	khit kan bàeng yâek phêht	คิดการแบ่งแยกเพศ
shade	tâi rôm	ใต้ร่ม
shape	rûup	รูป
to share	bàeng	แบ่ง
short (time)	mâi naan	ไม่นาน
short (height)	sân	สั้น
shortage	khwaam khàat khlaen	ความขาดแคลน
to shout	tàkohn	ตะโกน
to show	sadăeng	แสดง
shut	pit	ปิด
shy	aai	อาย

S

sick	pùay	ป่วย
side	khâang	ข้าง
sign	pâai	ป้าย
similar	khláai-khláai	คล้ายๆ
since	tâng tàe	ตั้งแต่
single (unmarried)	pen sòht	เป็นโสด
to sit	nâng	นั่ง
situation	sathǎanákaan	สถานการณ์
size	khanàat	ขนาด
sleep	nawn	นอน
sleepy	ngûang nawn	ง่วงนอน
slow	cháa	ช้า
slowly	cháa-cháa	ช้าๆ
small	lék	เล็ก
a smell	klìn	กลิ่น
socialism	látthí sǎngkhom níyom	ลัทธิสังคมนิยม
solid	khǎeng	แข็ง
some	baang	บ้าง
somebody	baang khon	บางคน
something	baang sìng	บางสิ่ง
sometimes	baang thii	บางที
song	phlehng	เพลง
soon	rehw-rehw-níi	เร็วๆนี้
sorry (I'm sorry)	sǎa jai	เสียใจ
souvenir	khǎwng thîi rálèuk	ของที่ระลึก
special	phí-sèht	พิเศษ
spicy	phèt	เผ็ด

I (don't) like it spicy.
  mâi châwp phèt   ไม่ชอบเผ็ด

sport	kiilaa	กีฬา
standard	mâatàráthaan	มาตรฐาน
start	tâng tôn	ตั้งต้น
stay	yùu	อยู่

DICTIONARY

258

| steal | khàmōhy | ขโมย |
| to stop | yùt | หยุด |

Stop here.
jàwt thîi nîi   จอดที่นี่

story (tale)	rêuang	เรื่อง
straight	trong	ตรง
strange	plàek	แปลก
stranger (person)	khon plàek nâa	คนแปลกหน้า
street	thanŏn	ถนน
strong	khǎeng raeng	แข็งแรง
stupid	ngôh	โง่
style	bàep	แบบ
suddenly	than thii than dai	ทันทีทันใด
sunglasses	wâen taa kan daet	แว่นตากันแดด
sure	nâe nawn	แน่นอน
surprise	tham-hâi pràlàat jai	ทำให้ประหลาดใจ
survive	râwt chiwit	รอดชีวิต
sweet	wǎan	หวาน
swim	wâai náam	ว่ายน้ำ

T

to take	ao	เอา
to talk	phûut	พูด
tall	sǔung	สูง
tasty	aràwy	อร่อย
tax	phaasěi	ภาษี
telephone	thohrásàp	โทรศัพท์
to telephone	thohrásàp pai	โทรศัพท์ไป
telephone book	samùt thohrásàp	สมุดโทรศัพท์
temperature	unhà-phum	อุณหภูมิ
tent	ten	เต็นท์

| to test | sàwp | ทดสอบ |
| Thai | thai | ภาษาไทย |

I can't speak Thai.

phŏm/dìi-chăn phûut phaasăa thai mâi dâi

ผม/ดิฉันพูดภาษาไทยไม่ได้

Thailand	meuang thaai	เมืองไทย
thank you	khàwp khun	ขอบคุณ
there	thîi nân	ที่นั่น
thick	năa	หนา
thief	khàmôhy	ขโมย
thin	phăwm	ผอม
thing	sìng	สิ่ง
think	khít	คิด
thirsty	hĕw náam	หิวน้ำ
ticket	tŭa	ตั๋ว
time	wehlaa	เวลา
on time	trong wehlaa	ตรงเวลา

What's the time?

kìi mohng láew? กี่โมงแล้ว

tip (gratuity)	khâa bawríkaan	ค่าบริการ
	(khâa thíp)	(ค่าทิป)
tired	nèuay	เหนื่อย
together	dûay kan	ด้วยกัน
toilet	sûam	ส้วม

Where are the toilets?

hâwng sûam yùu thîi năi? ห้องส้วมอยู่ที่ไหน

toilet paper	kràdàat cham-rá	กระดาษชำระ
tonight	kheun-níi	คืนนี้
too	dûay (mĕuan kan)	ด้วย(เหมือนกัน)
toothbrush	praeng sĕi fan	แปรงสีฟัน
toothpaste	yaa sĕi fan	ยาสีฟัน

torch (flashlight)	fai chăai	ไฟฉาย
to touch	jàp	จับ
tour	thâwng thîaw	ท่องเที่ยว
tourist	nák thâwng thîaw	นักท่องเที่ยว
toward	thaang pai	ตรงไป
town	meuang	เมือง
train	rót fai	รถไฟ
transit (in transit)	doen thaang phàan	เดินทางผ่าน
translate	plae	แปล
trekking	doen nai phuu khăao	เดินผ่านภูเขา
trip	thîaw	เที่ยว
true	jing	จริง
trust	wái jai	ไว้ใจ
try	phayaayaam	พยายาม

U

umbrella	rôm	ร่ม
uncomfortable	mâi sabaai	ไม่สะดวก
under	tâi	ใต้
understand	khâo jai	เข้าใจ

Do you understand?
  khâo jai măi   เข้าใจไหม

I (don't) understand.
  phŏm/dì-chăn (mâi) khâo jai   ผม/ดิฉัน(ไม่)เข้าใจ

unemployed	wâang ngaan	ว่างงาน
university	mahăa-witháyaalai	มหาวิทยาลัย
unsafe	mâi plàwt phai	ไม่ปลอดภัย
until	jon thĕung	จนถึง
up	bon	บน
upstairs	khâang bon	ข้างบน
to use	chái	ใช้
useful	mii pràyòht	มีประโยชน์

V

vacation	wan yùt	วันหยุด
vaccination	kaan chìit wáksiin	การฉีดวัคซีน
valley	hùp khǎo	หุบเขา
valuable	mii khâa	มีค่า
value	khâa	ค่า
very	mâak	มาก
view	wiw	วิว
village	mùu bâan	หมู่บ้าน
to visit	pai yîam	ไปเยี่ยม
to vomit	aa-jian	อาจารย์
vote	lêuak	เลือก

W

wait	raw (khawy)	รอ(คอย)
walk	doen	เดิน
to want (something)	yàak dâi	อยากได้
war	sǒngkhraam	สงคราม
warm	òp-ùn	อบอุ่น
to wash (clothes)	sák	ซัก
to wash (not clothes)	láang	ล้าง
to watch	duu	ดู
water	náam	น้ำ
boiled water	náam tôm	น้ำต้ม
bottled drinking water	náam dèum khùat	น้ำดื่มขวด
water purification tablets	yaa mét tham-hâi náam sà-àat	ยาเม็ดทำให้น้ำสะอาด
way	thaang	ทาง
wealthy	ruay	รวย
weather	aakàat	อากาศ
to welcome	tâwn ráp	ต้อนรับ
a well	bàw	บ่อ

| wet | piak | เปียก |
| what | a-rai | อะไร |

What's this made of?
nii tham dûay à-rai? — นี่ทำด้วยอะไร

| when | mêua-rai | เมื่อไร |

When will the ... leave?
... jà àwk kìi mohng? — ...จะออกกี่โมง

| where | thîi nǎi | ที่ไหน |

Where is the ...?
... yùu thîi nǎi? — อยู่ที่ไหน

Where are the toilets?
hâwng sûam yùu thîi nǎi? — ห้องส้วมอยู่ที่ไหน

| who | khrai | ใคร |

Who lives here?
khrai yùu thîi nîi? — ใครอยู่ที่ไหน

whole	tháng mòt	ทั้งหมด
why	thammai	ทำไม
wide	kwâang	กว้าง
wife	mia	เมีย
win	chaná	ชนะ
wire	sên lûat	เส้นลวด
wise	mii panyaa	มีปัญญา
with	kàp	กับ
within	phaai-nai	ภายใน
without	pràatsàjàak	ปราศจาก
wood	mái	ไม้
wool	phâa sàkàlàat	ผ้าสักหลาด
	(phâa khǒn sàt)	(ผ้าขนสัตว์)
to work	tham ngaan	ทำงาน
world	lôhk	โลก

THAI VOWELS

a	อะ
aa	อา
ae	แอ
ai	ไอ, ใอ
ao	เอา
aw	ออ
e	เอะ
eh	เอ
eu	เอิ, อึ
eua	เอือ
i	อิ
ii	อี
ia	เอีย
iaw	เอียว
iu	อิว
o	โอะ
oh	โอ
oe	เอิว
oei	เอย
u	อุ
uu	อู
ua	อัว
uay	อ่วย

THAI CONSONANTS

ก	k	ก.ไก่
ข	kh	ข.ไข่
ค	kh	ค.ควาย
ง	ng	ง.งู
จ	j	จ.จาน
ฉ	ch	ฉ.ฉิ่ง
ช	ch	ช.ช้าง
ซ	s	ซ.โซ่
ฌ	ch	ฌ.กระเฌอ
ญ	y	ญ.หญิง
ฎ	d	ฎ.ชฎา
ฏ	t	ฏ.ปฏัก
ฐ	th	ฐ.ฐาน
ฑ	th	ฑ.มณโฑ
ฒ	th	ฒ.ผู้เฒ่า
ณ	n	ณ.เณร
ด	d	ด.เด็ก
ต	t	ต.เต่า
ถ	th	ถ.ถุง
ท	th	ท.ทหาร
ธ	th	ธ.ง

THAI CONSONANTS

น	n	น.หนู
บ	b	บ.ใบไม้
ป	p	ป.ปลา
ผ	ph	ผ.ผึ้ง
ฝ	f	ฝ.ฝา
พ	ph	พ.พาน
ฟ	f	ฟ.ฟัน
ภ	ph	ภ.สำเภา
ม	m	ม.ม้า
ย	y	ย.ยักษ์
ร	r	ร.เรือ
ล	l	ล.ลิง
ว	w	ว.แหวน
ศ	s	ศ.ศาลา
ษ	s	ษ.ฤๅษี
ส	s	ส.เสือ
ห	h	ห.หีบ
ฬ	l	ฬ.จุฬา
อ	aw	อ.อ่าง
ฮ	h	ฮ.นกฮูก

A

aa	อา	aunt/uncle (father's younger sister/brother)
aachîip	อาชีพ	occupation (job)
aahăan cháo	อาหารเช้า	breakfast
aahăan thîang	อาหารเที่ยง	lunch
aahăan yen	อาหารเย็น	dinner
aahăan	อาหาร	food
aai	อาย	shy
aa-jian	อาจารย์	to vomit
aakàat	อากาศ	air

aakàat năo
อากาศหนาว   It's cold.

aakàat	อากาศ	weather
aam-nâat phadèht-kaan	อำนาจเผด็จการ	dictatorship
aang àap náam	อ่างอาบน้ำ	bath
àap náam	อาบน้ำ	bathe
àat jà	อาจจะ	maybe
aathít kàwn	อาทิตย์ก่อน	last week
aathít nâa	อาทิตย์หน้า	next week
aayú	อายุ	age
adiit	อดีต	past
ai	ไอ	a cough
amnâat	อำนาจ	power
antàraai	อันตราย	dangerous
anú-săa-wárii	อนุสาวรีย์	monument
anúyâat	อนุญาต	permission
anúyâat hâi	อนุญาตให้	to allow

(mâi) anúyâat hâi
ไม่อนุญาตให้   It's (not) allowed.

ao jing ao jang	เอาจริงเอาจัง	serious
ao	เอา	take
ao maa	เอามา	to bring
a-rai	อะไร	what
a-rai kaw dâi	อะไรก็ได้	anything
aràwy	อร่อย	delicious/tasty
àtànoh-máti	อัตโนมัติ	automatic
awfit	สำนักงาน	office
àwk	ออก	to depart
àwk bàep	ออกแบบ	to design

B

baa	บาร์	bar
bâa	บ้า	crazy/mad
bâan (reuan)	บ้าน(เรือน)	house
bâan meuang	บ้านเมือง	homeland
bâan	บ้าน	home
baang khon	บางคน	somebody
baang sing	บางสิ่ง	something
baang thii	บางที	sometimes
bâang	บ้าง	any
baang	บ้าง	some
bàek (nam pai)	แบก(น้ำหนัก)	to carry
bàeng	แบ่ง	to share
bàep	แบบ	style
bàet-toe-rii	แบตเตอรี่	battery
bai anúyâat	ใบอนุญาต	to permit
bai khàp khii	ใบขับขี่	driver's licence
bai sèht ráp ngoen	ใบเสร็จรับเงิน	receipt
banyaakàat	บรรยากาศ	atmosphere
bàt khrehdìt	บัตรเครดิต	credit card
bàt pràjam tua	บัตรประจำตัว	identification (card)
bàw	บ่อ	a well

bawrikaan sák rîit sêua phâa	บริการซักรีดเสื้อผ้า	laundry
bawrisàt	บริษัท	company
bàwy-bàwy	บ่อยๆ	often
bèua	เบื่อ	bored
beung (thaleh sàap)	บึง	lake
bin	บิล	account/bill
bon	บน	on/up
boraan	โบราณ	ancient
bòt phâaphayon	เอกสาร	a documentary
bòt sùat mon	บทสวดมนต์	prayer
bùkhálík	บุคลิก	personality
bùrìi sawng	บุหรี่ซอง	pack of cigarettes
bùrìi	บุหรี่	cigarettes

C

cháa	ช้า	slow
cháa-cháa	ช้าๆ	slowly
chaai daen	ชายแดน	border
chaai fàng	ชายฝั่ง	coast
chaai-hàat	ชายหาด	beach
chái	ใช้	to use
chalàat	ฉลาด	intelligent
cháná	ชนะ	win
chanít	ชนิด	kind (type)
cháo	เช้า	early
châo	เช่า	to rent
châwp	ชอบ	to like
(mâi) châwp phèt	ไม่ชอบเผ็ด	I (don't) like it spicy.
chêu	ชื่อ	name
chêuak	เชือก	rope

chíi	ชี้	to point
chìit yaa	ฉีดยา	injection
chiiwít	ชีวิต	life
chín	ชิ้น	piece
chôhk dii	โชคดี	lucky
chonátbòt	ชนบท	countryside
chūn	ชุน	damp
chuan	เชิญ	to invite
chûay	ช่วย	to help
chút wâai náam	ชุดว่ายน้ำ	bathing suit

D

dàan	ด่าน	customs (officials)
dâi	ได้	can (to be ableto)
dâi yin	ได้ยิน	hear
dam náam	ดำน้ำ	diving
dang	ดัง	loud
dao	เดา	to guess
dēaw níi	ตอนนี้	now
dèk	เด็ก	child
dèk àwn	เด็กอ่อน	baby
dèk chaai	เด็กชาย	boy
dèk phûu yēng	เด็กผู้หญิง	girl
dèum dâi	ดื่มได้	drinkable (water)
dèum	ดื่ม	to drink
deung	ดึง	pull
dii	ดี	good/nice
dii-chān chêu (f)	ดิฉันชื่อ	
dii kwàa	ดีกว่า	better
dii thîi-sùt	ดีที่สุด	best
din	ดิน	dirt
dìp (mâi sùk)	ดิบ	raw
doem	เดิม	original

doen nai phuu kháao	เดินผ่านภูเขา	trekking
doen thaang phàan	เดินทางผ่าน	transit (in transit)
doen	เดิน	walk
dohy	โดย	by
don-trii jáet	คนตรีแจ๊ส	jazz
don-trii	คนตรี	music
dûay	ด้วย	also
dûay (mĕuan kan)	ด้วย(เหมือนกัน)	too
dûay kan	ด้วยกัน	together
duu lae	ดูแล	to care (to take care of)
duu	ดู	to watch

E

èun	อื่น	other

F

fâai/sǎmlii	ฝ้าย/สำลี	cotton
faen	แฟน	boyfriend/girlfriend
fai	ไฟ	fire/light
fai chǎai	ไฟฉาย	flashlight/torch
fai fáa	ไฟฟ้า	electricity
fǎn	ฝัน	to dream
fang	ฟัง	listen
feun	ฟืน	firewood
fim	ฟิล์ม	film (roll of)
fǒn	ฝน	rain
fǒn tòk	ฝนตก	raining
frii (mâi khít ngoen)	ฟรี(ไม่คิดเงิน)	free (of charge)
fùn	ฝุ่น	dust

H

hǎa ngoen	หาเงิน	earn
hǎa yâak	หายาก	rare
hǎa	หา	to look for
hǎai jai	หายใจ	to breathe
hàang klai	ห่างไกล	remote
hâeng	แห้ง	dried
hâeng	แห้ง	dry
hâi phawn	ให้ผ่าน	to bless
hâi	ให้	give
hǎo	เหา	lice
hàw	หัว	package
hâwng náam	ห้องน้ำ	bathroom
hâwng sàdaeng silápà	การแสดงศิลปะ	art gallery
hâwng sûam	ห้องส้วมอยู่ที่ไหน	toilet

hâwng sûam yùu thîi nǎi?

	ห้องส้วมอยู่ที่ไหน	Where are the toilets?
hâwng	ห้อง	room
hèht-kaan	เหตุการณ์	event
hèht-phǒn	เหตุผล	reason
hěn kàe tua	เห็นแก่ตัว	selfish
hěw náam	หิวน้ำ	thirsty (be thirsty)
hǐw	หิว	hungry (be hungry)
hǔa boraan	หัวโบราณ	conservative
hǔa nâa	หัวหน้า	boss
hǔa ráw	หัวเราะ	laugh
hùp khǎo	หุบเขา	valley
hǔu nùak	หูหนวก	deaf

I

iik hók wan	อีกหกวัน	in (six) days
iik thii	อีกที	again

D I C T I O N A R Y

J

| iik | อีก | more |
| itsàrà | อิสระ | free (not bound) |

J

jàai	จ่าย	to pay
jàak	จาก	from
jâang	จ้าง	hire
jai kwâang	ใจกว้าง	generous
jam dâi	จำได้	remember
jam pen	จำเป็น	necessary
jang-wàt	จังหวัด	province
jâo khǎwng	เจ้าหนี้	owner
jâo nâa thîi	เจ้าหน้าที่	officer
jàp	จับ	to touch
jàt	จัด	organise
jawng	จอง	to book
jawng	จอง	to reserve

jàwt thîi nîi จอดที่นี่		Stop here.
jèp	เจ็บ	hurt
jèp	เจ็บ	painful
jing	จริง	true
jintànaakaan	จินตนาการ	imagination
jìt-jai	จิตใจ	the mind
jon thěung	จนถึง	until
jòp (sèht)	จบ(เสร็จ)	over (finished)
jòt-mǎai	จดหมาย	letter
jùt mǎai	จุดหมาย	destination
juup	จูบ	kiss

K

| kaan àwk | การออก | departure |
| kaan bàat jèp | การบาดเจ็บ | injury |

kaan bàeng-yâek kìit kan	การแบ่งแยกกิจการ	discrimination
kaan bawríhǎan ngaan	การบริหารงาน	administration
kaan chìit wáksiin	การฉีดวัคซีน	vaccination
kaan jawng	การจอง	reservation
kaan khàmǒhy	การขโมย	robbery
kaan khǎng khúk	การขังคุก	imprisonment
kaang kehng yiin	ก็เก็ยีนส์	jeans
kaan khòm hěhng	การข่มเหง	persecution
kaan khòm khěun	การข่มขืน	rape
kaan lên	เกมส์เล่น	game
kaan lêuak tâng	การเลือกตั้ง	election
kaan meuang	การเมือง	politics
kaan meuang fàai khwǎa	การเมืองฝ่ายขวา	right-wing
kaan meuang fàai sáai	การเมืองฝ่ายซ้าย	left-wing
kaan mii sùan rûam	การมีส่วนร่วม	participation
kaan pàtiwát	การปฏิวัติ	revolution
kaan phátthanaa	การพัฒนา	development
kaan pràthúang	การประท้วง	a protest/ demonstration
kaan ráp sên bon	การรับสินบน	corruption
kaan sàdaeng lákhawn sàt	การแสดงละครสัตว์	circus
kaan sàkòt jìt	การสะกดจิต	hypnotism
kaan sèuk-sǎa	การศึกษา	education
kaan sǒnthánaa	การสนทนา	conversation
kaan tàeng-ngaan	การแต่งงาน	marriage
kaan tàt mái tham laai pàa	การตัดไม้ทำลายป่า	deforestation
kaan tàt sǐn jai	การตัดสินใจ	decision
kaan tàw sûu	การต่อสู้	a fight

kaan tháeng	การแท้ง	abortion
kaan thiip rót jàkrayaan	การถีบรถจักรยาน	cycling
kaan tìt chúa	การติดเชื้อ	infection
kaan tìt yaa	การติดยา	drug addiction
kaan tìt	การติด	addiction
kaan tôh yáeng	การโต้แย้ง	argument
káat	แก๊ส	gas (natural)
kâew	แก้ว	glass
kai	ไกด์	a guide
kamlang jàlàp	กำลังจะหลับ	asleep
kào	เก่า	old (things)
kâo-îi	เก้าอี้	chair
kàp	กับ	with
kasèt-kam	เกษตรกรรม	agriculture
kàt	กัด	bite
kàwn	ก่อน	before
kehm khawmpiwtoe	เกมส์คอมพิวเตอร์	computer games
kèp wái	เก็บไว้	save
kèuap	เกือบ	almost
khâa bawríkaan (khâa thíp)	ค่าบริการ(ค่าทิป)	
khâa châo	ค่าเช่า	rent
khâa phàan pràtuu	ค่าผ่านประตู	admission (fee)
khâa pràp	ค่าปรับ	fine (penalty)
khâa	ค่า	fee/value
khâa	ฆ่า	to kill
khâai phák raem	ค่ายพักแรม	camp
khâai	ขาย	sell
khâam	ข้าม	across
kháan	ค้าน	against
khâang	ข้าง	side
khâang bon	ข้างบน	upstairs
khâang lâang	ข้างล่าง	downstairs

kháang lǎng	ข้างหลัง	at the back (behind)
khâang nai	ข้างใน	indoors
khâang nai	ข้างใน	inside
khabûan kaan	ขบวนการ	procession
kháeng raeng	แข็งแรง	strong
khǎeng	แข็ง	hard/solid
khàeng	แข่ง	race (contest)
khâi	ไข้	fever
kham náe nam	คำแนะนำ	advice
kham thǎam	คำถาม	a question
khàmōhy	ขโมย	robber
khàmōhy	ขโมย	steal
khàmōhy	ขโมย	thief

khan sùt-tháai jà àwk kìi mohng?
คันสุดท้ายจะออกกี่โมง
What time does the last vehicle leave?

khan	คัน	itch
khěan	เขียน	to write
khanàat	ขนาด	size
khanǒm bang	ขนมปัง	bread

khâo jai mǎi
เข้าใจไหม   Do you understand?

khâo jai	เข้าใจ	to understand
khâo phák	เข้าพัก	to check-in (hotel)
khao róp	เคารพ	respect
khào	ข่าว	news
khâo	เข้า	to enter/admit
khàp rót	ขับรถ	to drive
khâw khwaam	ข้อความ	message/information
khâw phìt	ข้อผิดพลาด	mistake
khâw sǐa prìap	ข้อได้เปรียบ	disadvantage

khǎw sàdaengkhwaam yin dii!
การแสดงความยินดี   Congratulations!

khǎw yeum	ขอยืม	borrow
khǎwng boraan	ของโบราณ	antique
khǎwng khwǎn	ของขวัญ	present (gift)
khǎwng thiam	ของเทียม	imitation
khǎwng thîi ráléuk	ของที่ระลึก	souvenir
khàwp khun	ขอบคุณ	thank you
kha-yà	ขยะ	garbage/rubbish
khem	เค็ม	salty
khêun	ขึ้น	to board (train, bus)
khêun	ปีน	to climb
khêun láew	ขึ้นแล้ว	aboard
kheun ngoen	คืนเงิน	refund
kheun-nii	คืนนี้	tonight
khîi kiat	ขี้เกียจ	lazy
khit	คิด	to think
khit thěung	คิดถึ	to miss (family etc)
khit thěung bâan	คิดถึบ้าน	homesick
khláai-khláai	คล้ายๆ	similar
khěm thít	เข็มทิศ	compass
khòm khěun	ข่มขืน	to rape
khom	ขม	bitter
khon	คน	people/person
khon diaw	คนเดียว	alone
khon kǎw thaan	คนขอทาน	beggar
khon liang dèk	คนเลี้ยงเด็ก	babysitter
khon phôeng rôem	คนเพิ่งเริ่ม	beginner
khón phóp	ค้นพบ	discover
khon plàek nâa	คนแปลกหน้า	stranger (person)
khon rák rûam phêht	คนรักร่วมเพศ	homosexual
khon tìt	คนติด	addict

khong jà	คงจะ	probably
khót	คด	bent/crooked
khrai	ใคร	who

khrai yùu thîi nîi?
ใครอยู่ที่ไหน Who lives here?

khráng nèung	ครั้งหนึ่ง	once
khrâwp khrua	ครอบครัว	family
khrêuang bin	เครื่องบิน	aeroplane
khrêuang dèum	เครื่องดื่ม	a drink
khrêuang khum kam-nòet	เครื่องคุมกำเนิด	contraceptive
khrêuang pân din phâo; khrêuang thûay chaam	เครื่องปั้นดินเ ผาเครื่องถ้วยชาม	pottery/ceramics
khrêuang	เครื่อง	machine
khrêua bawríkaan ngoen dúan	เครื่องบริการเงินด่วน	automatic teller (ATM)
khrêuang plaeng fai	เครื่องแปลงไฟ	adaptor
khrêung	ครึ่ง	half
khùat	ขวด	bottle
khúk	คุก	jail/prison

khun chêu arai?
คุณชื่ออะไร What is your name?

khunáphâap	คุณภาพ	quality
khûu	คู่	double/pair
khûu mán	คู่หมั้น	fiance
khûu meu thâng thîaw	คู่มือท่องเที่ยว	guidebook
khwǎa	ขวา	right (not left)
khwaam	ความเกี่ยวพันกัน	relationship
khwaam àp aai khǎai nâa	ความอับอายขายหน้า	embarrassment

khwaam chûay lĕua	ความช่วยเหลือ	aid
khwaam khàat khlaen	ความขาดแคลน	shortage
khwaam khít hĕn	ความคิดเห็น	opinion
khwaam khít kìaw-phan kan	ความคิด	idea
khwaam klua	ความกลัว	fear
khwaam òhp âwm aarii	ความโอบอ้อมอารี	hospitality
khwaam phìt	ความผิด	fault
khwaam plàwt phai	ความปลอดภัย	safety
khwaam ráp phìt châwp	ความรับผิดชอบ	responsibility
khwaam ráwn	ความร้อน	heat
khwaam rúu-sèuk	ความรู้สึก	feeling
khwaam sămphan	ความสัมพันธ์	relation
khwaam taai	ความตาย	death
khwaam yâak jon	ความยากจน	poverty
khwaam yúttitham	ความยุติธรรม	justice
kìi mohng láew? กี่โมงแล้ว		What's the time?
kiilaa	กีฬา	sport
kìit kan bàeng yâek phêht	คิดการแบ่งแยกเพศ	sexist
kìit kan bàeng yâek phĕw	คิดการแบ่งแยกผิว	racist
kii-taa	กีตาร์	guitar
kin (inf)	กิน	
klâa	กล้า	brave
klai	ไกล	distant/far
klâi	ใกล้	close (adj)
klâi	ใกล้	near

... klai thâo rai?
...ไกลเท่าไร | | How far is ...?

klap	กลับ	to return
klâwng thàai rûup	กล้องถ่ายรูป	camera
klàwng	กล่อง	box
klìat	เกลียด	to hate
klìn	กลิ่น	a smell
klom	กลม	round
klua	กลัว	afraid
kongsúun	กงสุล	consulate
kòt	กฎ	rule
kòt-kehn	กฎเกณฑ์	regulation
kòt-mãai	กฎหมาย	law
kràdàat	กระดาษ	paper
kràdàat cham-rá	กระดาษชำระ	toilet paper
kràdàat muan bùrii	กระดาษมวนบุหรี่	cigarette papers
kràdeum; pùm	กระดุม,ปุ่ม	buttons
kràdùuk	กระดูก	bone
kràpão thẽu	กระเป๋าถือ	handbag
kràpǎwng	กระป๋อง	a can
kràtham phìt	กระทำผิด	offend
kròht	โกรธ	angry
kun-jae	กุญแจ	a lock/padlock
kwâang	กว้าง	wide
kwaang	กวาง	deer

L

lãai	หลาย	several
lãai pii maa láew	หลายปีมาแล้ว	years ago
láang	ล้าง	wash (not clothes)
lâang	ล่าง	below
láe	และ	and
lâek plìan	แลกเปลี่ยน	to exchange

láew	แล้ว	already
lam lawng	ลำลอง	informal
lăng	หลัง	back (body)/behind
lăng jàak	หลังจาก	after
lăng-khaa	หลังคา	roof
láp	ลับ	secret
látthí khawm-miw-nít	ลัทธิคอมมิวนิสต์	communism
látthí naai thun	ลัทธินายทุน	capitalism
látthí săngkhom niyom	ลัทธิสังคมนิยม	socialism
lehn khawnthâek	เลนส์กันแตก	contact lens
lehw-kwàa	เลวกว่า	worse
lék	เล็ก	small
lék (náwy)	เล็ก(น้อย)	little (adj)
lên	เล่น	to play
lêuak	เลือก	to choose/vote
lêuat/loh-hìt	เลือด/โลหิต	blood
léuk	ลึก	deep
leum	ลืม	forget
líf	ลิฟท์	lift (elevator)
lôhk	โลก	Earth/world
lŏng thaang	หลงทาง	lost
long	ลง	down/to board (boat)
lót raakhaa	ลดราคา	discount

lót raakhaa dâi mái?
ลดราคาได้ไหม   Can you lower the price?

lûuk bawn	ลูกบอล	ball
lûuk kun-jae	ลูกกุญแจ	key
lûuk săo	ลูกสาว	daughter

M

| maa | มา | come |
| máa | หมา | dog |

mâak	มาก	many/plenty/very
mâatàráthaan	มาตรฐาน	standard
mahãa samùt	มหาสมุทร	ocean
mahãa-witháyaalai	มหาวิทยาลัย	university
mài	ใหม่	new
mái	ไม้	wood
mâi	ไหม้	to burn
mâi dii	ไม่ดี	bad
mâi jiing	ไม่จริง	false
mái khìit fai	ไม้ขีดไฟ	matches
mâi khoei	ไม่เคย	never
mâi mii a-rai	ไม่มีอะไร	nothing
mâi mii loei	ไม่มีเลย	none
mâi naan	ไม่นาน	short (time)
mâi plàwt phai	ไม่ปลอดภัย	unsafe
mâi sabaai	ไม่สะดวก	uncomfortable
mâi sadùak	ไม่สะดวก	inconvenient
mâi wâang	ไม่ว่าง	busy
mánút	มนุษย์	human
mao	เมา	drunk (inebriated)
mao khlêun	เมาคลื่น	seasick
máreun	มะรืน	day after tomorrow
mãw	หมอ	doctor
mêua rehw rehw níi	เมื่อเร็วๆนี้	recently
mêua waan níi	เมื่อวานนี้	yesterday
meuang	เมือง	city/town
meuang nâwk	เมืองนอก	overseas
meuang thai	เมืองไทย	Thailand
mêua-rai	เมื่อไร	when
mêua-rai kaw dâi	เมื่อไรก็ได้	anytime
mêut	มืด	dark
mia	เมีย	wife
mii	มี	have
mii aachíip	มีอาชีพ	professional

mii khâa	มีค่า	valuable
mii khan (mii tháwng)	มีครรภ์(มีท้อง)	pregnant
mii khwaam phìt	มีความผิด	guilty
mii khwaam súk	มีความสุข	happy
mii panyaa	มีปัญญา	wise
mii pràyòht	มีประโยชน์	practical
mii pràyòht	มีประโยชน์	useful
mii sùan rûam	มีส่วนร่วม	participate
mo\hŏh	โมโห	cross (angry)
mĕuan	เหมือน	like (similar)
mĕuan kan	เหมือนกัน	same
mum	มุม	corner
mùu bâan	หมู่บ้าน	village

N

náa	น้า	aunt/uncle (mother's younger sister/brother)
nâa	หน้า	next
nâa sŏn jai	น่าสนใจ	interesting
nâa thêung	น่าทึ่ง	amazing
nǎa	หนา	thick
naai jâang	นายจ้าง	employer
naai lŭang	ในหลวง	king
naaiyók ráthámontrii	นายกรัฐมนตรี	prime minister
naalikaa plùk	นาฬิกาปลุก	alarm clock
náam	น้ำ	water
náam dèum khùat	น้ำดื่มขวด	bottled drinking water
náam khǎeng	น้ำแข็ง	ice
naan láew	นานแล้ว	long ago
náam-man	น้ำมัน	oil
náam tôm	น้ำต้ม	boiled water

náam tôm	น้ำต้ม	boiled water
náam thûam	น้ำท่วม	flood
naanaachâat	นานาชาติ	international
naathii	นาที	minute
náe nam	แนะนำ	to advise/recommend
nâe nawn	แน่นอน	certain/positive/sure
nâen	แน่น	crowded
naew (sên)	แนว(เส้น)	line
nai	ใน	in
nàk	หนัก	heavy
nák thâwng thîaw	นักท่องเที่ยว	tourist
nák thôht	นักโทษ	prisoner
nák thúrakit	นักธุรกิจ	business person
nam khâo maa jàak tàang pràthêht	นำเข้ามาจากต่างประเทศ	to import
náng sĕu phim	หนังสือพิมพ์	newspaper
náng sĕu	หนังสือ	a book
nâng	นี้	to sit
năng	หนัง	film/movie
năng phâapháyon	หนัง,ภาพยนตร์ โรงภาพยนตร์	cinema (film)
năng-sĕu doen thaang	หนังสือเดินทาง	passport
năo	หนาว	cold (weather)
náp	นับ	to count
nâwk	นอก	out
nawliikaa	นาฬิกา	clock
nawn	นอน	sleep
náwy kwàa	น้อยกว่า	less
náwy	น้อย	few
nehn thêht	เนรเทศ	exile
nĕua	เหนือ	above
nèuay	เหนื่อย	tip (gratuity)

nèung	หนึ่ง	one
ngâai	ง่าย	easy
ngaan	งาน	job
ngaan bâan	งานบ้าน	housework
ngaan fěi-meu (hàttakam	งานฝีมือ(หัตถกรรม)	handicrafts
ngaan kaw-sâang	งานก่อสร้าง	construction work
ngaan paatîi	งานปาร์ตี้	party
ngaan silápà	งานศิลปะ	artwork
ngîap	เงียบ	quiet
ngoen pliik	เงินปลีก	change (coins)
ngoen	เงิน	money
ngoen	เก็บเงิน	cheque(bill)
ngôh	โง่	stupid
ngûang nawn	ง่วงนอน	sleepy

nîi tham dûay à-rai?
นี่ทำด้วยอะไร   What's this made of?

níyom	นิยม	to prefer
noen	เนิน	hill
nók	นก	bird
nùm	หนุ่ม	young

O

oh-kàat	โอกาส	chance/opportunity
ong-kaan	องค์การ	organisation
ong-sǎa	องศา	degree (temperature)
òp-ùn	อบอุ่น	warm

P

| pâa | ป้า | aunt (older sister of either parent) |
| pâai | ป้าย | sign |

pâai rót meh	ป้ายรถเมล์	bus stop
pai	ไป	go
pai (mâi) dâi ไป(ไม่) ได้		I can (not) go.
pai ... thâo rai? ไป...เท่าไร		How much to ...?
pai yîam	ไปเยี่ยม	to visit
panhǎa	ปัญหา	problem
parinyaa	ปริญญา	degree (academic)
pàtisèht	ปฏิเสธ	to refuse
pàtisèht	ปฏิเสธ	to deny
pàt-jùban	ปัจจุบัน	present (time)
pâwg kan	ป้องกัน	to prevent
pâwg kan	ป้องกัน	to protect
pêh sàphai lǎng	เป้สะพายหลัง	backpack
pen	เป็น	to know (how to do something)
pen kan aeng (thaan phêuan)	เป็นกันเอง	friendly
pen khon phí-kaan	เป็นคนพิการ	disabled
pen nîi	เป็นหนี้	to owe
pen pai mâi dâi	เป็นไปไม่ได้	impossible
pen sòht	เป็นโสด	single (unmarried)
pen sùan tua	เป็นส่วนตัว	personal
pen thaang kaan	เป็นทางการ	formal
pen wàt	เป็นหวัด	to have a cold
phâa hòm	ผ้าห่ม	blanket
phâa sàkàlàat (phâa khǒn sàt)	ผ้าสักหลาด(ผ้าขนสัตว์)	wool
phaai nâwk	ภายนอก	outside
phaai-nai	ภายใน	within
phâak	ภาค	region
phaasǎa	ภาษา	language

phaasăa angkrìt	ภาษาอังกฤษ	English
phaasĕi	ภาษี	tax
phàen din thalòm	แผ่นดินถล่ม	landslide
phàen din wăi	แผ่นดินไหว	earthquake
phàen din; tîi din	แผ่นดิน;ที่ดิน	land
phàen thîi	แผนที่	map
phaeng mâak แพงมาก		It costs a lot.
phaeng	แพง	expensive
phâi	ไพ่	cards (playing)
phák phàwn	พักผ่อน	to relax
phan mái	พรรณไม้	a plant
phasŏm	ผสม	to mix
phát lom	พัดลม	fan
phátsàdù	พัสดุ	parcel
phaw	พอ	enough
phăwm	ผอม	thin
phayaayaam	พยายาม	to try
phêht-phlawy	เพชรพลอย	jewellery
phèt	เผ็ด	hot (spicy)
phêuan	เพื่อน	friend
pheun	พื้น	floor
phêut	เพาะ	crop
phiphítháphan	พิพิธภัณฑ์	museum
phí-sèht	พิเศษ	special
phìt	ผิด	wrong
phìt kamnòt wehlaa	ผิดกำหนดเวลา	delay
phìt kòt-măai	ผิดกฎหมาย	illegal
phlaesatoe	พลาสเตอร์	bandage
phlàk	ผลัก	push
phlang ngaan pàrámaanuu	พลังงานปรมาณู	nuclear energy
phlehng	เพลง	song

phlìt	ผลิต	to produce
phloeng ngaan	พลังงาน	energy
phóe	เพ้อ	delirious

phŏm chêu ... (m)
ผมชื่อ...   My name is ...

phŏm/dì-chăn (mâi) khâo jai
ผม/ดิฉัน(ไม่)เข้าใจ   I (don't) understand.

phŏm/dì-chăn hĕn dûay
ผม/ดิฉันเห็นด้วย   I agree.

phŏm/dì-chăn mâi dâai tham
ผม/ดิฉันไม่ได้ทำ   I didn't do it.

phŏm/dì-chăn mâi hĕn dûay
ผม/ดิฉันไม่เห็นด้วย   I don't agree

phŏm/dii-chăn yàa
ผม/ดิฉัน   I want to go to ...

phŏn-lámái	ผลไม้	fruit
phóp	พบ	to find/meet
phót-jànaanúkrom	พจนานุกรม	dictionary
phrá	พระ	priest
phrá jâo	พระเจ้า	god
phráw wâa	เพราะว่า	because
phráwm láew	พร้อมแล้ว	ready
phû thaen	ผู้แทน	representative
phû òpháyóp	ผู้อพยพ	refugee
phûu dohy-sǎan	ผู้โดยสาร	passenger
phûu jamnai yaa sèhp tìt	ผู้จำหน่ายยาเสพติด	drug dealer
phûu jamnai	ผู้จำหน่าย	distributor
phuu khǎo	ภูเขา	mountain
phûu koh-hòk	พูดโกหก	liar
phûu mii aayú mâak	ผู้มีอายุมากกว่า	elder

phûu ráp jàai ngoen	ผู้รับจ่ายเงิน	cashier
phûu rûam ngaan	ผู้ร่วมงาน	colleague
phûu yài	ผู้ใหญ่	adult
phûu yĕng	ผู้หญิง	female
phûut	พูด	to talk
piak	เปียก	wet
pii	ปี	year
pit láew	ปิดแล้ว	closed
pit	ปิด	to close/shut
plae	แปล	translate
plàek	แปลก	strange
plàwt phai	ปลอดภัย	safe (adj)
plian rót	เปลี่ยนรถ	to change (buses, trains etc)
plùuk	ปลูก	grow
pòet	เปิด	to open/open
praakòt chát (hĕn ngâai)	ปรากฏชัด(เห็นง่าย)	obvious
pràatsàjàak	ปราศจาก	without
pràchaathípawtai	ประชาธิปไตย	democracy
praeng sĕi fan	แปรงสีฟัน	toothbrush
praisanii bàt	ไปรษณียบัตร	postcard
pràjam pii	ประจำปี	annual
pràjam wan	ประจำวัน	daily
pràkan	ประกัน	insurance
pràp aakàat	ปรับอากาศ	air-conditioned
pràsòpàkaan	ประสบการณ์	experience
pràthaan	ประธาน	president
prathêht	ประเทศ	country
pràthúang	ประท้วง	to protest
pràtuu	ประตู	door
pràtuu	ประตู	gate
pràwàt bùkhon	ประวัติบุคคล	biography
pràyàt	ประหยัด	economical

pràyòht	ประโยชน์	profit
prung aahǎan	ปรุงอาหาร	to cook
pùay	ป่วย	ill/sick

R

raai lá-ìat	รายละเอียด	detail
raakhaa	ราคา	price
raakhaa	ราคา	to cost
raai-kaan aahǎan	รายการอาหาร	menu
ráan aahǎan	ร้านอาหาร	restaurant
ráan kaafae	ร้านกาแฟ	café
ráan khǎai nǎng sěu	ร้านขายหนังสือ	bookshop
ráan khǎai yaa	ร้านขายยา	chemist (pharmacy)
ráan khǎai yaa	ร้านขายยา	pharmacy (chemist)
ráang kaai	ร่างกาย	body
râek	แรก	first
rák	รัก	love
rámát ráwang	ระมัดระวัง	careful
rao rao; pramaan	ราวราวประมาณ	approximately
rao tham dâi เราทำได้		We can do it.
rao tham mâi dâi เราทำไม่ได้		We can't do it.
ráthábaan	รัฐบาล	government
rátsaphaa	รัฐสภา	parliament
ra-waang	ระหว่าง	among/between
ra-wàang thîi	ระหว่างที	during
raw (khawy)	รอ(คอย)	wait
ráwn	ร้อน	hot (weather)
ráwng hâi	ร้องไห้	cry
râwt chiwít	รอดชีวิต	survive
rehw	เร็ว	fast/quick
rehw-rehw-níi	เร็วๆนี้	soon

rĕu	หรือ	or
reua	เรือ	boat
reua dohysǎan	เรือโดยสาร	ferry
rêuang	เรื่อง	story (tale)
rêuang talòk	เรื่องตลก	joke
reúduu bai mái rûang	ฤดูใบไม้ร่วง	autumn
rian	เรียน	to learn
rîip	รีบ	to hurry
rôem	เริ่ม	begin
rôhk eht	โรคเอดส์	AIDS
rôhk wàt	โรคหวัด	a cold
rohng nǎng; rohng phâapháyon	โรงหนัง	cinema (place)
rohng raem	โรงแรม	hotel
rôm	ร่ม	umbrella
rót fai	รถไฟ	train
rót jàkrayaan	รถจักรยาน	bicycle
rót meh	รถเมล์	bus
rót yon	รถยนต์	car
rûam meu kan	ร่วมมือกัน	cooperative
ruam tháng	รวมทั้ง	included
ruay	รวย	rich/wealthy
rûng cháo	รุ่งเช้า	dawn
rúu	รู้	to know (something)
rúujàk	รู้จัก	to know (a person)
rûup	รูป	shape
rûup (phâap)	รูป(ภาพ)	a photograph
rûup law	รูปหล่อ	handsome
rúu-sèuk	รู้สึก	to feel

S

(mâi) sǎmkhan	ไม่สำคัญ	It's important.
sà wâai náam	สระว่ายน้ำ	pool (swimming)

sǎa mǐi	สามี	husband
sa-àat	สะอาด	clean
sáai	ช้าย	left
sǎai (cháa)	สาย(ช้า)	late
sǎai kaan bin	สายการบิน	airline
sǎan	ศาล	court (legal)
sǎathaa-ráná	สาธารณะ	public
sǎathaa-ránárát	สาธารณรัฐ	republic
sàatsànǎa	ศาสนา	religion
sabaai	สบาย	comfortable
sadǎeng	แสดง	to show
sâe khǎeng	แช่แข็ง	to freeze
sáek fai	แสงไฟ	lighter
sák	ซัก	to wash (clothes)
sàksit	ศักดิ์สิทธิ์	holy
samǒe	เสมอ	always
sǎmphaará	สัมภาระ	baggage
sǎm-ràp	สำหรับ	for
samùt thohrásàp	สมุดโทรศัพท์	telephone book
sân	สั้น	short (height)
sànǎam tennít	สนามเทนนิส	court (tennis)
sǎn-châat	สัญชาติ	citizenship
sàng	สั่ง	to order
sěang dang	เสียงดัง	noise
sanǒe	เสนอ	to offer
sǎntiphâap	สันติภาพ	peace
sanùk sanǎan	สนุกสนาน	to enjoy (oneself)
sanùk	สนุก	fun
sǎnyaa	สัญญา	contract/promise
sâo jai	เศร้าใจ	sad
saphaan	สะพาน	bridge
sàphâap wâet láwm pen phít	สภาพแวดล้อมเป็นพิษ	pollution
sàt	สัตว์	animals

sathǎan thûut	สถานทูต	embassy
sathǎanákaan	สถานการณ์	situation
sathǎa-nii khǒn sòng	สถานีขนส่ง	bus station
sawàang	สว่าง	bright (light)
sawàt-dii (khráp/khâ)	สวัสดี(ครับ/ค่ะ)	hello (greetings)
sàwàtdikaan	สวัสดิการ	dole
sawng	ซอง,หีบ,ห่อ	packet
sàwp	ทดสอบ	to test
sàwy khâw meu	สร้อยข้อมือ	bracelet
sèhtákit	เศรษฐกิจ	economy
sĕa jai	เสียใจ	sorry (I'm sorry)
sêu	ซื้อ	to buy
sêu sàt	ซื่อสัตย์	honest
sêua khòht	เสื้อโค้ท	coat
sêua phâa	เสื้อผ้า	clothing
sĕi dam	สีดำ	black
sìang	เสี่ยง	risk
silápà	ศิลปะ	art
silápin	ศิลปิน	artist
sîn lûat	เส้นลวด	wire
sîn bon	สินบน	a bribe
sìng	สิ่ง	thing
sìng wâet láwm	สิ่งแวดล้อม	environment
sôh-pheh-nii	โสเภณี	prostitute
sòk-kápròk	สกปรก	dirty
sŏm-khuan	สมควร	perfect
sŏn jai	สนใจ	interested
sòng àwk nâwk pràthêht	ส่งออกนอกประเทศ	to export
sòng	ส่ง	to send
sŏngkhraam	สงคราม	war
sòt	สด	fresh (not stale)
sûam	ส้วม	together
sŭan	สวน	garden/park

sùan	ส่วน	part
sùan tua	ส่วนตัว	private
sùan yài	ส่วนใหญ่	majority
sŭay	สวย	beautiful/pretty
sŭun meuang	กลางเมือง	city centre
sŭung	สูง	high/tall
sùkhàphâap	สุขภาพ	health
sùsăan	สุสาน	cemetery
sùt	สุด	end (n)
sùt-tháai	สุดท้าย	last (adj)
sùutibàt; bai kòet	สูติบัตร,ใบเกิด	birth certificate

T

tŭa	ตั๋ว	ticket
taa bàwt	ตาบอด	blind
taai/sĭa	ตาย/เสีย	to die
taai láew; sĭa laew	ตายแล้ว,เสียแล้ว	dead
taam	ตาม	follow
tàang pràthêht	ต่างประเทศ	abroad/foreign
tàe	แต่	but
tàek	แตก	break
tàek láew	แตกแล้ว	broken
tàek ngâai	แตกง่าย	fragile
tàek tàang	แตกต่าง	different
tàeng-ngaan	แต่งงาน	marry
tâi	ใต้	under
tâi rôm	ใต้ร่ม	shade
tákhriw	ตะคริว	cramp
tàklà	ตะกละ	greedy
tàkohn	ตะโกน	to shout
talàat	ตลาด	market
talàwt kaan	ตลอดกาล	forever

talòk	ตลก	funny
tam-rùat	ตำรวจ	police
tâng tàe	ตั้งแต่	since
tâng tôn	ตั้งต้น	start
tàt	ตัด	to cut
tàt sĭn jai	ตัดสินใจ	to decide
tàw tâan nuukhlia	ต่อต้านนิวเคลียร์	antinuclear
tawn bàai	ตอนบ่าย	afternoon
tawn cháo	ตอนเช้า	morning
tawn khâm	ตอนค่ำ	night
tâwn ráp	ต้อนรับ	to welcome
tawn yen	ตอนเย็น	evening
tàwp	ตอบ	to answer
tem	เต็ม	full
tên ram	เต้นรำ	dance
ten	เต็นท์	tent
tèuk	ตึก	building
thâa	ถ้า	if
thàai rûup	ถ่ายรูป	to photograph
thaam pràkan	ทำประกัน	to insure
thăam	ถาม	ask
thaan (pol)	ทาน	to eat

thaan khâo láew rĕu yang?
Have you eaten yet? ทานข้าวแล้วหรือยัง

thaan láew
I've eaten already. ทานแล้ว

thaang	ทาง	way
thaang aakàat	ทางอากาศ	airmail
thaang boraanákhádii		
	ทางโบราณคดี	archaeological
thaang doen	ทางเดิน	path
thaang khâo	ทางออก	entrance

thaang pai	ตรงไป	toward
thaang rót fai	ทางรถไฟ	railway
thǎa-wawn	ถาวร	permanent
thai	ภาษาไทย	Thai
tháleh saai	ทะเลทราย	desert
tham	ทำ	to do/make

tham à-rai?
ทำอะไร   What are you doing?

tham dûay	ทำด้วย	made (to be made of)
tham hǎai	ทำหาย	lose
tham ngaan	ทำงาน	to work
thamachâat	ธรรมชาติ	nature
thamadaa	ธรรมดา	ordinary
tham-hâi pràlàat jai	ทำให้ประหลาดใจ	surprise
tham-laai	ทำลาย	destroy
thammai	ทำไม	why
than samǎi	ทันสมัย	modern
than thii	ทันที	instant
than thii than dai	ทันทีทันใด	suddenly/immediately
thanaakhaan	ธนาคาร	bank
thanai-khwaam	ทนายความ	lawyer
thǎng káet	ถังแก๊ส	gas cartridge/cylinder
tháng mòt	ทั้งหมด	all/whole
tháng sǎwng	ทั้งสอง	both
thanǒn	ถนน	avenue/street/road
thâo kan	เท่ากัน	equal
thâo-nán	เท่านั้น	only

thâo rai?
เท่าไร   How much?

thawng	ทอง	gold
tháwng phùuk	ท้องผูก	constipation

thâwng thîaw	ท่องเที่ยว	tour
thâwt	ทอด	fried
thêht sa kaan	เทศกาล	festival
thěung	ถึง	to arrive
thian	เทียน	candle
thîaw bin	เที่ยวบิน	flight
thîaw	เที่ยว	trip
thîi	ที่	at/place
thîi khìa bù-rìi	ที่เขี่ยบุหรี่	ashtray
thîi nǎai kaw dâi	ที่ไหนก็ได้	anywhere
thîi nǎi	ที่ไหน	where
thîi nân	ที่นั่น	there
thîi nîi	ที่นี่	here
thîi phák	ที่พัก	accommodation
thîi pòet khùat	ที่เปิดขวด	bottle opener
thîi pòet kràpǎwng	ที่เปิดกระป๋อง	can opener
thîi yùu	ที่อยู่	address
thìip rót jàkrayaan	ถีบรถจักรยาน	to cycle
thiw thát	ทิวทัศน์	scenery
thohrásàp pai	โทรศัพท์ไป	to telephone
thohrásàp	โทรศัพท์	a telephone
thôht	โทษ	to blame
thong	ธง	flag
thúk khon	ทุกคน	everyone
thúk wan	ทุกวัน	every day
thúk yàng	ทุกอย่าง	everything
thúk	ทุก	each/every
thǔng	ถุง	bag
thǔng yaang anaamai	ถุงยางอนามัย	condom
thûng naa	ทุ่งนา	farm
thúrákìt	ธุรกิจ	business
thùuk kòt-mǎai	ถูกกฎหมาย	legal
thùuk tâwng	ถูกต้อง	right (not wrong)

thùuk	ถูก	cheap
thûut	ทูต	ambassador
tiang nawn	เตียงนอน	bed
tìt sĕn bon	ติดสินบน	to bribe
tìt tàw kan	ติดต่อกัน	infectious
tìt tàw kan dâi	ติดต่อกันได้	contagious
tôh yáeng	โต้แย้ง	to argue
tòk-long	ตกลง	to agree
tòk náam	ตกน้ำ	overboard
tôm	ต้ม	boil
triam	เตรียม	prepare
trong	ตรง	straight
trong-trong	ตรงๆ	direct
trong khâam	ตรงข้าม	opposite
trong wehlaa	ตรงเวลา	on time
túkkàdaa	ตุ๊กตา	doll
tûu sehf	ตู้เซฟ	safe (for valuables)

U

ûan	อ้วน	fat
ùbàtihèht	อุบัติเหตุ	accident
unhà-phum	อุณหภูมิ	temperature
ùpakawn dam náam	อุปกรณ์ดำน้ำ	diving equipment
ùtsăahàkam	อุตสาหกรรม	industry

W

wâai náam	ว่ายน้ำ	to swim
wăan	หวาน	sweet
wâang ngaan	ว่างงาน	unemployed
wâang plào	ว่างเปล่า	empty
wâen taa kan daet	แว่นตากันแดด	sunglasses
wâen taa	แว่นตา	glasses (spectacles)

wái jai	ไว้ใจ	trust
wan	วัน	day
wan kòet	วันเกิด	birthday
wan seun	วานซืน	day before yesterday
wan thîi	วันที่	date (time)
wan yùt	วันหยุด	holiday
wăng	หวัง	hope
wehlaa nát	เวลานัด	appointment (time)
wehlaa yùt phák	วันหยุด	vacation
wehlaa	เวลา	time
wian hŭa	เวียนหัว	dizzy
witháyú	วิทยุ	radio
witthii kaan	วิธีการ	process
wiw	วิว	view
wong dontrii	วงดนตรี	band (music)
won-ùtháyaan hàeng châat	วนอุทยานแห่งชาติ	national park

Y

yaa aèt-saphairin	ยาแอสไพริน	aspirin
yaa bàti chii-wáná (aenthibai-awthik)	ยาปฏิชีวนะ	antibiotics
yaa kan malaeng	ยากันแมลง	insect repellant
yaa khâa chûua rôhk	ยาฆ่าเชื้อโรค	disinfectant
yaa khâa chéua	ยาฆ่าเชื้อ	antiseptic
yaa mét tham-hâi náam sà-àat	ยาเม็ดทำให้น้ำสะอาด	water purification tablets
yàa sèhp tit	ยาเสพติด	dope (drugs)
yaa sĕi fan	ยาสีฟัน	toothpaste
yaa	ยา	drugs
yâak	ยาก	difficult
yàak dâi	อยากได้	want (something)
yâak jon	ยากจน	poor

yâang	ย่าง	to barbeque
yàang-rai	อย่างไร	how
yâe	แย่	awful
yài	ใหญ่	big
yang	ยัง	yet/not yet
yao	ยาว	long
yawm ráp	ยอมรับ	to accept
yâwy sàlǎi dâi	ย่อยสลายดี	biodegradable
yin yan	ยืนยัน	to confirm
		(a booking)
yók lôek	ยกเลิก	to cancel
yók thôht	ยกโทษ	to forgive
yók yâwng	ยกย่อง	to admire (people)
yûng yâak sáp-sáwn	ยุ่งยากซับซ้อน	complex (adj)
yùt	หยุด	to stop
yùt phák	หยุดพัก	to rest
yùu	อยู่	stay
yùu khâai phák raem	อยู่ค่ายพักแรม	to camp
yùu khâang	อยู่ข้าง	beside
yùu thîi	อยู่ที่	to live

... yùu thîi nǎi?
...อยู่ที่ไหน

Where is the ...?

INDEX

NOTES

NOTES

NOTES

Phrasebooks

L onely Planet phrasebooks are packed with essential words and phrases to help travellers communicate with the locals. With colour tabs for quick reference, an extensive vocabulary and use of script, these handy pocket-sized language guides cover day-to-day travel situations.

- handy pocket-sized books
- easy to understand Pronunciation chapter
- clear & comprehensive Grammar chapter
- romanisation alongside script for ease of pronunciation
- script throughout so users can point to phrases for every situation
- full of cultural information and tips for the traveller

'...vital for a real DIY spirit and attitude in language learning'
– *Backpacker*

'the phrasebooks have good cultural backgrounders and offer solid advice for challenging situations in remote locations'

– *San Francisco Examiner*

Arabic (*Egyptian*) • Arabic (*Moroccan*) • Australian (*Australian English, Aboriginal and Torres Strait languages*) • Baltic States (*Estonian, Latvian, Lithuanian*) • Bengali • Brazilian • British • Burmese • Cantonese • Central Asia • Central Europe (*Czech, French, German, Hungarian, Italian, Slovak*) • Eastern Europe (*Bulgarian, Czech, Hungarian, Polish, Romanian, Slovak*) • Ethiopian (*Amharic*) • Fijian • French • German • Greek • Hill Tribes • Hindi & Urdu • Indonesian • Italian • Japanese • Korean • Lao • Latin American Spanish • Malay • Mandarin • Mediterranean Europe (*Albanian, Croatian, Greek, Italian, Macedonian, Maltese, Serbian, Slovene*) • Mongolian • Nepali • Pidgin • Pilipino (*Tagalog*) • Quechua • Russian • Scandinavian Europe (*Danish, Finnish, Icelandic, Norwegian, Swedish*) • South-East Asia (*Burmese, Indonesian, Khmer, Lao, Malay, Tagalog Pilipino, Thai, Vietnamese*) • South Pacific (*Fijian, Fijian Hindi, Hawaiian, Kanak, Maori, Niuean, Pacific French, Pacific Englishes, Rapanui, Rarotongan Maori, Samoan, Spanish, Tahitian, Tongan*) • Spanish (*Castilian; also includes Catalan, Galician and Basque*) • Sri Lanka • Swahili • Thai • Tibetan • Turkish • Ukrainian • USA (*US English, Vernacular, Native American languages, Hawaiian*) • Vietnamese • Western Europe (*Basque, Catalan, Dutch, French, German, Greek, Irish*)

COMPLETE LIST OF LONELY PLANET BOOKS

AFRICA Africa – the South • Africa on a shoestring • Arabic (Egyptian) phrasebook • Arabic (Moroccan) phrasebook • Cairo • Cape Town • Central Africa • East Africa • Egypt • Egypt travel atlas • Ethiopian (Amharic) phrasebook • The Gambia & Senegal • Kenya • Kenya travel atlas • Malawi, Mozambique & Zambia • Morocco • North Africa • South Africa, Lesotho & Swaziland • South Africa, Lesotho & Swaziland travel atlas • Swahili phrasebook • Trekking in East Africa • Tunisia • West Africa • Zimbabwe, Botswana & Namibia • Zimbabwe, Botswana & Namibia travel atlas
Travel Literature: The Rainbird: A Central African Journey • Songs to an African Sunset: A Zimbabwean Story • Mali Blues: Traveling to an African Beat

AUSTRALIA & THE PACIFIC Australia • Australian phrasebook • Bushwalking in Australia • Bushwalking in Papua New Guinea • Fiji • Fijian phrasebook • Islands of Australia's Great Barrier Reef • Melbourne • Micronesia • New Caledonia • New South Wales & the ACT • New Zealand • Northern Territory • Outback Australia • Papua New Guinea • Pidgin phrasebook • Queensland • Rarotonga & the Cook Islands • Samoa • Solomon Islands • South Australia • South Pacific phrasebook • Sydney • Tahiti & French Polynesia • Tasmania • Tonga • Tramping in New Zealand • Vanuatu • Victoria • Western Australia
Travel Literature: Islands in the Clouds • Sean & David's Long Drive

CENTRAL AMERICA & THE CARIBBEAN Bahamas and Turks & Caicos • Barcelona • Bermuda • Central America on a shoestring • Costa Rica • Cuba • Dominican Republic & Haiti • Eastern Caribbean • Guatemala, Belize & Yucatán: La Ruta Maya • Jamaica • Mexico • Mexico City • Panama
Travel Literature: Green Dreams: Travels in Central America

EUROPE Amsterdam • Andalucía • Austria • Baltic States phrasebook • Berlin • Britain • British phrasebook • Central Europe • Central Europe phrasebook • Croatia • Czech & Slovak Republics • Denmark • Dublin • Eastern Europe • Eastern Europe phrasebook • Edinburgh • Estonia, Latvia & Lithuania • Europe • Finland • France • French phrasebook • Germany • German phrasebook • Greece • Greek phrasebook • Hungary • Iceland, Greenland & the Faroe Islands • Ireland • Italian phrasebook • Italy • Lisbon • London • Mediterranean Europe • Mediterranean Europe phrasebook • Paris • Poland • Portugal • Portugal travel atlas • Prague • Provence & the Côte D'Azur • Romania & Moldova • Russia, Ukraine & Belarus • Russian phrasebook • Scandinavian & Baltic Europe • Scandinavian Europe phrasebook • Scotland • Slovenia • Spain • Spanish phrasebook • St Petersburg • Switzerland • Trekking in Spain • Ukrainian phrasebook • Vienna • Walking in Britain • Walking in Italy • Walking in Ireland • Walking in Switzerland • Western Europe • Western Europe phrasebook
Travel Literature: The Olive Grove: Travels in Greece

INDIAN SUBCONTINENT Bangladesh • Bengali phrasebook • Bhutan • Delhi • Goa • Hindi/Urdu phrasebook • India • India & Bangladesh travel atlas • Indian Himalaya • Karakoram Highway • Nepal • Nepali phrasebook • Pakistan • Rajasthan • South India • Sri Lanka • Sri Lanka phrasebook • Trekking in the Indian Himalaya • Trekking in the Karakoram & Hindukush • Trekking in the Nepal Himalaya

COMPLETE LIST OF LONELY PLANET BOOKS

Travel Literature: In Rajasthan • Shopping for Buddhas

ISLANDS OF THE INDIAN OCEAN Madagascar & Comoros • Maldives • Mauritius, Réunion & Seychelles

MIDDLE EAST & CENTRAL ASIA Arab Gulf States • Central Asia • Central Asia phrasebook • Iran • Israel & the Palestinian Territories • Israel & the Palestinian Territories travel atlas • Istanbul • Jerusalem • Jordan & Syria • Jordan, Syria & Lebanon travel atlas • Lebanon • Middle East on a shoestring • Turkey • Turkish phrasebook • Turkey travel atlas • Yemen
Travel Literature: The Gates of Damascus • Kingdom of the Film Stars: Journey into Jordan

NORTH AMERICA Alaska • Backpacking in Alaska • Baja California • California & Nevada • Canada • Florida • Hawaii • Honolulu • Los Angeles • Miami • New England USA • New Orleans • New York City • New York, New Jersey & Pennsylvania • Pacific Northwest USA • Rocky Mountain States • San Francisco • Seattle • Southwest USA • USA • USA phrasebook • Vancouver • Washington, DC & the Capital Region
Travel Literature: Drive Thru America

NORTH-EAST ASIA Beijing • Cantonese phrasebook • China • Hong Kong • Hong Kong, Macau & Guangzhou • Japan • Japanese phrasebook • Japanese audio pack • Korea • Korean phrasebook • Kyoto • Mandarin phrasebook • Mongolia • Mongolian phrasebook • North-East Asia on a shoestring • Seoul • South-West China • Taiwan • Tibet • Tibetan phrasebook • Tokyo
Travel Literature: Lost Japan

SOUTH AMERICA Argentina, Uruguay & Paraguay % Bolivia • Brazil • Brazilian phrasebook • Buenos Aires • Chile & Easter Island • Chile & Easter Island travel atlas • Colombia • Ecuador & the Galapagos Islands • Latin American Spanish phrasebook • Peru • Quechua phrasebook • Rio de Janeiro • South America on a shoestring • Trekking in the Patagonian Andes • Venezuela
Travel Literature: Full Circle: A South American Journey

SOUTH-EAST ASIA Bali & Lombok • Bangkok • Burmese phrasebook • Cambodia • Hill Tribes phrasebook • Ho Chi Minh City • Indonesia • Indonesian phrasebook • Indonesian audio pack • Jakarta • Java • Laos • Lao phrasebook • Laos travel atlas • Malay phrasebook • Malaysia, Singapore & Brunei • Myanmar (Burma) • Philippines • Pilipino (Tagalog) phrasebook • Singapore • South-East Asia on a shoestring • South-East Asia phrasebook • Thailand • Thailand's Islands & Beaches • Thailand travel atlas • Thai phrasebook • Thai audio pack • Vietnam • Vietnamese phrasebook • Vietnam travel atlas

ALSO AVAILABLE: Antarctica • Brief Encounters: Stories of Love, Sex & Travel • Chasing Rickshaws • Not the Only Planet: Travel Stories from Science Fiction • Travel with Children • Traveller's Tales

LONELY PLANET

FREE Lonely Planet Newsletters

We love hearing from you and think you'd like to hear from us.

Planet Talk

Our FREE quarterly printed newsletter is full of tips from travellers and anecdotes from Lonely Planet guidebook authors. Every issue is packed with up-to-date travel news and advice, and includes:

- a postcard from Lonely Planet co-founder Tony Wheeler
- a swag of mail from travellers
- a look at life on the road through the eyes of a Lonely Planet author
- topical health advice
- prizes for the best travel yarn
- news about forthcoming Lonely Planet events
- a complete list of Lonely Planet books and other titles

To join our mailing list, residents of the UK, Europe and Africa can email us at go@lonelyplanet.co.uk; residents of North and South America can email us at info@lonelyplanet.com; the rest of the world can email us at talk2us@lonelyplanet.com.au, or contact any Lonely Planet office.

LONELY PLANET OFFICES

Australia
PO Box 617, Hawthorn,
Victoria 3122
☎ (03) 9819 1877
fax (03) 9819 6459
email: talk2us@lonelyplanet.com.au

USA
150 Linden St, Oakland,
CA 94607
☎ (510) 893 8555
TOLL FREE: 800 275 8555
fax (510) 893 8572
email: info@lonelyplanet.com

UK
10a Spring Place,
London NW5 3BH
☎ (020) 7428 4800
fax (020) 7428 4828
email: go@lonelyplanet.co.uk

France
1 rue du Dahomey, 75011 Paris
☎ 01 55 25 33 00
fax 01 55 25 33 01
email: bip@lonelyplanet.fr
minitel: 3615 lonelyplanet
(1,29 F TTC/min)

**World Wide Web: www.lonelyplanet.com *or* AOL keyword: lp
Lonely Planet Images: lpi@lonelyplanet.com.au**